Edmund Kirke

Personal recollections of Abraham Lincoln and the Civil War

Edmund Kirke

Personal recollections of Abraham Lincoln and the Civil War

ISBN/EAN: 9783337224066

Printed in Europe, USA, Canada, Australia, Japan

Cover: Foto ©ninafisch / pixelio.de

More available books at **www.hansebooks.com**

PERSONAL RECOLLECTIONS

OF

ABRAHAM LINCOLN

AND

THE CIVIL WAR

BY

JAMES R. GILMORE

(EDMUND KIRKE)

AUTHOR OF "AMONG THE PINES,"
"JOHN SEVIER, THE COMMONWEALTH BUILDER,"
"THE LIFE OF JAMES A. GARFIELD," ETC.

Illustrated

BOSTON
L. C. PAGE AND COMPANY
(INCORPORATED)
1898

CONTENTS.

CHAP.		PAGE
I.	My First Interview with President Lincoln	9
II.	A Cabinet Session on a Momentous Occasion	23
III.	The Great Uprising	33
IV.	My First Acquaintance with Horace Greeley	39
V.	The Conception of the Emancipation Proclamation	49
VI.	The Genesis of the Book "Among the Pines"	65
VII.	The Emancipation Proclamation	75
VIII.	My Connection with the New York Tribune	86
IX.	The Dissatisfaction with President Lincoln	95
X.	Travel in War Time	104
XI.	With "Old Rosey"	114
XII.	Rosecrans Declines the Presidential Nomination	137
XIII.	Conferences with President Lincoln	148
XIV.	The Tribune in the Draft Riots	167
XV.	The Proposed Recession of North Carolina	206
XVI.	The Preliminaries to the Peace Mission of 1864	230
XVII.	Our Visit to Richmond	248

ILLUSTRATIONS.

ABRAHAM LINCOLN	*Frontispiece*
WILLIAM H. SEWARD	20
HORACE GREELEY	40
W. S. ROSECRANS	101
JAMES A. GARFIELD	118
JAMES F. JAQUESS	138
U. S. GRANT	226
JEFFERSON DAVIS	261

ILLUSTRATIONS.

ABRAHAM LINCOLN	*Frontispiece*
WILLIAM H. SEWARD	20
HORACE GREELEY	40
W. S. ROSECRANS	101
JAMES A. GARFIELD	118
JAMES F. JAQUESS	138
U. S. GRANT	226
JEFFERSON DAVIS	261

PREFACE.

AMONG the many disclosures that are now being made in regard to the men and events of our recent Civil War, none are more interesting than those which relate to the eminent man who guided the country through that great crisis. Each fresh disclosure reveals him in some new aspect, and they all deepen the impression that he was a "providential man," singularly endowed, and specially commissioned, for the vast work which he did in American history.

It was my good fortune to know him well, and to be, at an early period in his administration, the depositary of his confidential views on national policy, and also his trusted agent in the attempted carrying out of some of his more important plans in connection with the Civil War. Therefore it has been represented to me that it would deepen the universal affection and reverence for this great and good man, if I were to make public what I know of the inner history of some of the important events of the war before I go hence and can no longer speak face to face with my countrymen. For this reason these sketches are now published. Some of them appeared during the war in the columns of the *Atlantic Monthly* and the New York *Tribune*, but the larger part are now freshly produced from notes made while the events were transpiring, and from a somewhat retentive memory. All conversations with Mr.

Lincoln it was my habit to write down in my note-book within twenty-four hours after they occurred, and hence I am able to reproduce, after the lapse of more than thirty years, his very words, and his peculiarities of speech and manner. The same is true of what I report of my interviews with Generals Grant and Rosecrans, but the remark does not apply to what I relate of Horace Greeley and the Hon. Robert J. Walker, I having been in such frequent intercourse with those gentlemen as to render such accuracy of verbal statement both unnecessary and impracticable. I have aimed to correctly report the opinions and sentiments they expressed on the occasions that are mentioned, but the language used is my own, though it doubtless has a certain verisimilitude that might enable it to pass as their own phraseology.

A valued friend, who ranks as one of the ablest of American critics, to whom I have submitted these "Recollections" for the purpose of deciding whether they should, or should not, be given book publication, has just written me as follows: "I have read the entire manuscript with very much interest and pleasure. It contains a great deal that is new to me and, I venture to say, that will be new to nine hundred and ninety-nine out of a thousand of the generation who took no active part in the affairs of the country in war times. Valuable side-light is thrown by your disclosures on some of the hidden springs and inner workings of the times, and it appears to me that it is worthy to be preserved on account of its intrinsic value."

In the hope that the reader may concur in the opinion of this most excellent gentleman, this volume is given to the public.

JAMES R. GILMORE.

LAKE GEORGE, N. Y., MAY 24, 1898.

PERSONAL RECOLLECTIONS
OF
ABRAHAM LINCOLN
AND
THE CIVIL WAR.

CHAPTER I.

MY FIRST INTERVIEW WITH PRESIDENT LINCOLN.

ON Saturday, the 13th of April, 1861, I was at Willard's Hotel, Washington, lured there by a restless desire to learn something of the probable course of the Lincoln administration in the tremendous crisis that was then upon the country. The city was aflame with excitement over the attack upon Fort Sumter, accounts of which were appearing almost hourly in "extras" of the daily journals; and having secured a copy of the latest "extra," I retired to the smoking-room of the hotel, directly after I had breakfasted, to gather the news, and to speculate upon the influence which this breaking out of actual war would have upon my private fortunes; for, however devoted a man may be to his country, his first thought, in the face of any great calamity, is of himself and of those who are dependent on him.

While thus absorbed in gloomy forebodings, I became conscious that I was undergoing the scrutiny of a gentleman who sat near me, also engaged in the morning newspaper. I gave him only a casual glance, but that was enough to show that he was a man past middle life, and of striking personal appearance. He was of the medium stature, with broad shoulders, a deep chest, and a capacious head that was about all forehead. His features were prominent, his eyes deep and piercing, and they had the look of conscious power that belongs to born leaders of men. At any other time I should have given him more attention, but just then I was absorbed in the question, "Are not those cannon of Beauregard sending up in smoke the work of my lifetime?"

Soon the gentleman I have referred to rose from his seat, and, coming directly to me, said: "Your beard disguises you, but I know you, and I think you have not forgotten me."

I gave him a quick glance, then sprang to my feet, and, grasping his extended hand, exclaimed: "I shall never forget you. I have followed your every step since I was a boy, and I thank God that you are left to serve the country."

With a stronger grasp of the hand, he said: "The boy is father of the man, — you are the same enthusiastic youth who came to me at Natchez some twenty years ago."

"Enthusiastic? Yes, when there is anything to enthuse over. I shouted myself hoarse when you checkmated Buchanan's attempt to saddle the Lecompton Constitution upon Kansas. That act alone entitles you to a national monument."

"It gratifies me to have you say so," he said. "But tell me about yourself; how has the world fared with you these dozen years?"

I told him; but as I propose to sink the personal pronoun in these sketches, as far as possible, what was said is here omitted.

The gentleman who had thus accosted me was the Hon. Robert J. Walker, who was the predecessor of Jefferson Davis in the United States Senate from Mississippi, and became famous by his able management of the Treasury Department during the administration of President Polk.

If the reader will consult any encyclopædia published in this country since 1850, he will find there an outline of this gentleman's remarkable career. He there will learn that from Feb. 22, 1824, when, a young man of only twenty-three, he brought about in the Harrisburg Convention the nomination of Andrew Jackson for the presidency, until the 9th of April, 1865, when Lee surrendered at Appomattox, — a period of more than forty years, — he originated very many, and advocated all, of the great movements that have contributed to the progress and expansion of this country. Then, if he will turn to the debates in the United States Senate between 1836 and 1843, and read the speeches which he, a Southern Senator, representing a State in close affiliation with South Carolina, had the courage to utter in defence of the Union and in denunciation of John C. Calhoun, the great giant of Nullification, he will learn something of the rare qualities of the man, his lofty purpose, his breadth of view, and his serene intrepidity in the face of an almost overwhelming antagonism. Those speeches stirred my blood when a boy; but nothing in Mr. Walker's whole career ever thrilled me with such enthusiastic admiration as his long and single-handed struggle with the Calhoun heresy in Mississippi. In November, 1832, the State was ready to follow South Carolina in its repudiation of the laws of the United States, but Robert J. Walker mounted the "stump," and by his single voice held it back from a mad plunge into Nullification. He followed this up in 1833 by a series of articles in the Natchez *Journal* that won the enthusiastic approval of ex-President Madison; and he kept up the agitation until January, 1836, when Mississippi came fully over to his side, and sent him to continue the conflict with Calhoun on the floor of the United States Senate. In all the history of this country there is nothing more magnificent than this single-handed struggle of Robert J. Walker, not merely with the one giant, Calhoun, but with all the forces of Nullification in the entire Southern country.

His whole career had been disinterestedly patriotic, and it was not surprising that at the opening of our great civil conflict he should part company with many of his former political associates, and come out openly, strongly, and uncompromisingly in support of the Union. I was in familiar intercourse with him when I was but a stripling, but at this time I had not met him for several years. There was, therefore, something to say between us of a personal character. When this had been gone over, he asked: "What do you think of the present situation?"

"That we are among the rocks on a lee shore, with neither Robert J. Walker nor Andrew Jackson to keep us from the breakers. I have recently been through the interior, from Charleston to Key West, and every man I met was jubilant over the prospect of being soon rid of the Yankees. If Sumter falls, — as it inevitably will, — and Lincoln attempts to recover it, — as he is bound to do, — we shall have to encounter the entire seaboard people."

At this point Mr. Walker rose, and beckoned to a gentleman who had just entered the room and was closely regarding us. He was a tall, spare man, of about Mr.

Walker's age, and he had a shrewd, thoughtful appearance. Negligently clad in a loose-fitting suit of gray, he looked more like a much-engrossed man of business than a statesman; but Mr. Walker introduced him to me as Secretary Cameron of the Lincoln administration. As he took a chair near us, Mr. Walker said: "Mr. Cameron, this gentleman is just the one you want to meet. He knows every acre of the cotton-growing country, and, except Texas, has recently been over all the States in secession. He can tell you the feeling of the seaboard people, and their probable course in this emergency."

Mr. Cameron remarked that he was very glad to meet me; but expressed a fear that an interview in so public a place would attract attention, and suggested that we should adjourn to some private apartment. Then "Governor" Walker — as Mr. Cameron styled him — secured such a room at the hotel office, and soon we were seated there in a conversation that lasted something more than two hours. I shall not attempt to detail it; I kept no notes of what was said; the substance of it, however, was repeated soon afterwards in an interview with Mr. Lincoln, of which I entered a full account in my note-book. This interview was requested by Mr. Cameron, and arranged for by him for two o'clock that afternoon.

At two o'clock precisely, Governor Walker and I were ushered into Mr. Lincoln's private room at the White House. Mr. Cameron was there, and near him, seated in a large armchair, was a tall man, in an ill-fitting suit of black, whom I recognized from his portraits to be Mr. Lincoln. He rose as we entered, and, greeting Mr. Walker with great cordiality, he said: "So, Governor, this is the gentleman who knows all about the South, and can tell us how high that raccoon is going to spring."

"He can give you a very shrewd guess, Mr. President," said Mr. Walker, "for he knows the South thoroughly."

While this was being said, I scanned somewhat closely Mr. Lincoln's personal appearance. He was exceedingly tall, and so gaunt that he seemed even above his actual height of six feet, four inches; but he was not — as very tall men often are — ungainly in either manner or attitude. As he leaned back in his chair, he had an air of unstudied ease, a kind of careless dignity, that well became his station; and yet there was not a trace of self-consciousness about him. He seemed altogether forgetful of himself and his position, and entirely engrossed in the subject that was under discussion. He had a large head, covered with coarse dark hair that was thrown carelessly back from a spacious forehead. His features also were large and prominent, the nose heavy and somewhat Roman, the cheeks thin and furrowed, the skin bronzed, the lips full, the mouth wide, but played about by a smile that was very winning. At my first glance he impressed me as a very homely man, for his features were ill-assorted and none of them was perfect, but this was before I had seen him smile, or met the glance of his deep set, dark gray eye, — the deepest, saddest, and yet kindliest, eye I had ever seen in a human being. I had been prejudiced against him, but with the first words he addressed to me the prejudice vanished, and, feeling perfectly at my ease, I answered his request to tell him all I knew about the South, by saying: "It is a large subject, Mr. Lincoln; where shall I begin?"

He said: "Wherever you like; and take your own time and way about it."

"Then, sir, permit me to give you a general opinion of the Southern people from one who was born among them, — Mr. Bennett Flanner, of Wilmington, N. C. He was a shrewd observer of men and things, a most excellent man, and a class-leader in the Methodist Church. He had consigned his produce to our Boston house from time immemorial, and every summer he came on and spent a fortnight with our senior partners. The firm owned a tract of about a hundred thousand acres of timber land in Maine, and one summer the senior partners asked Mr. Flanner to go down with them and take a look at it. He went, and when he returned he came to me and said: 'Ah, my boy, I've seen them all now,—all the Yankees. I had seen the York Yankees and the Boston Yankees, and now I've seen the down-east Yankees,—they're all a right cute sort of folk; but, after all, the damnedest Yankees on the face of the earth are the Southern Yankees.'"

"Then," said Mr. Lincoln, with the smile that made his homely features good-looking, "you agree with Mr. Flanner that the Southern people are the highest style of Yankees?"

I answered that I did; that they were of the same race as ourselves, but unmixed with our degraded foreign element, and with our every trait intensified in consequence of having a servile race to support them in idleness. Of course, there is every variety of character among them, but they are all like Jeremiah's figs,—"the good very good, the bad not fit to feed the pigs." As politicians, the meanest man among them had not his equal in the Northern States.

"And what is the feeling of those people towards the Government?" asked Mr. Lincoln.

I then went on to say that I thought the masses—not the politicians—were, until a little time before, quite indifferent as to the extension or non-extension of slavery; that the slave-owners, who were the inciters of the present trouble, were a very small minority of the Southern people, numbering, all told, only about 200,000. The small slaveholders were mostly planters, and many among them believed, what I had often told them, that they could raise their produce cheaper by hired than by slave labor. And the non-slaveholders were generally satisfied to let things go on as they were, not caring very much which party was in power; but when he was nominated for the presidency, they were told that he was an Abolitionist, and worse, that he had negro blood in his veins; and that both from blood and principle he was bound to go to the length of freeing the slave, and placing him on a political equality with the white. Political equality, in many districts of the South, would mean negro domination, — and the domination of the lowest type of negro, — which no Southern, or even Northern, white man would submit to.

"Do you think the Southern people believe such absurdities?" asked Mr. Lincoln.

I answered that I knew it to be the general opinion among what are called the masses. They were fairly intelligent men, the bone and sinew of the South; but the most of them were never a hundred miles from home, never saw a decent Yankee, and never read anything but what the politicians chose to tell them in the Southern newspapers. Let a Northern army be sent among them, and every man of them would become a soldier, and would fight to the last gasp in defence of his fireside. They had no idea of any allegiance to the General Government. They had been reared in the doctrine of State Rights, and so when their States secede they would go with them, feeling sure that they were doing their duty to their country.

"Then," said Mr. Lincoln, "our only hope is in conciliating the leaders. Would not one good, decisive victory bring them to their senses?"

"No, sir," I replied, "not ten victories. The leaders have gone into this struggle to win, at any cost of time and treasure. Those who are not self-seeking scoundrels, like Toombs and Wigfall, are fanatics, like Jeff Davis and Alexander Stephens, and both words and concession would be wasted upon them. They have planned this thing for over thirty years, — ever since our friend Mr. Walker and General Jackson scotched the snake, Nullification. They could not kill it, and it soon came to life again, in the form of Secession. The only way to bring the South to its senses is to put down the Secession leaders."

"Then," said Mr. Lincoln, "we must separate one class from the other. Are not their interests the same?"

I answered that they were not; that the leaders were all slave-owners. The great body of the Southern people were not slave-owners; their property was in lands, houses, and merchandise, and if they employed slaves, they paid wages to their masters; and they would pay the same to the slaves if they were emancipated. I knew hundreds of cotton and turpentine producers who used altogether hired slave labor. I also knew as many slave-owners whose entire income was from thus hiring out their slaves. So long as it would be as cheap to the producer to pay wages to the slave as to the master, he could have no interest in secession. If he were at that time opposed to the Government, it was only because he believed its policy was to put the negro on an equality with the white man.

"Then," remarked Mr. Lincoln, "the Abolitionists are right in saying that slavery is the root of the whole evil."

"They are, sir. The slave-owners control the South,— control it because of their wealth, and their wealth is in their slaves. A man in the South is not worth so many dollars, but so many negroes. They have gone into the rebellion to protect that kind of property, and you can't put it down until you deprive them of it."

"But you are aware that I have no constitutional right to abolish slavery."

"Except as a war measure. But seven States have already declared themselves independent, and begun a war in Charleston harbor."

"Yes," he answered, "such doings look like war; but whether we have had cannon-balls enough to justify extreme measures is the question. We won't discuss that. But tell me, Mr. Gilmore, what would you do if you were in my place, — bound as I am to support the Constitution?"

"Pardon me, Mr. Lincoln, I think you have invited me here to give you facts, and not opinions. Governor Walker is the one to answer such a question."

"I know he's our American Solon. He's in favor of cutting straight across lots; but it's safer to go around by the road, and, sometimes, you get there just as soon. The Governor is a statesman; you are a man of the people, and that is just the reason I want to know what you would do in the present circumstances."

"Well, Mr. Lincoln, as you put it on that ground I will answer your question. If I were in your place, sir, I should announce at once to the seven States in secession that if they did not return to their allegiance within a specified time — say ninety days — I would free every one of their negroes. And I should give a like notice to every State that follows them into secession. The result would probably be the freeing of every slave in the South; but for that you would be in no way responsible. The slaveholders would have brought it upon themselves."

"And do you suppose the North would sustain me in any such measure? Don't you know that the Abolitionists have been working for thirty years to bring the North to that way of thinking? And with what result? A corporal's guard, and not a party."

"I can only judge of others by myself, Mr. Lincoln. For more than twenty years I have been in the closest relations with the South; my best friends are there; and four-fifths of all I have in the world will go up in smoke if we have a war of any considerable duration; but I would rather see it all go than leave to my children a disorganized and disunited country. Other men feel as I do, and they will require you to remove from the nation this apple of perpetual discord."

"They may, if they are brought to see things as you see them. And they would find me willing — I may say eager — to listen. But you must bear in mind that I have no right to emancipate the slaves, except for the preservation of the Union."

"I understand, — it must be a war measure, forced upon you by the pressure of positive necessity."

"Or the overwhelming sentiment of the North," said Mr. Lincoln. "That I should heed, and heed gladly. I am, you know, only the servant of the people. Educate them up to such a measure, and I will do their and your bidding."

"It seems to me, sir, that nothing more can now be expected of you. Anything so revolutionary as the emancipation of the slaves might be allowed to wait until the intentions of the Southern people are more fully developed. You can dismiss all thought of conciliating the politicians; but you can hope for an amicable adjustment of affairs, and a restored Union, by showing both by word and act a friendly disposition towards the Southern people. Therefore, I should suggest no invasion of their homes, and, in your military operations, a strictly defensive policy. But all your friendly professions they will regard as false so long as Mr. Seward is a member of your Cabinet. They regard him as their arch enemy; and from his prominence and ability they will believe that he is really the soul and brains of your administration."

"Then they consider Seward as the King-devil?" said Mr. Lincoln, smiling.

"Yes, sir," I answered; "both politicians and people regard him as the incarnation of all evil, — a man of ability, but false, hypocritical, time-serving, and cowardly. If the leaders had not thought him a coward, I question if they would have fired upon Fort Sumter. They would not have done so, had such a man as Andrew Jackson or Robert J. Walker been in your Cabinet."

"Come, come, Mr. Gilmore," said Mr. Walker, hastily, "omit any reference to me."

"None is necessary, Governor," I said, "for it is plain that Mr. Lincoln has the opinion of you that I have. But he has asked me here to tell him what I know and think; now, I *know* that I have expressed the Southern opinion of Mr. Seward, and I *think* that if Mr. Lincoln listens to the timid advice which Mr. Seward, from his extreme caution, is sure to give him, he will run the country upon the rocks, where no earthly power can save it from going to pieces."

"But you would not have me discard a wise councillor at the bidding of a mob, and a Southern mob at that?" said Mr. Lincoln.

"Is he a wise councillor, sir, if Mr. Cameron is right in saying that he thinks this storm will blow over in ninety days? If he can say that, after a dozen years' intimate intercourse with the Southern leaders, is his judgment to

be trusted? Understand me, Mr. Lincoln; I have no personal antagonism to Mr. Seward. I have never met him. I doubt if I should know him if we were to meet upon the street."

"Well, well," remarked Mr. Lincoln, with his peculiar smile, "I guess the Southern people would hang Seward if they should catch him. But now tell me how you would go to work to put down this rebellion?"

I smiled broadly, as I answered, "First, you ask me, sir, a question that only a statesman can answer; and now one fit for only a military man. Do you ask this, also, because I am one of the people?"

"No," he answered, again smiling. "I ask this because you are a practical man, — one, I take it, who never meets an obstacle without seeking a way to overcome it. You must have thought a good deal on the subject; now give me the result of your thinking."

"Well, sir, I was very much struck in reading awhile ago the plan of the British Cabinet for subduing the revolted colonies. It was brought to my attention by my former business partner, Mr. Frederic Kidder, of Boston, a man twenty years my senior, of very sound judgment, and thoroughly acquainted with the South. The British commanders tried to put it in execution on three distinct occasions, and on each occasion they were thwarted only by what we call accidental circumstances. But for these circumstances — over which neither Washington nor the Continental Congress had any control whatever — they would have succeeded, and we probably have been to-day no nearer a national existence than Canada. The plan was to divide the Southern colonies by a line running westward from Charleston, also to separate New England from the middle colonies by the Hudson River, and to crush each section separately. I have never seen the plan fully stated except in a 'History of the American War,' by Stedman, a prominent officer under Cornwallis; but it may be distinctly traced in the operations of the British armies."

Mr. Lincoln then said: "The principle is right,—'divide and conquer,'—but how would you apply it to our present circumstances?"

I then went on to give him Mr. Kidder's ideas,—stating that they were his and not my own, and that he had given a good deal of thought to the subject. He and the others frequently interrupted me with questions, but the discussion was too lengthy to be here repeated. I need here only say that the plan was in effect executed by General Sherman in his "march to the sea," and that Mr. Lincoln intended to carry it out in 1863 by swinging North Carolina out of the Confederacy, as I shall relate hereafter.

At the end of a long two hours Governor Walker and I took our leave, Mr. Lincoln inviting me to call on him when I was again in Washington. As we left the White House the newsboys were crying. "Fort Sumter on fire—the barracks burning;" and a few hours later Major Anderson lowered the flag of the Union at the bidding of the Confederates.

CHAPTER II.

A CABINET SESSION ON A MOMENTOUS OCCASION.

A BRIEF telegraphic account of the surrender of Fort Sumter appeared in the Washington newspapers on the following morning, and I had just finished the reading of it when Robert J. Walker laid his hand upon my shoulder, saying: "The blow has fallen! What mortal man can foresee the consequences?"

"I cannot," I replied. "But it seems to me that much will depend upon the prompt action of the Government. Any weakness shown now will be fatal."

"Well," he said, "we must possess our souls in patience until to-morrow. They may talk things over to-day, but will take no action on Sunday. Meanwhile, suppose we go to church and get our minds into a submissive mood."

A little after noon on the following day he came to me again at Willard's Hotel, saying: "The Cabinet must by this time have finished its session, and I am impatient to hear what action they have decided on. Come, go with me to Cameron; I don't like to bother Mr. Lincoln."

We found Mr. Cameron at his desk in his private room at the War Department, and, looking up, he said: "Ah, gentlemen, I am glad to see you. Be seated. I know what you have come for, and I'll be through in a few minutes, — as soon as I draft this telegram."

Soon he looked up again, and said to Mr. Walker:

"Governor, let me read this to you,—you are more familiar with these things than I am. It is a call on the States for 75,000 troops."

Mr. Walker pronounced the paper in proper form, and then Mr. Cameron, ringing for a subordinate and telling him to see that the despatches were sent off at once, turned about on his chair and told us that the President had decided to issue a call for 75,000 men, and a proclamation convening Congress for an extra session on the 4th of July. At the Cabinet meeting he, Cameron, had proposed a call for 500,000 men; a close blockade of the Southern ports; the capture of Charleston and New Orleans, and the giving of freedom to all slaves who should desert their masters and join the Union armies; but his suggestions had been strongly opposed by Mr. Seward, on the ground that such decisive measures would close the door for any reconciliation with the seceded States. Mr. Lincoln had coupled the call for Congress and for 75,000 troops together, as a compromise between the views of Mr. Seward and Mr. Cameron, remarking that the Congress would be fresh from the people, and would represent the public will; which he should be ready to heed if it demanded an energetic war and a call for half a million, or even a million, of men. It was clear to Mr. Cameron that his suggestions would have been adopted but for the strenuous opposition of Mr. Seward.

"Well," said Mr. Walker, "he has probably made us miss our only chance. This action will have no more effect than the letting off of a boy's cannon. Of course, you said all that could be said against it?"

Mr. Cameron said that he had; and then went on to give, at Mr. Walker's suggestion, a pretty full report of the Cabinet meeting. There was, he said, a full attendance,

A CABINET SESSION.

and when all had come together, Mr. Lincoln turned to him, and said: "Well, Cameron, war seems to be upon us. Now, what do you propose to do about it?" Mr. Cameron answered that he had given a good deal of thought to that plan of the British for subduing the American colonies, which was discussed in the President's room on the previous Saturday, and he had concluded it was entirely applicable to the present situation.

Mr. Lincoln remarked: "The plan seems to be a good one; but how are we to carry it out, — where get the ships, the men, and the money?"

Mr. Cameron answered that we should not need many ships; small coasting-vessels, armed with a single gun, would largely serve the purpose, and five hundred of these would be idle in the Northern ports the moment a blockade was proclaimed. Quite a number were then in the Southern ports, and would, of course, be seized upon by the Confederates and armed with the guns Mr. Floyd had provided for the occasion; but he had no fear that they would do us any material damage; for, whatever the Southerner might be on land, on the water he would be no match for our Yankee seamen.

Mr. Lincoln said that he could believe that. But he asked: "How many men will be needed — soldiers and seamen — to carry out this programme?"

Mr. Cameron answered that he did not know; it would depend on the Confederate operations. To uniformly whip them, he thought we should need twice their number wherever they might assail us; not because they were better men than ours, but better trained and accustomed to the use of the rifle. However, whether the men were needed or not, he should recommend the calling out at once of half a million; it would require all of that number to convince the Confederates that the Government was in earnest.

Mr. Lincoln looked incredulous, as he asked: "Would the North respond to any such call? Would not the people laugh at us, — say we had been struck with a panic?"

Mr Cameron thought no one could have that opinion who reflected that the Government was coolly doing its duty in the very hotbed of Secession, and with Baltimore between it and any safety. As to the country responding to a call for 500,000 men, he thought New England and the West would respond for their quota before a day was over. Governor Andrew, of Massachusetts, alone had 5,000 men, equipped and ready to march at an hour's notice, and the West was a tinder-box, that would blaze up the moment a match was applied to it. That match would be the fall of Fort Sumter, which would prove a boomerang to the South. They might as well have let it alone! They only meant to fire the Southern heart, but they forgot that it might have a like effect upon the North. His only doubt was about New York. The interests of its people were largely interwoven with those of the South. They felt friendly to it, and would dislike to see it coerced. But Robert J. Walker could straighten that State out in a fortnight. The fact that he, a Southern man, the predecessor of Jeff Davis in the United States Senate, the prime mover in the annexation of Texas, and in all great Southern projects, except the extension of slavery, for the last third of a century, — the fact that *he* counselled a patriotic support of the Union, would have immense weight with the timid and temporizing at the North.

Evidently gratified, Governor Walker interrupted Mr. Cameron, by saying: "I thank you for thinking of me, —

I am ready to do my duty in any capacity. But go on. What did Mr. Lincoln say to this?"

"He said that there might be something in what I said; but he asked: 'Having got your half a million men, and money to handle them, what would you do?' I answered that I would first secure Washington, and the route to it from its base of supplies,—the North. Then I would put the few forts we still hold in the seceded States in an impregnable position, and recover and rebuild Sumter,— which we must do, or admit that we are not a government. That done, I would capture Charleston and New Orleans, and hermetically seal up the seven seceded States till they fretted themselves into submission to the Constitution.

"'I see,' said Mr. Lincoln, 'you would carry out that British plan. I think it would be easier said than done. How would you do it?'

"I answered that, with Charleston as a base, I would throw a line of army posts along the Tennessee line to the Mississippi, which river I would hold with a strong patrol of gunboats. Then I would withdraw the United States mails, and close every seaboard and gulf port from Charleston to the Rio Grande by a blockade, through which not a bale of cotton could go out, nor an ounce of powder come in.

"'In that case,' said Mr. Lincoln, 'you imagine the fire to be confined to the Cotton States?'

"I answered, 'No. The fire is already lighted in the Border States. Virginia is preparing to secede, and, if she does, she will doubtless carry others.'

"'Then,' remarked Mr. Lincoln, 'with all the Slave States in rebellion, what would you do?'

"I replied that I would simply extend the plan of isolation. It is vital that we hold Maryland. Added to that, we would need to defend the line of Pennsylvania and the Ohio River. This done, we would have the Cotton States closed up; the Border States also closed up and between two lines of fire; and it seems to me that, if we did not invade their territory, they would have nothing to do but to lash themselves to pieces in their own fury.

"'You don't propose, then,' said Mr. Lincoln, 'to invade the sacred soil beyond running a cordon of army posts from Charleston to the Mississippi?'

"I said: 'That is all, except to establish such bases of supply as would be needed by our army and navy. I should bear in mind, Mr. Lincoln, the distinction between the politicians and the people which was brought to our attention on Saturday. The Southern leaders will fight us anywhere and everywhere; invade us if they have the power,—Toombs has threatened to call the roll of his slaves on Bunker Hill. The people, I think, will not fight us unless we invade their country. All men will defend their firesides, but I question if the majority of the Southern people will willingly go into a neighboring State, and much less come North to attack us in our homes. I should avoid any unnecessary invasion of the Southern territory.'

"'Then we must act wholly on the defensive?' said Mr. Lincoln.

"'Yes, sir, I should do so at first, and until we are attacked, as we probably shall be. Then I should be careful to have two men to their one. A Yankee may be as good a man as a Southerner, but our armies would not be altogether Yankee. In them there would be a foreign element, not in any way the equal of the Southerner.'

"'It is a gigantic plan,' said Mr. Lincoln, 'and with the men and the money it might be feasible. What do you think of it, Mr. Seward?'

"Mr. Seward thought it radically defective in one important feature, — the means to carry it out. It would require not only half a million of men, but a hundred millions of dollars, and we could not get the money. 'In October last, when Cobb tried to float a loan of ten millions, he got only seven millions, and had to sell treasury notes at a discount of from six to twelve per cent.; Dix, only two months since, was obliged to sell bonds to pay current expenses at a reduction of nine and ten per cent.; and when Mr. Chase opened his bids for eight millions not a fortnight ago, he found only about three millions of offerings at less than six per cent. discount. No, Mr. Lincoln, you can't get the money for any such operations.'

"Mr. Lincoln then turned to Mr. Chase, saying: 'You hold the bag, Mr. Chase. Can we get the money?'

"Mr. Chase answered: 'If the fall of Sumter should have the effect on the North that Mr. Cameron anticipates, you could get the men, and I the money. I should appeal to the country, and it would support the war with its last dollar.'

"Then Mr. Seward took another tack, and said it would be rash and dangerous to resort to extreme measures; that we should thereby exasperate the South beyond reconciliation, and make hopeless our ever coming together again. All but Mr. Chase and myself seemed to be of this opinion, and finally Mr. Lincoln, saying that in the multitude of councillors there is wisdom, decided to call Congress together, and throw the responsibility upon the country."

When Mr. Cameron concluded, he turned to Mr. Walker, and asked: "Governor, what is to be the outcome of all this?"

"A long war," answered the Governor. "A war that will last till one section or the other is completely ex-

hausted. I know the Secession leaders; every one of them will die in the last ditch, and Jeff Davis, particularly, is the most obstinate man I ever encountered. He thinks he is right, and he will fight till he has not a leg to stand on. There will be a holocaust of lives, rivers of blood, millions of wasted property; but we shall emerge from the conflict with the stain of slavery wiped from the country.

"This decision of Mr. Lincoln — which will give the Secession leaders time to mature their plans, and thoroughly organize their forces — satisfies me that God's time has come for destroying the accursed thing. The North is not ready for immediate emancipation. Mr. Lincoln is right, — the Abolitionists, after thirty years of agitation, are merely a corporal's guard, and not a party. They have appealed to the moral sentiment of the people, and the people, absorbed in money-getting, have given the old answer: 'Am I my brother's keeper?' — an answer which is wrong both in fact and theory; for no part of a political body can be diseased without the malady affecting the entire system. The North has thought to escape the infection by confining slavery within certain limits; but that cannot be done; from its very nature slavery demands room, and it would overleap any barrier that might be set against it. This being so, Providence seems to have resolved upon its extermination, and, as the only way to bring it about, has allowed the South to attack the Union, knowing that the North would fight to sustain our nationality when it would not to destroy slavery."

"Then you are convinced that slavery will be destroyed. But will the Union survive the convulsion?"

"It may be for a time disrupted; that will depend on the spirit of the Northern people, and the energy of the General Government. If Mr. Seward's counsels prevail, it seems to me that the South may be temporarily successful, and the present Union go to pieces. But only for a time, for disunion is opposed to the physical laws of this continent. No two or more nations, divided only by lines of latitude, could exist long upon it. Canada is separated from us by the lakes and the St. Lawrence, yet, were slavery once exterminated, it would soon seek admission to the Union. The Rocky Mountains are our only natural barrier, and for that reason I have for years advocated the building of a Pacific railroad. With Europe it is different. That continent seems designed by nature to be the nursery of different nationalities. If you look upon the map you will observe that Great Britain, Spain, Italy, Norway, and Sweden are mostly, or altogether, surrounded by water, while France is naturally separated by the Alps and the Rhine from Italy and Germany. The only lack of a natural boundary is that between Germany, Austria-Hungary, and Russia; and hence the first two of these nations will eventually have to unite to balance the overshadowing power of Russia. In Europe, thus parcelled out geographically, the various nations of the Aryan race could grow up distinct in language and institutions, but the time was to come, in the providence of God, when all these peoples should be welded together to form a higher type of man,— a race that should build up a free, enlightened, all-powerful country, to lead the van in the great march of the nations. God had, I think, that purpose in view when he led Columbus across the ocean; when he decided, on the Plains of Abraham, that the dominant race on this continent should be the Anglo-Saxon; and when he enabled Washington to strike from our limbs the shackles of an effete feudalism. As I read history, he has meant to create here a great united people, who shall become by their example and their effort the regenerators and Christianizers of the whole world. This being his design, we cannot suppose that he will permit it to be thwarted by a handful of slave-drivers, who seek to build themselves up on the blood and sweat of their fellow men, and the ruin of their country. They may prevail for a day, but only for a day; for all the good forces of the universe will be arrayed against them, and, sooner or later, they will go down in defeat and dishonor. What now is most needed is to arouse the North to the fact that the destruction of slavery is vital to the preservation of the Union. Every Northern statesman sees it; but it is necessary it should be seen by the people. When they once realize it, they will insist on continuing the war until slavery is utterly exterminated."

CHAPTER III.

THE GREAT UPRISING.

I RETURNED to New York from my brief visit to Washington on the morning of Tuesday, the 16th of April, 1861, and as I rode up-town to my house on Thirty-fourth Street, I nowhere observed any indications of popular excitement. No gatherings of people were on the avenues, and only the customary throng of men and women were passing, with their usual quietude, to their daily vocations. When I went down-town later in the day, and mingled somewhat with the men of affairs, I found among them the same apathetic feeling. All seemed to have heard the comforting assurance of Mr. Seward, " It is a tempest in a teapot; it will soon blow over," and the president of the great Mutual Life Insurance Company said to me, " That remark is authentic, — Mr. Seward has made it to me himself; and if he, a member of the Government, feels no alarm, why should we trouble our heads about it? At any rate, *we* are safe, for our securities are largely New York real estate."

I answered him, " Mr. Winston, Mr. Seward's opinion is not worth a bad half-dollar; his strong desire for peace blinds him to facts; and you can't afford to hug yourself in fancied security; for if the Union goes, all will go with it. In that event your New York mortgages will not realize you fifty cents on the dollar." When, a few weeks later, Mr. Winston put the name of his company down for several millions of the first Government loan, I was told that he said, "We might as well take this, for if the Union goes, we shall all go with it."

But this was not the feeling prevalent among New York men of business on the 16th of April, three days after the fall of Fort Sumter. They were not Secessionists, though they tolerated a mayor, Fernando Wood, who strenuously advocated the secession of New York, and its erection into a free city; and also had allowed, without protest, the publication, by his brother, of the New York *News*, a widely circulated journal, as virulent in its denunciation of the Union as any Southern newspaper. They were simply engrossed in their own affairs, and lulled to sleep by the oracular utterances of William H. Seward, so that they did not properly feel the insult to the nation in the lowering of its flag at Fort Sumter. They began to awake from this somnolent condition when, two days later, that identical flag, battle-rent and smoke-begrimed, was landed with its heroic defenders in New York, and they also saw marching along Broadway, on its way to Baltimore, the Sixth Massachusetts Regiment, its men shouting:

"John Brown's body lies a-mouldering in the grave,
But his soul is a-marching on."

It was the soul of John Brown which first roused them from sleep; but it was the voice of Robert J. Walker that fired them with a fixed determination to stay the fratricidal hands which were lifted against their country. He arrived in New York that same evening, and on Saturday morning was waited upon by several leading citizens, who requested him to address a mass-meeting to be held within a few hours, in Union Square, in support of the Government. He gladly assented. It was beyond all comparison the largest gathering of men that ever came together for peaceful discussion on this continent. By those accustomed to estimating crowds the number assembled was set at a hundred thousand; but as I looked over the immense throng from the stand near the Washington statue, I could readily have believed it to be far more numerous. Mr. Walker had been allowed no time for preparation, but he spoke like a man inspired. Other speakers were there, — Governor Dix, William M. Evarts, Senator Baker, Daniel S. Dickinson, and O. M. Mitchell, — all famous for their eloquence, and their words were interrupted by literal thunders of applause; but when Mr. Walker rose, and was introduced by Governor Dix as a "Southern man, a lifelong Democrat, and the predecessor of Jefferson Davis in the Senate from Mississippi," a deep stillness fell on the vast assemblage, and all ears were strained to catch his lightest utterance. It was as though they thought that this man could tell them the truth, and point out the right action to take in the great crisis that was upon the country. This he did, and what he said was received with such profound attention that his words seemed to make a deeper impression than all else spoken at the meeting. It was that meeting, following so closely on the fall of Fort Sumter, that fully aroused the State of New York to its duty to the Union.

On the Monday following his great speech in Union Square, Mr. Walker spoke in Brooklyn. Then he returned to Washington, saying to me as he went away: "I have not talked with a single individual who would not, for the sake of peace, take the South back with slavery, and all our old disagreements unsettled. If we do that, this war will have to be fought over again. The people must be made to see this, — that we can have no permanent peace without the destruction of slavery, and that it is for the interest of sake of the white man." He was spending his strength for naught. I was planting my diminishing substance in a porous soil, where every ounce of compost went through to the Antipodes.

One of the maxims of the wise old gentleman who had given me my business education was, "Never waste your money on the unattainable," and I was deliberating on a counter-revolution in the conduct of the *Knickerbocker* when one day it occurred to me to try the experiment of putting new wine into new bottles. Hence, I decided to bring out a new magazine with the beginning of the year, which should picture the social system of the South as it actually was, and show the North that the removal of slavery was essential to the salvation of the Union, addressing not merely the moral sentiments, but also, and mainly, the spirit of nationality among the people. The magazine should be equal in ability to the *Atlantic Monthly*, and I would furnish a free copy to every leading newspaper throughout the North. This might indoctrinate the organs of public opinion with our views, and so, in time, revolutionize public sentiment. Some money would have to be sunk to establish such a publication; but in my then state of mind money was not an all-important consideration. Having decided upon this, I went on to Washington to secure the coöperation of Robert J. Walker. He not only pledged his aid to the enterprise, but promised me such early advices as to the intentions of the Government as would give to the magazine a semi-official character.

CHAPTER IV.

MY FIRST ACQUAINTANCE WITH HORACE GREELEY.

ON the day following the disastrous battle of Ball's Bluff, I made the acquaintance of Horace Greeley. The loss of Colonel Baker, more than the sore defeat and loss of a thousand men, was felt as a national calamity, and the news had overspread New York City with gloom. His death brought to me personally a realizing sense of the terrible nature of the struggle; for I had been introduced to him at the immense gathering in Union Square, and had sat beside him during the delivery of his great speech on that occasion, — the best, I thought, then spoken, with the sole exception of that of Robert J. Walker. That he, so brave, so eloquent, so well equipped for rousing the country to the situation, should be cut off thus early in the struggle, was to me an inexplicable mystery. Did it portend that the stars in their courses were about to fight against Sisera? I could not tell; but, whatever might be the end, I resolved to do what little I could to serve my country. These thoughts were in my mind when I called upon Mr. Greeley.

I had provided myself with a letter from an intimate friend of his, which briefly stated the object of my visit; and, armed with this, I clambered up to the fourth story of the old *Tribune* building, on the afternoon of that day, and was ushered into the sanctum of the great editor. He was seated at his desk, writing in a most ungainly attitude, — the desk being so high that he had to sit bolt upright, his right arm extended in a horizontal direction. He paid me no sort of attention, and taking a seat on a dilapidated sofa at his back, I awaited his leisure. After awhile, without turning around, he said, " Well, sir, what can I do for you ? "

" This letter will tell you, sir," I answered, rising, and placing it, open, on the desk before him. " A glance at it will save your time and mine."

He cast his eye upon the letter; then brushed it aside, and resumed his writing, not having yet shown me the light of his countenance. Then, when he had written, perhaps a short paragraph, he said, " So, you are going to start a new magazine, — do you expect to make any money by it ? "

" No, sir; I expect to lose money."

" You do!" he exclaimed. " Then why do you start it ? "

" Because we have something to say which the country ought to hear."

" You think so, — what is it ? "

" That the Union can't be saved without destroying slavery."

" Bosh! That idea was broached before you were born."

" Yes," I answered, " by Abolitionists who openly advocated disunion. We shall approach the subject from a different standpoint."

" Who are *we ?* " he asked.

" The best literary men in this country, outside of the *Atlantic* circle, with Robert J. Walker as political, and Charles Godfrey Leland as literary, editor."

Until this moment he had kept on writing; now he dropped his pen, turned about on his seat, and scanned me closely, saying, " Robert J. Walker! Why, he's the greatest man we've had since Ben Franklin; and Charley Leland, — if he'll write for us, we will pay him five times as much as you can afford to. Now, take my advice: save your money, and let your men write for the *Tribune*. We can give their ideas a hundred times the circulation that you can."

" I don't know about that, Mr. Greeley. We shall aim to indoctrinate the whole press of the country. I shall start with an exchange list of at least three thousand."

" That's a good idea; but it will cost you money. You can reach the same result, at no expense, through the *Tribune*."

" Allow me to doubt it. We should reach only *Tribune* readers, and the majority of them are in no need of conversion. I should prefer your writing for us, to our people writing for you."

" Well, that might be better, inasmuch as you want new converts, and they'll have to come mainly from the Democratic ranks. But what shall I write? Not politics, — you'll prefer to have that done by Walker."

" Write whatever you please, and long or short, at your pleasure."

" Then, suppose I give you my trip across the Continent, in two or three chapters?"

" That would do very well. Now, what shall we pay you? I'd rather have that understood."

" That is right. I can't afford to write without pay. I am poor, and now that we are all going to the devil, I shall have to look closely after the dimes. Would it be out of the way if I should name $25 an article?"

"Not at all. It is precisely one-half of what I expected to pay. But, Mr. Greeley, please tell me why you think we are all going to the devil?"

Leaning back against his desk, he surveyed me for a moment with a look of childlike helplessness. Then he said, "I am surprised that you ask such a question, when for half a year we have had one continued succession of disasters, — Big Bethel, Bull Run, Wilson's Creek, and now Ball's Bluff, and the loss of Baker, — with nothing to offset but a few insignificant victories in West Virginia, — and all owing to the supineness and stupidity of the people at Washington. Six months! and we worse off than when we began! Why, six weeks of such a man as Jackson would have stamped the whole thing out: and now it must go on till both sections are ruined, and all because we have no sense or energy in the Government. It pains, it grieves me to think of it; for I feel in a measure responsible for it. For you know it is said that but for my action in the convention, Lincoln would not have been nominated. It was a mistake, — the biggest mistake of my life."

"I can't see how it was a mistake, when your choice lay between only two men; of the two, Lincoln is infinitely preferable to Seward. If Seward has his way he will send the country to destruction."

"What do you know about Seward?"

"Nothing personally; however, of my own knowledge I can say that it was he who brought about the call for 75,000 men, when a majority of the Cabinet would have called for 500,000, and also have favored Lincoln's proclaiming freedom to all slaves who should desert their rebel masters. He opposed energetic measures, on the ground that they would close the door of reconciliation with the seceded States."

"Reconciliation!" he exclaimed, "when those fellows have been preparing for this thing for years! But, how did you get the facts about that Cabinet meeting?"

"I can't tell you without a breach of confidence; but you may rely upon the facts. I was in Washington, and had them direct within an hour after the Cabinet adjourned."

"If I had known them at the time I would have unseated Seward," he said, in a regretful way.

"Pardon me, Mr. Greeley, if I doubt your ability to do that. Mr. Lincoln has an overestimate of Seward, — a sort of blind confidence in his judgment. I told him distinctly that if he listened to the advice which Seward, from his extreme timidity, would be sure to give him, he would run the country upon the rocks where no earthly power could save it. Moreover, I told him that if Robert J. Walker had been in Seward's place, the Confederates would not have dared to fire upon Fort Sumter. But all I said had no more effect upon him than water upon a duck's back."

"How was it that you had a chance to say such things to him?"

"He sent to me, through Secretary Cameron, for a confidential interview, and I went to him with Governor Walker; I volunteered nothing, merely answered his or Cameron's questions."

"Are you in intimate relations with Walker?"

"Well, he likes me, and I like him. When I was a boy of about twenty he did me a service that had a decided influence on my subsequent fortunes. We like those to whom we have done a favor; that, I suppose, accounts for his having a kindly feeling for me."

"And what is your impression of Lincoln?"

"I have met him but once. I think him thoroughly honest, and anxious to do his duty."

"And could you not so win his confidence that he would disclose to you, from time to time, his views on certain lines of policy?"

"I don't think I could, for, if I read him aright, he is a very politic man,— one of the hear-all-and-say-nothing sort. It amused me to see how adroitly he drew out of me just what I was most anxious to tell. He could have no motive for confiding his views to me; but with Governor Walker it will be different. Mr. Lincoln has the highest opinion of his judgment, and will naturally seek his advice on all important subjects that may, from time to time, come up. He will be forced to be open with him, and thus I shall know all the inner workings of the administration."

"For Walker will tell you all such things?"

"Of course. He has Mr. Lincoln's permission to do so. Now, Mr. Greeley, you have asked my impressions of Lincoln, and I have told you only the half. He has the reputation of being the frankest of men, but there never was a bigger mistake. With all his apparent transparency, he is as deep as a well. I don't know that you are as deep as Lincoln, but you are asking me a number of questions with some hidden object. Please to tell me what it is before we go any farther."

He took one knee in his two hands, and, swaying himself back and forth, laughed heartily. Soon he said: "Well, I'll tell you; I want to do you and Walker a good turn,— to save you from throwing your money away on that magazine. While we've been talking, I've been thinking how I could do it, and this is my plan: to take Leland upon our staff with a handsome salary; you and I to put our heads together, and get Walker into Seward's place; and, as for yourself, — you to go to Washington as manager for the *Tribune*, — not to write, but to keep posted on inside things, and report everything to me promptly. Your pay should be satisfactory, and the position would, no doubt, be a permanent one, for I think you are a man to tie to."

I answered: "I feel very sensibly the compliment you pay me, Mr. Greeley, but there are difficulties in the way, which, if you will allow me, I will state frankly. No doubt, Leland would be flattered by any such proposal from the *Tribune*, but his heart is in the magazine project, and any salary you might offer him would be no temptation. He has refused to accept any pay whatever from me until the magazine shall have made the money. As to Mr. Walker, if he were in the Cabinet I should feel that the Union would be saved; but I doubt very much if either you or I could influence Mr. Lincoln on the subject; and I do not know that Governor Walker would accept any position in the Government; but, if you please, I will speak to him about it, and then do whatever he may desire. As to myself: since I was twenty I have never held a subordinate position, and I should not work well in double harness with even so kindly a man as you are. You would expect me to devote myself heart and soul to the *Tribune*, and I shouldn't care a hill of beans for it, except as it served my present purpose, which is to set squarely before the American people the enormity of slavery, and the absolute necessity of exterminating it if we are to have a permanent Union. When that is done, 'Othello's occupation will be gone.'"

He answered: "I can understand your position and feelings; but if we can't work together, in what you call double harness, we may be of mutual help to each other, — you can, when it will be allowable, give me prompt information, and, if you start the magazine, I can aid you materially. Suppose you talk this over with Walker, and report to me what he thinks about my suggestion. You may tell him that he can count on me to the extent of my ability."

"I will do that as soon as I can get to Washington; and I have no doubt he will approve of our coöperating with you in all ways in our power."

"I infer from your speaking of showing up slavery that you know something about the South,— is there any chance of a peaceable solution of this question?"

"I have known the South since boyhood, and have been in more or less intimate relations with all classes of its people, — more particularly with the producers. The people would be friendly enough with us but for their leaders. *They* are bent upon separation, that they may control and perpetuate slavery. We can, I think, have no peace now without disunion."

"Then had we better not let them go, and save all this bloodshed and waste of property? Seward, as you say, has made Lincoln miss our only opportunity; and shall we not be forced to let them go at last? I have thought a good deal on the subject, and I'm not able yet to see how twenty millions, disunited, accustomed only to peaceful pursuits, and fighting on the outside of a circle, can subdue ten millions, united, trained to arms, and fighting on the inside of the circle. I don't know of such a thing being ever done in history. Do you?"

"No, I do not, and still I firmly believe it will be done, and we shall yet be a great, united, and free people. Shall I tell you why? and will you allow me to be a little personal?"

"Certainly, be as personal as you please. I'm not thin-skinned, though I never did like unjust censure."

"I shall not tread upon your corns; I'll merely give you a little of your own history. You were a homespun boy, born among the stony hills of New Hampshire, but when only six years old you announced your intention to print a newspaper, — which shows that the thing was born in you. At the age of eleven you tried to get into a printing-office. They rejected you because of your youth, but at fourteen you succeeded, and then went to work, night and day, to perfect yourself as a printer. I need not speak of your subsequent career, — I only wish to refer to your life-purpose, so early formed and persistently followed in the face of every discouragement, until going on, step by step, you, twenty years ago, on a thousand dollars borrowed capital, started the *Tribune*. Then came out what was in you, — a lofty purpose to educate and elevate the American people, and in particular the working classes. And how wonderfully you have succeeded! Your name is a household word everywhere in this country, and you are known all over Europe. Your thoughts are pondered daily by a million of people. No king upon his throne ever wielded the power that you do; and your power has been always for good; your cry, 'Land for the landless,' passed the 'Homestead Bill,' and gave homes to thousands, — I don't know but to millions; and your 'Go West, young man,' has filled a vast territory with a hardy, industrious population who are now the glory, and will soon wield the power, of this great nation. I want to speak within bounds, but I fail to find in all history any single man who has done so much, by his unaided effort, in his own lifetime, for the uplifting of the race as you have."

He had sat through the whole of this, his back resting against his desk, his hands clasped about his knee, looking at me intently; but now his lips quivered, and a mist came into his eyes; but he said nothing, and I went on:

"Now, what would you think of the man who, when a tow-shirted boy, formed that high purpose, and, through nearly forty years of the hardest kind of struggle, pursued it till he had built up this great beneficent power called the *Tribune*, — what would you think of him if he should suddenly come down here some morning, close his doors, put up his shutters, throw his type out of the windows, and tell the country to go to the devil?"

He laughed as he said: "The thing is unthinkable, — inconceivable."

"Of course it is; and to me it is inconceivable that God has been at work for nearly four hundred years, building up this country, just for the pleasure of knocking it to pieces. I do not think he is a bigger fool than Horace Greeley."

"Probably not," he said, taking my hand as I rose to go, "and if I didn't feel the force of your argument I should be an atheist. Good-by. Don't fail to report to me when you have seen Walker."

CHAPTER V.

THE CONCEPTION OF THE EMANCIPATION PROCLAMATION.

I WAS not able to again visit Washington till the latter part of November, 1861, when public excitement was at its height over the *Trent* affair. I then related to Mr. Walker my interview with Horace Greeley, to which he listened with interest, saying, at the close: "I think a good understanding with Mr. Greeley is very important: we can keep him from going off upon tangents, and I can give you, from time to time, information that will be of value to him. But you will need to be discreet, and never disclose anything that might do harm if published. Greeley is too ready to take the public into his confidence. To us he can be of great service by helping you to make the magazine known, and by giving me the use of his columns on special occasions. Every way the arrangement will be admirable. May I speak of it in confidence to Mr. Lincoln?"

I assented to this, and at once he sent a note to the President asking at what hour we could have an interview. The messenger soon returned, with a narrow slip of paper, addressed to "His Highmightyness, Governor Walker, late of Kansas Territory." On it was written in pencil: "I shall be glad to see you both, — come at 3 P.M. A. L."

While the man was away, I said to Mr. Walker: "Now, what do you say to Greeley's suggestion about your being made a Cabinet minister?"

"I have told Mr. Lincoln that it would not be wise. I will tell you about it, but what I say must be in the strictest confidence. Mr. Lincoln broached the subject to me, a few days after the battle of Bull Run, something in this manner : 'Governor,' he said, 'do you remember that your Yankee friend said that if you had been in my Cabinet, the rebels would never have dared to fire upon Fort Sumter; and that they never would have confidence in me so long as Seward was my adviser?'

"I said I remembered it very well, and then he asked: 'Don't you think that he was about right?'

"To that I answered that you overestimated me, — always had, — but that you correctly stated the Southern opinion of Mr. Seward. Then he said : 'Well, what would you say to my repeating his remarks to Seward, laying stress upon the point your friend made, that there never can be a reconciliation with the South while he is in my Cabinet? Then, if he should be patriotic enough to resign, would you take his place?'

"I told Mr. Lincoln promptly that I thought it would not be wise to do so. That things had changed, — the opportunity had passed for conciliating the Southern people; that now it was war, till one or the other side was exhausted; that he needed all the strength he had, or could get, at the North; and that Mr. Seward had a large following, and however he might personally feel about being cashiered, his friends would certainly object to it and fall away from a zealous support of the Government. But I added that while I should urgently advise him to avoid a rupture with Mr. Seward, I was ready to serve him and the country in the position suggested or otherwise; but that I could be of most use in a private capacity, — acting as I do now as special adviser to Mr. Chase in the management of the Treasury Department. All now hinges on a proper conduct of the finances. It is that which may soon send me to Europe."

"I think you have acted both patriotically and wisely; but," I added, "speaking of Seward reminds me to tell you that Leland — who has gone into the magazine project with genuine enthusiasm — has arranged with Oakey Hall for a series of articles to be called 'Cabinet Sessions,' the papers to represent the imaginary sittings of the Cabinet, and to report the discussions, and give the individual views of the various members on all important subjects as they arise, — such, for instance, as this *Trent* affair. Seward is a warm friend of Mr. Hall, and he has promised to give him, from time to time, the facts on which to build the articles. It strikes me they would be of value as serving to show that the magazine has a sort of semi-official character. The people now are greedy for reliable information as to the purposes of the Government."

"Yes, that is so," he answered, "but the papers should be reliable; and are you sure that Seward might not mislead you?"

"I might send you the proofs, — that would guard against any false diplomacy."

"You had better do that," he said; "and don't pay too much for the articles, for I could do them myself."

"They will cost nothing. Leland has offered Mr. Hall pay, and he has peremptorily declined it. Hall is very much in earnest, and a thorough gentleman."

"That will do; but be sure to send me the proofs, for it just now occurs to me that Seward may conceive an ill will towards me. I do not know it, but I strongly suspect that Mr. Lincoln has rapped him over the knuckles on two or three occasions lately, and Seward may conclude that I am the cause of his waning influence. He is disposed to have his own way,—he considers himself the administration, and I think Mr. Lincoln has been obliged to give him a back seat. Now, who have you got to write your sketches of the South? They should be well done, and show that you know what you are talking about."

I answered, "Richard B. Kimball, who wrote that strong serial in the *Knickerbocker*. He has lived in Texas; was president of the Galveston and Houston Railroad, and founded a town on the Brazos River."

"He ought to be competent; but scan everything closely, and whenever you are in doubt about a manuscript, send it to me. Never forget that you have set out to educate the people on a subject that is vital to them and the country. Pardon me, if my tone is somewhat dictatorial. I want you to succeed, and you always seem to me that young fellow who came to me more than twenty years ago."

"Never mind the tone; I am not as old, nor as wise, as you are, and never shall be."

Among public men, I never knew one so punctual to appointment as Robert J. Walker. He used to say that the hours and half-hours, which most men throw away, through a lack of promptness, would make them all rich; for time is money.

The clocks were striking three when we were ushered into Mr. Lincoln's private room at the White House. He received Mr. Walker with a cordial hand-shake and "I'm glad to see you, Governor." To me he said: "I scarcely thought you'd come again,—I've profited so little by your suggestions."

"That matters not, Mr. Lincoln," I replied. "You know it is said there is a divinity that shapes our ends; if so, whatever is, is right."

"But whatever has been, since you were here, has not been right,— it's been all wrong. I am glad that you and the Governor haven't lost heart, and are stripping for the fight. You still think it will be a long one?"

"I do, sir," I replied, "and that its issue will largely depend upon the war spirit being kept up at the North. I shall do my part to that end, for I think that war is the only way to a satisfactory settlement."

Mr. Walker then remarked: "We will detain you, Mr. President, for but a few moments. Mr. Gilmore has had an interview with Horace Greeley, and I've told him he had better relate it to you."

"Go on, Mr. Gilmore," responded Mr. Lincoln. "Tell me how Horace feels."

I then detailed the interview, and at the close Mr. Lincoln said, "It strikes me this is important. What do you think, Governor?"

"I think it is, sir, highly important; and with your permission I'll write a note to Mr. Gilmore, approving of the arrangement, and saying I will keep him informed on all important matters, with liberty to communicate them to Mr. Greeley. This would be for him to show to Greeley."

"That would be well," said Mr. Lincoln; "and suppose that I should write a letter to you suggesting your note to Gilmore? That would show Greeley that you were acting with my knowledge and approval."

"That would be better yet; and let me suggest that you do it now, so Mr. Gilmore can take them both with him when he goes home to-night."

"That's wise — that's wise," said Mr. Lincoln. "It will give Greeley absolute confidence in Gilmore." Saying this, he turned about to his desk, and after awhile read to us the following letter:

Dear Governor: — I have thought over the interview which Mr. Gilmore has had with Mr. Greeley, and the proposal that Greeley has made to Gilmore, namely, that he (Gilmore) shall communicate to him (Greeley) all that he learns from you of the inner workings of the administration, in return for his (Greeley's) giving such aid as he can to the new magazine, and allowing you (Walker) from time to time the use of his (Greeley's) columns when it is desirable to feel of, or forestall, public opinion on important subjects. The arrangement meets my unqualified approval, and I shall further it to the extent of my ability, by opening to you — as I do now — fully the policy of the Government, — its present views and future intentions when formed, — giving you permission to communicate them to Gilmore for Greeley; and in case you go to Europe I will give these things direct to Gilmore. But all this must be on the express and explicit understanding that the fact of these communications coming from me shall be absolutely confidential, — not to be disclosed by Greeley to his nearest friend, or to any of his subordinates. He will be, in effect, my mouthpiece, but I must not be known to be the speaker.

I need not tell you that I have the highest confidence in Mr. Greeley. He is a great power. Having him firmly behind me will be as helpful to me as an army of one hundred thousand men. That he has ever kicked the traces has been owing to his not being fully informed. Tell Gilmore to say to him that, if he ever objects to my policy, I shall be glad to have him state to me his views frankly and fully. I shall adopt his if I can. If I cannot, I will at least tell him why. He and I should stand together, and let no minor differences come between us; for we both seek one end, which is the saving of our country. Now, Governor, this is a longer letter than I have written in a month, — longer than I would have written for any other man than Horace Greeley.

Your friend, truly,

ABRAHAM LINCOLN.

November 21, 1861.

P. S. — The sooner Gilmore sees Greeley, the better, as you may before long think it wise to ventilate our policy on the *Trent* affair.

When Mr. Lincoln had finished reading the foregoing, he said, " Now, Governor, will that do ? "

" It is admirable, Mr. Lincoln," answered Mr. Walker. " You are the ablest diplomatist I ever knew."

" I beg your pardon, — I can't hold a candle to one Robert J. Walker. Is not that so, Mr. Gilmore ? "

" I'd rather not say, Mr. Lincoln, for I want to get into your good graces; but I will tell you what Horace Greeley thinks of Mr. Walker. He told me that he was the greatest man we've had since Ben Franklin."

" Greeley is right," said Mr. Lincoln. " The country doesn't know half his worth or ability."

That subject being disposed of, Mr. Lincoln alluded to the *Trent* affair, and asked if I had observed, from our exchanges, that the war feeling extended throughout the country.

I told him that if the newspapers were a criterion of popular sentiment, it extended everywhere; and undoubtedly the popular feeling was intensely bitter towards England.

" You are a sensible man," he said. " You don't share this feeling, or, if you do, you wouldn't just now act upon it."

" I don't like the English aristocracy, sir; I never did. But I think it would be unfortunate to have a serious quarrel with England at present, for doubtless she and France would at once acknowledge the independence of the South. If that should be done, would it not so dispirit the North that the people would fail to give you the proper support ? "

" Very likely it would have a discouraging effect. I see what you mean, — you think this *Trent* affair will give Palmerston the pretext he wants. But has not the Governor told you the course he advises me to take to checkmate that gentleman ? "

"He has not, — we have not discussed the subject."

"Then I'll tell you, in confidence, what it is: To disavow the action of Captain Wilkes, give up Mason and Slidell, and say to Palmerston that we do it in accord with the principle on which we fought the War of 1812, — a denial of the right of search. To be ahead of them, Seward has already written Minister Adams to that effect, and instructed him to say to Earl Russell that we are merely waiting the British demand for the Confederate gentlemen. This will probably stave off France and England for the present. They will, doubtless, soon seek some other pretext; if they should, the Governor and I have hit upon a plan that will keep their hands off for all time to come. But that we shall use only as the very last resort."

The Governor then said, "Mr. President, would it not do to let Mr. Gilmore know the course you have decided upon? He is bent upon going into an unprofitable enterprise, and if he knew your intentions he might decide to save his time and money."

"But, Governor," said Mr. Lincoln, "his enterprise is likely to serve our purpose. However, it seems but fair that he should know our intentions; then he will lose his money with his eyes open. But, Mr. Gilmore, this thing is known to only the Governor and myself, and if it should leak out prematurely, it might detract from its effect on the country, and give me no end of embarrassment. The Governor says you are water-tight; but can we trust you absolutely?"

"You can, sir, if you don't tell me your plan. If the plan is of prime importance I prefer not to know it; for, should some one else let it out, you couldn't then shake your brown locks at me, and say I did it."

He uttered a quiet, pleasant laugh as he said, "You

CONCEPTION OF EMANCIPATION. 57

ought to know Shakespeare better; but I'll tell you the plan, for I'd like to know how it strikes a man of average intellect and intelligence. You'll be a criterion of how it would take with the country."

It was now my turn to laugh, and I did so, saying, "You remind me of Judge Edmonds, who, whenever he writes a brief, or an opinion on some knotty or intricate legal point, always calls his daughter — who is entirely ignorant of law — into his room, saying, 'I want to read this to you, for if you can understand it, any one can.'

"Well," said Mr. Lincoln, "I think you can understand my policy. When Wilkes, in an excess of zeal, took those Southern gentlemen out of a British vessel, it occurred to me at once that he had done exactly what England and France wanted, — given them a pretext for acknowledging the Confederacy, and opening its ports for England to get its cotton, France the tobacco it has stored at Richmond. I lay awake all night, contriving how to get out of the scrape without loss of national dignity. Seward was for fight, and went so far as to concoct a savage despatch to Adams; but I told him that one war at a time was enough, and sent for the Governor. He reminded me that we fought the War of 1812 in denial of the right of search, and that in this *Trent* affair we had violated our own principles. Then my course was as clear as noonday. I could disown the act of Wilkes with perfect consistency. Until the Governor gave me that idea I could see no way out of the difficulty, but by an open avowal that the real issue between the North and the South was slavery, and by issuing an immediate proclamation declaring free every slave in the States now in rebellion. Of course, the proclamation, so far as the South is concerned, would be a Pope's bull against the comet, — inoperative except within the lines of our armies, — but it would tie the hands of England, for no British Government could stand for a day, that sided with the slave-owners after the issue between slavery and freedom had been distinctly stated. To checkmate England would be to checkmate France, for Louis Napoleon would not dare to take a single step without Palmerston. Then we could say, ' We are fighting for the rights of man against a slave-driving oligarchy that would rivet chains upon unborn millions;' and on that platform the whole civilized world — except the slaveholders and the copperheads — would have been with us."

"You certainly," I said, "would have created a moral force that would ostracize the Confederacy among civilized nations. Why have you not issued the proclamation?"

"I'll tell you," he replied, "and this is what you are to keep absolutely confidential. It is because the Governor has opposed it. I got so enamored of the idea, from intently brooding upon it, that I was disposed to take the bull by the horns and make the proclamation at once, at the same time that I disavowed the blunder of Wilkes, but the Governor said: ' You must not do it. It would be premature. You don't know how it would affect the North. Keep this in reserve; the disavowal of Wilkes will serve your present purpose.' He made a speech on the occasion, and it impressed me so strongly that I can repeat every word of it. He said: ' Mr. President, such a proclamation issued now, pending a settlement of the *Trent* affair, will lose all its moral force. Palmerston and the English aristocrats will infer that we see ourselves on the brink of ruin, and are playing our last card. I know Palmerston personally, — he is astute, clear-sighted, but pig-headed and tenacious as his own bulldog. He would say to his Cabinet: "This is merely a Yankee trick, and any fool can see through it.

They are coming the moral dodge,—as if the world was governed by moral ideas. You and I, gentlemen, know better. It is governed by British cannon and British common sense, and — damn the Yankees, damn the niggers — those Southerners are gentlemen, and we will recognize them at the first favorable opportunity." This, Mr. Lincoln, is the view that Palmerston would take of such a proclamation. We must show him a bold front. The only argument he can understand is brute force. First get this *Trent* affair out of your way, and then come out squarely for the right, giving no more heed to Palmerston and that bogus Bonaparte than if they were not in existence. The negro must be freed; we can have no permanent peace until it is done. And you will have to do it; but first make sure that you have the North behind you!' Now, Governor, have I reported you correctly?"

"I recognize my ideas," said Mr. Walker. "But I was not aware that my tone was quite so dictatorial."

"You were simply in earnest; it's a way you have which I don't at all object to. Now, Mr. Gilmore, I am holding back a proclamation of emancipation for such an emergency. How do you think one would be received at the North?"

I answered: "If one were issued to prevent the interference of England, or any other foreign power, I think it would meet with universal approval; if issued without such a necessity, and merely as a humanitarian measure, I question if it would have much popular support. You told me eight months ago that, after thirty years of agitation, the Abolitionists were merely a corporal's guard, and not a party; and you were right. The Abolitionists have failed to get converts because they have advocated disunion; you have got soldiers because you were trying to save the Union.

A majority in the North would welcome an emancipation proclamation, if they were fully convinced that the Union could not be saved without destroying slavery. Convince them of that, and you will be the saviour of the country."

"You are going to help me do that by appealing, the Governor says, to the spirit of nationality among the people. Now, Mr. Gilmore, you know if such a proclamation should once be issued, we should have to stand by it, and refuse any settlement with the South that did not recognize the freedom of the slaves. Is the negro fit for freedom?"

"That depends, Mr. Lincoln, on what you consider fitness. If you ask if he would be self-supporting, I should answer that he had supported his master, and could undoubtedly support himself; if you ask if he is fit to have the suffrage, or to govern the smallest community of even his own color, I should say most decidedly that he is not, — confining the remark to the vast majority of the present slaves. I would give the negro freedom, — let him own his own body and his own soul, — but not allow him to control the bodies and souls of other men."

"But in this country a man is not a man unless he has the right to vote."

"I admit that; but we do not give the suffrage to minors, and some of the best-governed States deny it to all who cannot read their Constitution. The great majority of the slaves are merely children, and scarcely one in a thousand can read and write. You will have to give them freedom; but if you couple suffrage with it, you will sow a crop of dragon's teeth in the South that will yield no end of trouble. It will produce antagonism between the races. In some sections the negro is in the majority, and no white man will submit to the domination of the black. The fear that it may be coming is what makes the Southern rank and file fight us so desperately."

"Well," remarked Mr. Lincoln, "we will manage to get across that stream if we ever come to it. Speaking of dragon's teeth, I think they were sown when the first cargo of negroes was brought into Jamestown in 1620. You believe in Providence, — will you tell me why he allowed the African to be made a slave in this country?"

"I believe in Providence, Mr. Lincoln, because I read history, and see one far-reaching, all-embracing plan running through it, that can have emanated from only an overruling mind that has all things in control; but I am not a member of the Almighty's Cabinet, and cannot always perceive the reason for some of his doings. I can put facts together, and draw conclusions; but I cannot wholly grasp a plan that stretches across a thousand centuries. I hope to solve some problems when I get to the other side of Jordan. It is very certain that if I am then alive and well, I shall ask some questions."

Mr. Lincoln laughed, saying: "Very likely, if you have managed to keep out of the fire. But you needn't wait that long to answer my question, — you must have questioned why a Benevolent Being has allowed the blacks to exist here in abject servitude for now two hundred and forty years."

"I have, and the question always staggered me until I saw some of Lamar's recent importations. They were fresh from the jungles of Africa, — about nine-tenths animal, and one-tenth human being. I was tempted to buy one, and send him to Darwin as the 'missing link' that scientists have so long been in search of. They showed me what the American negro had risen from, and then I saw the wisdom of Providence in permitting African slavery. It was to elevate and Christianize the race so it might enter the future life at a far higher level than it would have taken had it gone there from its native Africa. From that view-point, slavery has been an unspeakable blessing to the negro; and I take it that God has both worlds in view when he shapes the destiny of men and nations. He allowed slavery to benefit the blacks; he has permitted it to continue until it has demoralized the whites, and they would make it universal; and now he is bringing it to an end to save both whites and blacks. And the end is coming in the same blood and struggle that have marked every forward step in human progress."

"There are four millions of blacks here,—there are far more in Africa. Are they to be left in their low-down, animal condition?"

"I think not. Speke and Grant, Baker and Livingstone have already opened the door of that continent, and before many years the white man will go there with the spelling-book, the railroad, and the telegraph, and ere long 'Ethiopia will stretch out her hands unto God.' But those people will not reach civilization through the purgatory of slavery. They will come to it owning their own bodies and their own souls, and I suspect their souls are of as much real account as ours. The Captain of the Lord's Host has planned this war, Mr. Lincoln, and so I have faith in the end, and I believe you will do your part in it like a true soldier."

"I shall try to," he said, "God being my helper. Now, good-by. Come to see me whenever you are in Washington."

I called upon Mr. Greeley on the following afternoon, and found him, as usual, at his desk writing. He turned around as I entered, and, without rising, held out his hand, saying, "I'm glad to see you. Have you been to Washington?"

"Yes, sir," I answered, "and I'll detain you but a few moments. Here are a couple of letters that will tell you the whole story."

He glanced over them, and then re-read that from Mr. Lincoln, carefully, his face beaming with a simple joyousness. Then he said: "He is a wonderful man,—wonderful. I never can harbor a thought against him, except when I keep away from him. You must let me keep this letter."

"I doubt if I can, Mr. Greeley. You notice what he says about the arrangement being confidential. Of course it would come out if the letter were seen by any one."

"It shall not be seen. I want it just to look at when I am downhearted. The approval of such a man is worth having."

"Then, sir, keep it until I again see Mr. Lincoln. If he objects, I shall have to reclaim it. I propose to be absolutely frank with you, Mr. Greeley; that and the other letter were written to give you confidence in me, and to assure you that they would strictly keep their part of the agreement."

"So I understand it; and about this *Trent* affair. Did the Governor tell you what their intentions are?"

"No, but Mr. Lincoln did in the Governor's presence."

I then repeated to him, word for word, what the President had said about it, when he remarked: "Those are precisely my views. Shall I state them in the *Tribune*, omitting the intentions of the Government?"

"I would suggest that you wait until I hear from Mr. Walker."

"Very well. What does Walker say as to his being Secretary of State?"

"That it would not be wise, — that he can serve the country better in a private capacity, just as you do. But I infer, from what the Governor said, that Seward's influence is waning with Lincoln; Walker, I know, he regards very highly."

"Thank God for that, — it will prevent any evil Seward might do. And you, — are you resolved to go on with your money-spending adventure?"

"Yes, until the money gives out."

"When it does, come to me, and I'll make a berth for you."

CHAPTER VI.

THE GENESIS OF THE BOOK "AMONG THE PINES."

It was late in November, 1861, and to conform to the custom of the periodical trade the January number of the new magazine had to be in the hands of the public by the middle of December. All of it was in type and ready to be printed except the first of a series of Southern sketches that had been promised by Richard B. Kimball, when one morning that gentleman entered my private office and announced to me that he could not possibly have his article ready for our first number. His mind had been engrossed with some important negotiations; and, though he had tried, he had not been able to get into the mood for sketch-writing. I remonstrated with him, told him the sketch was a positive necessity, that the magazine without it would be the play of Hamlet with Hamlet omitted; but it was all to no avail, his mental machinery, he said, was out of gear, and to make it work was impossible.

Sitting with me at the time was Mrs. Caroline M. Kirkland, the distinguished woman who was the originator and efficient manager of the great "Sanitary Commission," of which Dr. Henry W. Bellows was president. I had been fortunate enough to secure her as a contributor, and having heard the conversation, she said: "Pardon me, but why don't you write the sketch yourself? You know the South better than Mr. Kimball. He is acquainted with but one of the States; you know them all."

"But," I replied, "I am not a magazine writer. Besides, I don't know what to say, — where to begin or to end."

"Begin anywhere, — tell some of those stories about the South that you've told to me; your trip up the Waccamaw would do to commence with, — that time you swam the river with a horse and wagon, and slept all night in a room with a grass widow and her beautiful daughter, whose only garment was a linsey gown. Describe that family, — you couldn't better illustrate the ruinous influence of slavery upon the Southern whites. Write out the story just as you have told it to me, and I will throw it into shape so it will pass muster. Now do this. You can make your knowledge of service to the country, — if you can't shoulder a musket, you can blow a bugle."

I acted on her suggestion, and the letter which she subsequently wrote me, thanking God for having put it into her head to suggest to me the writing of "Among the Pines," is now preserved in the historical library of the Johns Hopkins University. She was one of those grand women who are the glory of our country.

Two mornings after the foregoing interview I handed to Mr. Leland the sketch I had written. In a short time he came into my room with the manuscript, saying, "This is admirable, — just what we want."

"I am glad you like it," I replied. "I'll take it at once to Mrs. Kirkland, and have her put it into shape."

"No, you won't," he said, coolly thrusting the manuscript into his pocket. "And to make sure of that, I'll take it myself to the printer."

In due time the initial number of the magazine was issued, and about one-third of an edition of 10,000 copies, with "Please exchange" stamped upon each, was sent to the leading newspapers throughout the North. Soon returns began to come in, and, to my inexpressible delight, I observed that we were already making an impression. Some of the ablest journals, both East and West, commented favorably upon Leland's article, approving of his position, and several of them quoted my sketch entire, — among them the *Weekly Tribune*, — giving credit to the *Continental Monthly*, which was the best sort of an advertisement.

In great glee I wrote Mr. Walker: "Glory hallelujah! Our little leaven will soon leaven the whole lump, and every Northern man will turn into a musket."

He replied: "I am rejoiced at your success, and the magazine deserves it. The article on 'The Situation' (which I suppose is Leland's) is admirable. Horace Greeley's is good. 'Among the Pines' is excellent. I see that it is the first of a series. I like the ring of that man; hold on to him. The article on the 'Slave Trade in New York' is timely; but the best thing in the magazine is that 'Universal Cotton-gin' in the Editor's Table. The writer must know Jeff Davis. His description of him is perfect, and his rendering of Davis's stilted talk is admirable:

> "'A haggard man of sallow hue,
> Upon his nose the goggles blue,
> And in his cart a model U-
> Niversal Nigger Cotton-gin.'

"I read it last night to a dinner-party of about twenty, — mostly Senators and Representatives, — and they literally roared with laughter, as did Mr. Lincoln when he called my attention to it the other morning. He says he will pay that man's fare if he'll come on and spend an evening with him. Keep the writer at that sort of work, — such things are very effective. By the way, Mr. Lincoln suggests that it had better not be known just yet that I feel any special interest in the magazine. So, if you have told Leland, ask him to say nothing; also Horace Greeley, — the reason I leave you to guess. Please read the enclosed to Greeley, and write me what he says."

The "enclosed" was a memorandum of what had best be said in the *Tribune* on some matter of public interest; but what it was I cannot now remember, and I did not retain the manuscript. I replied to Mr. Walker that Greeley would follow his suggestion, and that I had written the "Cotton-gin," but must decline Mr. Lincoln's invitation on conscientious grounds, — not thinking that at the present price of potatoes he could afford to be so lavish on a limited salary.

The circulation of the *Continental* increased monthly, and it was in reality a good magazine, — made so by the unwearied zeal of Charles G. Leland, and the ability displayed by its contributors. Among its articles none pleased me more than several from my former business partner, Mr. Frederic Kidder, of Boston; and none displayed more ability than two contributed by A. Oakey Hall, then District Attorney, and subsequently Mayor of New York during the time of the "Tweed ring," when he became the victim of scoundrels. This for a moment cast a shadow upon his name; but through it all his friends knew — what has since been proved — that a more upright, incorruptible man, or a purer, more disinterested patriot than he never held office in this country.

Oakey Hall's first article was on Mr. Seward's recent diplomacy; his second was the first of the projected "Cabinet Session" series, for which Mr. Seward was to furnish the facts to be written out by Mr. Hall. This last article excited great public interest, and I looked eagerly for the second of the series. The manuscript not arriving in due time, Mr. Leland wrote Mr. Hall urging its prompt delivery. The *data* had not been forwarded by Mr. Seward, and Mr. Hall informed him of Mr. Leland's inquiry. The answer, which came by due course of mail, was, "Damn Leland and the *Continental;*" which illustrates the wisdom of not counting one's chickens until they are hatched. Leland had suggested to me that an announcement of the series might aid the circulation of the magazine; but I had replied: "No, no! The Indian remarked that the white man is uncertain, and the nigger will steal."

Despite the disfavor of Mr. Seward, the *Continental* was a success, — not in a money way, but in a higher field where money is counted as dross, and men shed their blood freely for a principle. It roused the country to a sense of the gravity of the situation. I never took up one of our exchanges — and I watched them narrowly — but I saw some of its thoughts filtered through the pen of some local editor, or uttered in the bugle tones of Charles Godfrey Leland. It was a great force in the awakening of the country. I can say this with no sham expression of modesty, for though I footed its bills, Leland was the *Continental Monthly.*

Leland was an all-accomplished literary man, with a knowledge absolutely encyclopædic, and so fully at command that he could write on any ordinary subject at a moment's notice. He wrote verse with as much facility as he did prose. His "Cavalry Song," which stirred the blood of the country like the peals of a bugle, was dashed off at a single sitting; and I have known him to write ten or twenty lines of perfect rhyme, to fill a vacant space, while the messenger who brought the proof was in waiting. He spoke a number of modern languages, and

Ralph Waldo Emerson once told me that he was the best German scholar in this country. But he was more than a scholar or a mere literary man. He was a large-hearted, large-minded lover of his country; and he loved it, not simply because he was born in it, but because he believed it to be the chosen nursery of freedom, where the working-man is to come into his rights, and be given the means to develop himself up to what nature has intended him. Born the son of a rich man, his strongest sympathies were with the poor. It is an instinct of human nature to feel for the "under dog." This with most men is an inactive sentiment; with Leland it was an active principle, and it led him to work, and, if occasion required, to fight, for the less fortunate, of whatever race or nationality. This he showed during the French Revolution of 1848, when, a young student in Paris, he fought, stripped to the waist, a red bandanna about his head, all day in defence of one of the barricades. When the fight was over, he called, at the head of a delegation of workingmen, on the Lamartine Government; and I know of nothing more picturesque than the cartoon which was then made of him and plastered upon nearly every wall in Paris. He was a magnificent character and a most lovable man. I have known few, very few, for whom I have conceived so strong and abiding an affection; and I still count it among the fortunate things of my life that he was for about two years my almost daily associate.

About May, 1862, the increasing business of the new magazine demanding more attention to details than I cared to give it, I arranged with George P. Putnam, the well-known publisher, to attend to its business, through Mr. Charles T. Evans, his agent for managing the *Rebellion Record*, and now, I think, Secretary of the Baptist Publication Society. Accordingly my headquarters were removed to his establishment in Broadway, and there, one morning, Richard B. Kimball, who was then writing for the *Continental* his novel, "Was He Successful," came into my room, having in his hand the magazine which contained my description of a negro funeral. He was one of the very few who knew that I was the writer of the series of papers entitled "Among the Pines," and now he said to me: "You must finish these sketches for book publication. They will take with the public, — my publisher, Carleton, would be glad to publish them."

Acting on this suggestion, I got together the sketches, so far as published, and called upon Mr. Carleton, offering to have the work completed, and to accept for it the usual royalty of ten per cent., *after* he had realized enough from sales to reimburse him for the cost of the stereotype plates. He took the copies of the magazine for examination, and in a few days reported to me that "Paper is high, times are dull, and people won't buy books when things look so squally," — in short, he declined the book in the usual style, "with thanks," and I went back to my office a "rejected author," but congratulating myself that Carleton did not know that I had written the book.

At the office I told Mr. Evans that we must dismiss all thought of book publication. In reply, he said, "I have had an estimate made on the cost of the plates and printing, and, with paper at twenty-five cents a pound, we can get out an edition of two thousand for $600. Let me publish it in your name."

"No, no," I said, "I am behind on the magazine nearly $3,000, and, even now, am losing $300 a month. I can't go into any side speculations."

"But you will consent, if I sell in advance a thousand

copies for enough to cover the cost of the whole edition?"

"Of course I will; and as a reward of merit, and to send your name down to future generations, I will have it placed on the title-page."

On the following day he reported to me that he had sold to Mr. M. Doolady, a prominent bookseller, whom he described as a "dyed-in-the-wool Democrat of the Copperhead variety," one thousand copies of a 12mo book, to be called "Among the Pines." The price would cover the disbursements on an edition of two thousand, and that same day the two-thirds of the work already written was sent to a printing-house to be stereotyped.

The book was kindly received by the critics. In the *Tribune* was a long and laudatory notice, though neither Mr. George Ripley (the literary editor) nor Horace Greeley knew me to be its author. During the first thirty days, the edition of two thousand copies was disposed of, and then the orders began to pour in like a rushing stream, fifty, one hundred, and even two hundred, in a day, until, by the end of the second thirty days, they had run up, if I remember aright, to over nine thousand copies. As, from time to time, Mr. Evans said to me, "We need to print another thousand," I answered, "Go ahead, I have a few dollars in bank; enough to last until collections come in."

But collections did not come in. The books had been sent to the ends of the country, and sold for cash; but cash meant, at that time, thirty or sixty, or even ninety days; and by the latter period, from the constant stream of orders, I was scudding under bare poles, — that is, with a bank account leaner than Pharaoh's lean kine, and with the printer's bill for the *Continental* coming due within a fortnight. "This will never do," I said to Mr. Evans. "Tell Putnam he must take the book."

"He can't," he answered; "he has not yet settled with his creditors. More than that, he can't command the money."

"Then the book must stop,—I won't be bothered with cramped finances."

"That would be a pity," said Mr. Evans. "Rather than do that you'd better go to Carleton."

I knew Mr. Carleton well, and thus needed no special business as an excuse for strolling into his establishment; but having in mind his refusal of the book, I intended that any overture for its publication should come from him, and not from me. He did not at once observe my entrance, but, as soon as he did, he came to where I was examining the new books upon his counter, and taking my hand, said, "What a dunce I was, not to have taken that book, 'Among the Pines.'"

"Not a dunce, Carleton," I answered, "you simply made a mistake. However, it is not too late to remedy it, if you are so disposed; for the book has made me poorer than a church mouse."

"Is that so,— do you own the plates?"

On my answering in the affirmative, he said, "Well, I'll take at cost what unfinished stock you have on hand; let you have what money you want, and pay you a royalty of twenty-five per cent."

My answer was, "Very well. It is a bargain."

In half an hour the contract was signed, and then he said, "What money shall I give you?"

"A thousand dollars will do," I answered; but on looking at the check which he handed me, I noticed it was for two thousand.

An account which is now before me shows that during the succeeding six months Mr. Carleton paid me, for royalty on that book, forty-seven hundred and fifty dollars. My total profits upon it were something over thirteen thousand; and they were nearly as much on another book, "My Southern Friends," which also grew out of the *Continental*. My total loss upon the magazine was sixty-three hundred dollars, and all my publishing friends had predicted it would be twenty thousand. I went into the enterprise counting upon a loss; but having "cast my bread upon the waters," it returned to me "after many days."

CHAPTER VII.

THE EMANCIPATION PROCLAMATION.

THE book "Among the Pines" was published in June, 1862, and as soon as it was issued I forwarded a dozen copies of it to Robert J. Walker; and being in Washington in the August following, he told me that he had given a copy to Mr. Lincoln, who had read it, and desired to talk with me about it. A messenger was then sent to the White House, and he soon returned with the request that we would call there at half past two. Meanwhile, Mr. Walker had said to me: "I have good news for you, but it must be strictly confidential, — the Emancipation Proclamation is decided upon."

"That *is* good news," I answered. "But why have you not let me know of it? It would have saved all the recent discontent of Mr. Greeley. When was it decided on?"

"When McClellan abandoned the siege of Richmond, and entrenched himself on the James River. On the 3d of July he telegraphed to the War Department that he had not over 50,000 men left with their colors, and asked for 100,000 more. Mr. Lincoln then decided to go down to Harrison's Landing to ascertain what had become of the magnificent army of 160,000 which McClellan had taken to the Peninsula. McClellan had previously written the President that any expression of radical views upon slavery would rapidly disintegrate our armies, and during this visit he plied him with arguments to the same effect. They had no other result than to make Mr. Lincoln think more and more seriously upon the subject; and on his return he said to me, 'We are beaten — we must change our tactics. I think the time has about come to strike that blow against slavery.' I told him I agreed with him, and that I thought it would turn the tide. Two days later he handed me his first draft of an Emancipation Proclamation. There was not a word or a line in it to alter, and I suggested its being at once submitted to the Cabinet, and published to the country. Mr. Lincoln delayed a few days to give fuller consideration to some features of the document, and then read it to his Cabinet. All the members were present, and all approved of it; but Mr. Seward objected to its immediate publication. He thought that given out in the midst of our present disasters, it would seem a cry of despair, a confession of the utter exhaustion of the Government; and he advised that its issue should be postponed till some decided victory should have relieved the public mind of its present depression."

"That," I remarked, "was in July, and it is now the 18th of August, and our condition is worse rather than better. Would not the Proclamation improve things, — be of itself such a change of front as would be equivalent to a victory?"

"It might be so," he said, "and I am inclined to think it would be; but Mr. Lincoln thinks it best to wait a little longer. He is hoping for some encouraging action from General Pope and the new Army of Virginia."

"I think that all of Mr. Greeley's impatience would be removed if he knew these facts. Shall I be at liberty to tell him?"

"We had better ask Mr. Lincoln. I have suggested it, but he has been fearful Greeley would let it leak out."

At half past two precisely, we were shown into Mr. Lincoln's private room at the White House. On no previous occasion had he seemed so attractive to me as then, both in manner and appearance. His deep-sunk, dark gray eye had a soft, kindly expression, and I never knew a smile so positively captivating. It transfigured his whole face, making his plain features actually good-looking, so that I could agree with Caroline M. Kirkland, who not long before had told me that he was the handsomest man she had ever seen. When he had motioned us to a couple of seats, he said to me: "Well, Mr. Edmund Kirke, do you know it is a long time since I beheld the light of your countenance. Since then how many volumes of prose and poetry have you written?"

"One volume of prose, Mr. Lincoln. I never write poetry."

"Don't you call 'The London *Times* on American Affairs' poetry?" Then leaning back in his chair, he repeated, with correct pronunciation, and an indescribably comic expression, the following:

> "John Bull vos a-valkin' his parlor von day,
> Ha-fixin' the vorld wery much his hown vay,
> Ven igstrawnary news cum from hover the sea,
> Habout the great country vot brags it is free.

> "Hand these vos the tidin's this news it did tell,
> That great Yankee Doodle vos goin' to — vell,
> That he vos a-volloped by Jefferson D.,
> Hand no longer some punkins vos likely to be."

"That thing," he said, "expresses my sentiments exactly; and if it isn't poetry, be kind enough to tell me what it is."

"It is doggerel, sir; but there is poetry in the latter

part, which was written by Leland. When I took it to him he said it wasn't finished, — that I should have killed the *Times.* Then I told him to do that himself, and in five minutes he wrote the last half-dozen stanzas. But allow me to say, Mr. Lincoln, you have a remarkable verbal memory."

"Well," he answered, "I can remember any jingle that strikes me; and that chimed in with my feelings, for I felt mightily like twisting the lion's tail. But now I want to ask you a few questions."

As he said this, he took from the drawer of his table a copy of "Among the Pines," every few leaves of which had a page turned down. Then looking at me searchingly, he asked, "How much of this book is true?"

I answered that in a certain sense all of it was true; that the book was made of detached experiences, put together to form a symmetrical whole. Every incident in it occurred as I related it, and under my own observation; but not in the sequence or localities represented.

"This old darky's sermon, did you hear that?" he asked.

I answered that I did, twenty years before; but I had repeated merely the substance of it, — the actual sermon was far better than I had reported it."

"Then," he said, "your memory is as good as mine. I can remember words that I heard but once, twenty and thirty years ago."

I said that his verbal memory was doubtless better than mine. If I should attempt to report the present interview at a future time, however distant, I could do it truthfully, so that he would pronounce it accurate, and yet he might have to correct some of my words and phrases. But persons, occurrences, and even abstract ideas, I never forgot.

My memory as to these things had been helped by an early habit of thinking in subjects, — placing a new fact with others of the same kind already in my brain, and pigeon-holing them, as it were, so that I could recall events in their order, and as they actually happened.

"Then, in describing, you simply recall the scene, and describe it as it lies in your memory. But I want to ask you a few more questions."

Then opening the book again, he went, in order, through the turned-down pages, asking me question after question in rapid succession, and saying at the close, "You say that Colonel J—— is an actual character! What was his social position, — how was he thought of in the community?"

I answered, "He stood very high, — exceptionally so. He was what is styled 'very popular.'"

"And yet this man, so passionate, so lost to self-control, so reckless of human life, had absolute power over two hundred of his fellow beings!" exclaimed Mr. Lincoln, with a tone of intense earnestness.

"The man was the product of the institution, Mr. President," said Governor Walker. "I have known many like him, only not so manly and kind-hearted; and I could tell you of at least half a dozen who live openly, as he did, with two wives, one their slave, and both mothers to their children. Mr. Gilmore has not overdrawn a single picture in the book."

I said then that I could tell things far worse than any told there, but I had avoided anything too bad to be believed. Besides, long association had given me a kindly feeling for the Southern people. I had seen that the fault lay not so much with them, as with the system which had blunted their humane feelings in their relations with the negro. They had come to regard him as a mere animal, to be fed and driven. "We have," I said, "rogues and human brutes in the North, but they are restrained by public sentiment; at the South there has been no public sentiment to restrain the white man from dealing as he pleases with the black man or woman."

"It is horrible — horrible," said Mr. Lincoln. "One can realize its enormity when such things are told by an eye-witness, and you tell them in a way to command belief. Governor, is it not about time that action was taken on this subject?"

"It is high time," answered Mr. Walker. "I fear we shall have no success until you issue that proclamation."

"Mr. Gilmore, tell me," said Mr. Lincoln, "who wrote that article, 'What shall be the end?' in your magazine, a little time back?"

I answered, "Judge John W. Edmonds."

"I felt sure it was written by some lawyer or jurist. It is the ablest statement of the subject that I've seen. He says that the men who are in armed rebellion against the Constitution and the Union must make up their minds to take what the fortune of war gives them. That this rebellion should be handled without gloves. The North should permit nothing to stand in the way of a complete and permanent triumph; and he recognizes the absolute necessity of the total extinction of slavery. How was that article received by your exchanges?"

I replied that it was very generally approved, and had been copied entire by many of the leading journals. I thought it expressed the almost universal opinion of loyal people, — that the real issue was between slavery and freedom, and that the Union could be saved only by the destruction of slavery.

"I think," he answered, "that you put it a little too

strong. I should be satisfied with a majority. But the Governor tells me that he is going into the magazine with you. Do you reflect that he is a man of imperious temper, and bound to rule things? What is it, Governor, that Pope said of Addison?"

"That he, like the Turk, would brook no rival near the throne," answered Mr. Walker, smiling.

"No, sir," responded Mr. Lincoln, "I assert it was 'Bear, like the Turk, no brother near the throne,' and I haven't read the line in twenty years. So you see the sort of editor you will get."

"I am not influenced by his erudition," I said. "I take him because he is anxious to share with me a loss of three or four hundred dollars a month."

"Well, he can do that as well as any one; and I suspect he wouldn't feel it, should it be ten times as much. But speaking of editors, — I infer from the recent tone of the *Tribune* that you are not always able to keep Brother Greeley in the traces."

I told him that I had never tried to do that, — that I had merely read to Mr. Greeley, from time to time, such memoranda as Mr. Walker had sent me for that purpose. I answered questions when he asked them, but never volunteered an opinion. I saw from the very first that any direct attempt to influence him would have no effect. With Sidney Howard Gay, however, my course had been different. He had been for five years associated with Mr. Greeley, and had more influence with him than any other person. He was my intimate friend, and to him, since April, 1862, when he was made managing editor to succeed Mr. Dana, I had taken the liberty to show Mr. Walker's despatches, and I thought he had softened Mr. Greeley's wrath on several occasions.

"What is he wrathy about?" asked Mr. Lincoln.

"The slow progress of the war, — what he regards as the useless destruction of life and property, and especially your neglect to make a direct attack upon slavery. On this last point I am told by Mr. Gay that he is now meditating an appeal to the country, which will force you to take a decided position. This Mr. Gay told me just as I left New York; I have not seen Mr. Greeley within a fortnight."

"Why does he not come here and have a talk with me?" said Mr. Lincoln. "Did you not show him my letter to the Governor?"

I replied that I had left it in his hands, stipulating, however, for its return if he should desire it; and that Mr. Gay had very recently suggested such an interview, but Greeley had objected to allowing the President to act as advisory editor of the *Tribune*.

"I have no such desire," said Mr. Lincoln. "I certainly have enough now on my hands to satisfy any man's ambition. Does not that remark show an unfriendly spirit in Mr. Greeley?"

I said that I thought not; that it was simply impatience with the slow movement of things. I had heard him express the strongest personal regard for the President; but he could not understand why, with our immense army and enormous expenditure, so little had been accomplished. He thought that our magnificent force of more than 200,000 men should have captured Richmond within a month. He had not understood the situation.

At this point Governor Walker remarked that he had explained to me the annoyance that McClellan had caused by his tardiness and disobedience of orders; and also that a Proclamation of Emancipation had been drawn and was only waiting a favorable moment for its publication, and he asked, " Shall he not be allowed to tell all this to Mr. Greeley?"

"I have only been afraid of Greeley's passion for news. Do you think he will let no intimation of it get into his paper?" said the President.

I answered that he would not if he gave his word to that effect; but I suggested that he should permit me to tell the same thing to Mr. Gay, who attended to the making up of the *Tribune*, and was not so absent-minded as Mr. Greeley.

To this Mr. Lincoln assented, and then I remarked that I would leave for home that night, to be in advance of Greeley's threatened " Appeal to the American people." Soon afterwards I bade Mr. Lincoln good-by, and late that night I took my departure from Washington.

Arriving in New York on the following morning, I looked into the *Tribune*, and the first thing that met my eye was Horace Greeley's " Prayer of Twenty Millions." It was addressed personally to Mr. Lincoln, and did not ask, as I had expected it would, for the issue of a proclamation freeing the slaves, but merely for the rigid enforcement of the " Confiscation Act," already passed by Congress. In it Mr. Greeley said: " What an immense majority of the loyal millions of your countrymen require of you is a frank, declared, unqualified, ungrudging execution of the laws of the land, more especially of the Confiscation Act. That act gives freedom to the slaves of rebels coming within our lines, or whom those lines may at any time enclose. We ask you to render it due obedience by publicly requiring all your subordinates to recognize and obey it."

That same day I communicated to Mr. Greeley the fact that an Emancipation Proclamation had already been drawn and approved of by Mr. Lincoln's Cabinet, and he was only waiting a favorable time to publish it to the country. He expressed great gratification with the news, but regret that he had not known it before, remarking: "If Mr. Lincoln were not so very cautious and reticent we should get along much better together; but I could forgive him all and everything, if he would infuse a little more energy into affairs; he seems to forget there is a possibility of exhausting the patience as well as the resources of the country."

Three days later Mr. Lincoln replied to the "Prayer of Twenty Millions" by a letter addressed personally to Mr. Greeley, and containing the famous sentence, "My paramount object is to save the Union, and not either to save or destroy slavery." This letter surprised Mr. Greeley, but his only comment on it — in my hearing — was, "It is no answer to my 'Prayer.' He had prepared it in advance, and took the occasion to get his views before the public. But I'll forgive him everything if he'll issue the proclamation."

The fortune of war continued against the Union armies. Pope was defeated at Bull Run late in August, and then things looked darker than ever. Meanwhile Mr. Lincoln had anxiously watched the progress of events, adding or changing a word or a line in his proclamation, till on Sept. 17, 1862, came the battle of Antietam, — which was rather a drawn battle than a victory. "Then," as he said in a conversation with Frank B. Carpenter, the artist, "I determined to wait no longer. The news came, I think, on Wednesday, that the advantage was on our side. I was then staying at the Soldiers' Home (three miles out of Washington). Here I finished writing the second draft of the preliminary proclamation; came up on Saturday, called the Cabinet together to hear it, and it was published on the ensuing Monday."

Thus the idea that slavery must be destroyed to bring

about a permanent restoration of the Union had at last triumphed; and it was with supreme gratification that I heard the chorus of rejoicing which arose from our numerous "exchanges" throughout the country. I regarded this, and it doubtless was, an expression of the feeling of a majority of the Northern people.

None more sincerely rejoiced over the proclamation than Horace Greeley. At our first meeting after its publication he said: "Do you remember what Victor Hugo says of Waterloo, — that it was not a battle, but a change of front of the universe? So this action of Mr. Lincoln is a change of front of the country. Henceforth and forever we shall be a free people." At the same interview he gave me an article he had written for the *Continental*, which closed with the following prophetic words: "Yet a little while, and the authority of the Nation will be acknowledged by its now revolted citizens, and the rebellion will subside as suddenly as it broke upon us. Yet a little while, and ours will be again a land of peace, returning joyfully to the pursuits of productive industry, and radiant with the sunlight of Universal Liberty."

CHAPTER VIII.

MY CONNECTION WITH THE NEW YORK TRIBUNE.

THE purpose for which I had established the *Continental Monthly* was accomplished by the issue of President Lincoln's Emancipation Proclamation. The North had at first taken up arms to maintain the Union, regardless of the extension or non-extension of slavery; but gradually a majority of the people had come to the conclusion that the life of the nation could not be preserved without the total extinction of the "peculiar institution." Of this I had been convinced by the general acclaim with which the Northern press had greeted the Emancipation Proclamation; but I soon had stronger evidence of it from personal contact with the people through a series of lectures that I delivered before literary associations in all the larger cities of the North. This revolution in public sentiment had been mainly brought about by the irresistible "logic of events," — the slow progress of the war, and the long series of disasters that had attended the Union armies; but though the people had thus been schooled by events, they had, doubtless, been largely influenced by the bold utterances of Charles G. Leland in the *Continental Monthly*, which had been scattered broadcast over the North. Clear-sighted statesmen had from the beginning seen that the real issue was the permanent establishment, or the entire extinction, of slavery; but Leland was the first to tell this truth to the people, and he told it in words that rang through the

North like the notes of a bugle. With his whole heart and soul he had entered the conflict. His friends had counselled him to moderate his tone; William H. Seward had rewarded his zeal with the elegant anathema, "Damn Leland and the *Continental;*" and even Robert J. Walker had said to me, "Had you not better hold him in a little?" To this injunction I had answered, "No, no! Let him alone. His words are doing their work. According to Wendell Phillips, to split a rock you need a charge of gunpowder." Thus I had stood by Leland when no one else would stand by him; and that is the sole credit I take to myself for the important work that was done by the *Continental Monthly.* He did it without pay or any hope of reward, and for it he deserves to be honored by the whole people, North and South, who are now reaping the fruits of the policy he so early and so manfully advocated.

The country thus aroused, and the Government fully committed to the policy of Emancipation, it seemed to me that the magazine had done its work, and could now gracefully withdraw from the arena. I had borne the brunt of its expenditures, and up to this period had realized but a small part of the extraordinary returns which I subsequently received from my books. To be sure, Mr. Walker was to share with me the further disbursements of the magazine; but a connection with it involved my time, which then was equivalent to money, — and money which, in the tied-up condition of my diminished resources, was absolutely needed for my personal requirements.

These considerations I laid before Mr. Walker, proposing to him the suspension of the *Continental.* To this he strongly objected, remarking that the magazine had not done half its work, for the war was not half over; that the financial strain upon the Government was already great, and soon would be terrific, — the public debt being then nearly a thousand millions, and inevitably to be at the end of the year two thousand millions; and that the *Continental* would be needed to promulgate and defend the financial policy of the administration. And he added that he was about to make his long-deferred visit to Europe as the financial agent of the Treasury Department, to raise all the money possible towards meeting the emergency. This last remark decided me, for I saw that his absence would throw upon me even a greater amount of work than I had anticipated; and though he remarked that my financial necessities might be easily provided for by some appointment under the Government, I kindly, but firmly, said: "If any provide not for his own, he is worse than an infidel, and I cannot consent to be a pensioner upon the Government." Our separation I made as easy as possible by conveying to him my entire interest in the *Continental*, and agreeing to finish, without charge, the book, "My Southern Friends," which was then running in the magazine.

He went to Europe in March, 1863, and did not return until November, 1864, meanwhile conducting the magazine under the editorship of his accomplished sister, Martha Walker Cooke, Mr. Leland having decided to resign on my withdrawal from the ownership. Leland was the ablest magazinist I have ever known, — not excepting even James T. Fields, — and had he continued to manage the *Continental* it would doubtless be alive to-day, and among the most successful of similar publications.

While in England Mr. Walker effected a sale of two hundred and fifty millions of the United States 5-20 bonds, and, what was quite as important, he defeated the second Confederate loan of seventy-five millions. He was, in my view, the ablest financier this country has produced since Alexander Hamilton. From my intimacy with him I was led to regard him as the real soul of the Treasury Department, and as the one most entitled to the credit of the financial policy which carried the country through the terrific strain of the Civil War. He was a great man. Among those whom I regard as "my masters," I have held but one other in higher honor. By Robert J. Walker I was taught to take broad views of things; to look on all sides of a subject; to seek in every detail for general principles; and to ever remember that "the things seen are temporal, and the things unseen, eternal;" and thus to square my life, as far as mortal man may, by laws of righteousness that are unchanging, — immutably fixed in the nature of things. I was not again in close relations with him, but our friendship lasted until his death in 1869.

I had consulted with Sidney Howard Gay in regard to withdrawing from the *Continental*, and not long after the foregoing interview with Mr. Walker I was seated in his room in the *Tribune* building one afternoon, when Mr. Greeley entered it to pass through to his "sanctum." Perceiving me, he paused, and accosted me, to the best of my recollection, somewhat as follows: "Well, Sub Rosa,[1] I am glad to hear that you've come to your senses at last."

"Then you think that up to this time I have been somewhat crazy?" I said, smiling broadly.

"I do," he answered; "mad as a March hare in wasting time and money to get the Emancipation Proclamation. What good has it done us?"

---

[1] When Mr. Greeley first asked me who wrote the sketches called "Among the Pines," I told him the writer's name was Sub Rosa. Subsequently, when the book had been issued, and the *Tribune* was about to publish a low-priced edition of it, Mr. Gay told him that I was its author; and afterwards Mr. Greeley usually addressed me by the above title.

At this point, Mr. Gay rose from his high-legged stool, and closed the door into the larger editorial room. Evidently he would not have the remarks of his chief heard by his subordinates.

I answered, "It has checkmated France and England, and set the true issue squarely before the country."

"Yes, and the people have disapproved of the proclamation,—every State election has gone against the Government."

"I think that merely expresses dissatisfaction with the results of the war. From meeting the people personally in all parts of the country, I have concluded that a majority heartily approve of the proclamation. I think you approved of it: when it was first issued you told me it was such a change of front as would make us forever a free people."

"Well, I thought so; and I hoped it would turn the tide of disaster, but what have we had? The slaughter of Fredericksburg, and Grant's bloody hammering at Vicksburg since November."

"I know," I replied, "and I am as much disappointed as you are. I think we both forgot that proclamations do not create generals."

"But who," he asked, "put Burnside in command when he protested his incompetence?"

"Lincoln, of course; but you will not condemn him for one mistake. The old backwoodsman said to Henry Clay, 'Pick your flint and try again.'"

He remarked that it had not been one mistake, but one unbroken series of blunders. The only good thing Lincoln had done was to issue the Emancipation Proclamation, which had to be forced from him; and that had come too late to save the country. The people held him, he said, responsible for the administration, and he intended to repudiate the whole concern.

"If you do that," I answered, "you will do the country more damage than twenty Fredericksburgs. You do not realize your power with the people. They know you are clear-sighted and disinterested. They trust you and look to you for guidance. If you open your batteries upon Lincoln, the country will lose confidence in him, and the Union will go to pieces."

Up to this time he had been leaning against the door of his "sanctum." Now he shambled up and down the room, a look of impotent distress upon his face as he exclaimed, "And they hold me responsible, and I — I can't justify myself without doing damage to the country."

"They do not hold you responsible. They know you had to take Lincoln, and they are beginning to like and trust him as they do you. If you two act together you will save the Union; if you don't, the rebel leaders will accomplish their ends."

"But how can I act with him if he won't act at all, or is always a day too late? He is under the control of Seward, and Seward would thwart my views merely because they were mine."

"I don't know it as a fact, but I believe that Seward has lost all influence with Lincoln. He keeps him merely because of his idea that he strengthens his administration at the North. You remember what he said in that letter to Mr. Walker, — that if you would come to him, and state your views frankly and fully, he would adopt them if he could. I think he would overturn his entire Cabinet rather than lose your support and friendship."

"Then suppose you go to him, and tell him that I think if Walker were in Seward's place, and Rosecrans in Stanton's, there would be some chance of saving the country. Stanton is energetic enough, but he is a mere lawyer, and lacks military knowledge."

"It would be more effective if that came from you personally. If I were to tell him that you distrust him, it would only add to his burdens, and he is now loaded down to the water's edge."

"If I were to go," he rejoined, "he would simply twist me around his finger; he always does. So we must peg along as we are; but it is hard to fight in a hopeless cause. Don't things look to you altogether hopeless?"

"Not by any means. Let me give you an idea from the prophet Isaiah. He says there is a God who rules this planet. He seems to have formed this country without natural divisions that it might be possessed by one great, united people. He meant they should be free, and a light to all other nations, to thereby lift the whole of humanity to a higher and better civilization. But the Deity has to work by human means, and man is a greedy animal,— greedy for gold; and to get more of it than they could by their own labor, the Virginia planters enslaved the negro, and set him to raising tobacco. The evil thing grew, and the Almighty permitted it,— probably with an eye to the future of Africa,— until the Slave Power threatened to dominate the whole country, and thus subvert the very purpose of its creation. Then the great Overruler said,— I am not now giving you Isaiah, but Robert J. Walker,— 'Thus far have I allowed you to go, but go no farther. I'll not let my plans be thwarted by a handful of slave-drivers.'

"He said this, and as he never does anything by halves, he resolved to pull up the evil thing by the roots. To do so he had to array the North against the South, and thus bring waste and death into nearly every household. I marvelled that a benevolent Deity could do this, until I reflected that in his view real wealth is of the spiritual sort, and human life is not bounded by a narrow horizon of seventy years, but has a limitless duration. The North has been slow to see his purpose, and at no time before the proclamation would it have refused a peace that provided for the perpetuation of slavery, — in his letter to you, Lincoln said that distinctly, — and even now nearly one-half of the people would accept any terms with the Rebellion. So, the war must go on, and disaster follow disaster, until the whole North is fully resolved to exterminate the accursed thing."

"How long can we stand this immense waste of life and property?" asked Mr. Greeley, who had listened to me with apparent interest.

"I don't know; but the South will be the first to become exhausted, — the waste of property is heavier on them than on us, and their loss of life is as great as ours, as is shown by the reports of every one of the battles. With peace the waste of property will soon be restored, and the loss of life you can't consider of much account, for you don't believe in hell-fire, and count that a man will be better off for getting into a cozy corner of the invisible country."

Mr. Greeley laughed one of those quiet laughs of his that used to ripple over his huge frame, giving an expression of genuine enjoyment. "Well, Sub Rosa," he said, "a Methodist parson was lost in you. Now that you've abandoned the *Continental* you had better preach theology through the *Tribune.*"

"What!" I exclaimed, "allow you to run your blue pencil through my best thoughts! No, thank you, Mr. Greeley. I should esteem it an honor to be associated with you, for I consider you the greatest of journalists, living or dead, but your views don't accord with mine."

"But," he said, "I have resigned the blue pencil. You would not report to me, but to Gay; and he is of your way of thinking."

"That is another part of speech," I remarked, turning to Mr. Gay. "Is he not jesting?"

"He is not jesting," he replied. "He has agreed that I shall direct the policy of the paper. You and I would not disagree; we shall urge an energetic prosecution of the war."

This was true. From the resignation of Charles A. Dana, early in 1862, until the close of the war, Mr. Gay controlled the course of the *Tribune*, and in all that time he did what no other man — except Mr. Dana — ever did or could do, — he held Mr. Greeley's great powers to the steady support of the Union.

Some details were then talked over, and it was agreed that I should become connected with the *Tribune* in a quasi-editorial capacity, not attached to the office, but going and coming at my pleasure, and doing my work wherever I chanced to be. I was to furnish a certain number of editorials weekly on such subjects as seemed to me timely, with full liberty to express my personal opinions, Mr. Gay reserving the right to toss my views into his waste-basket when they did not accord with those of the *Tribune*. The connection would give me free and frequent access to our armies at the front, and keep me in close touch with current events, and these were my main motives in accepting the position.

CHAPTER IX.

THE DISSATISFACTION WITH PRESIDENT LINCOLN.

My first visit to the front, after my connection with the New York *Tribune*, was to the Army of the Potomac, then under command of General Hooker, and on my way I had a brief interview with the President. Robert J. Walker had sailed for Europe, but Mr. Lincoln received me cordially, and expressed decided gratification when I told him of my loose-jointed connection with the *Tribune*. In answer to his question, "How does Horace feel now?" I merely said that he was somewhat downhearted; but I thought his spirits would revive with the first substantial victory. He answered, "We can reasonably look for one soon, now that we have 'fighting Joe Hooker' in command in Virginia. What troubles me most are our slow operations against Vicksburg." He spoke freely of Hooker, expressing the same view of him that is contained in the letter which he wrote to that officer on giving him his appointment. "He brags a little," he remarked to me, "but he has shown himself a good fighter."

At Hooker's headquarters I was introduced to him by the *Tribune* correspondent, and when told that I was one of the *Tribune* staff, he received me with decided cordiality. Very soon he launched into a glorification of his army, — "the finest on this continent," — and boasted of what he should do with it, — "have it in Richmond within three weeks, with a death-blow struck at the Rebellion." I met him several times, and on each occasion he talked in the same strain of overweening self-confidence. He seemed to forget that one of the most consummate generals of this age lay between him and the realization of his ambition.

James Redpath once told me that he never could write well unless he was "in a red-hot fury." I was strongly disgusted with Hooker's bombast, and deeply grieved at the blindness of Mr. Lincoln in placing such momentous interests in the hands of an inflated braggart; and my mingled indignation and regret I put into an article which I sent off to Mr. Gay on my return to Washington. It made no direct reference to Hooker, nor any censure of Mr. Lincoln, but the paper probably was as severe on the conduct of the war as any that might have been written by Mr. Greeley. I looked for it in the *Tribune* on my arrival in New York on the following day, and, not finding it there, I went down to the office, as soon as I thought Mr. Gay would be at his post, to urge its publication. "I held it back to show it to Horace," he said to me, "for I didn't expect quite so much red pepper from you. He is mightily pleased with it, — says that he knew you would come to your senses."

The article had gone into type, and I was reading the proof, when Mr. Greeley, apparently much absorbed, entered the room and passed into his private office. He gave me merely a casual recognition, but soon reappeared in his doorway, saying he would like to talk with me for a few moments. I kept no notes of the conversation that followed, and cannot at this distance of time repeat his language, but the substance of what he said is very distinctly impressed on my memory.

He began by remarking that he inferred from the editorial I had sent on from Washington that I was now convinced the Union could not be saved by the present administration.

I answered that I had begun to have decided fears on that subject; and then he went on to say that Lincoln — who seemed to be his own war minister — had shown a remarkable talent at putting the wrong men in the right places; that he had pitted such soldiers as McClellan, Burnside, and Hooker against the ablest general of the Confederacy; and given them magnificent armies only to be slaughtered, while he had sent Grant and Sherman, with but 33,000 men, to take Vicksburg, in the face of Pemberton and Johnston with 60,000; and left Rosecrans, our ablest general, and the only one who had shown himself a match for Lee, in the heart of Tennessee, unable to move for the want of a few thousand cavalry horses. With such management how could we expect anything but disaster?

I admitted that the conduct of the war had been bad; but was it right to put the whole responsibility upon Mr. Lincoln? He was not a military man, and of necessity had to depend upon his military advisers. I knew that he had felt every defeat as a personal calamity. With the right men about him I felt sure all would yet go well. I said that I knew nothing of Rosecrans, except that he had outgeneralled Lee in West Virginia, and won three important battles solely by his personal bravery. But if he (Greeley) felt sure that Rosecrans was the man to manage the war, I was confident Mr. Lincoln would give him the War Department, and also call Walker back from Europe to take the place of Seward. To accomplish this he had only to see Mr. Lincoln personally and set the necessities of the situation squarely before him.

Mr. Greeley shook his head, saying, "Suppose I did see him, and he did consent to such changes as I think vital, what guaranty should I have that he would not change his mind, find some pretext for evading his word, the moment my back was turned? How can I trust him after the way he has kept his agreement to give me early information? He has allowed Walker and you to tell me only what everybody knew. All important facts he has kept from me till they came out officially. Witness the Emancipation Proclamation, which you yourself had to entreat him to make known to me after it was wholly written, and approved of by all his Cabinet. Then, right on the heels of that, he added insult to injury by answering my 'Prayer of Twenty Millions,' which asked only for the honest enforcement of an existing law, as if it had been a demand for the abolition of slavery; thus adroitly using me to feel the public pulse, and making me appear as an officious meddler in affairs that properly belong to the Government. No, Sub Rosa, I can't trust your 'honest old Abe.' He is too smart for me. He thinks me a d——d fool; but I am never fooled twice by the same individual."

The above report repeats, I think, very nearly Mr. Greeley's exact language, and he spoke with a good deal of feeling. I answered that Mr. Lincoln was very far from considering him a fool; that I had heard him style him (Greeley) a great man, and a great power, worth more to the Union than an army of a hundred thousand men. However, Mr. Lincoln was a born diplomatist,— Walker had told me that he was the shrewdest politician he had ever known,— and he, doubtless, did write his famous letter merely to test public sentiment on the question of emancipation; but I could not believe that he had intended to in any way belittle or wound Mr.

Greeley. As to his failure to give him the earliest information, I thought he had fully meant to do so; but Mr. Greeley should remember that he had agreed to give him the "intentions" of the Government only when they were "formed," and that I believed his decision to issue the proclamation was not fully formed, except as a means to stave off England, until a day or two before its publication. I had watched the growth in his mind of the emancipation idea, from April, 1861, when he had told me that he would be found willing and eager to free the slaves whenever the country should demand it. I had never met him, after that time, when he did not ask me the feeling of the people on that subject. His hand seemed to be ever on the pulse of the public, and he anxious to note the rising popular sentiment in favor of emancipation. He was afraid of going too fast, and so had probably sometimes gone too slow, though he was undoubtedly right in putting his foot upon the Fremont and Hunter proclamations. I closed what I had to say with "But, Mr. Greeley, we are obliged to have Lincoln for another two years, — can't you bring your mind to the point of going to him, and demanding that he shall put competent men into his Cabinet?"

He answered that he could not, — that Lincoln had given no heed to the few suggestions he had already made, and he had shown a like disregard to every recommendation of the prominent men of his party. Lincoln had imbibed Henry Wilson's idea that God was managing the war, and he thought himself his vicegerent, to be infallibly led in the right direction. Hence, he was following his own impressions, in spite of the almost unanimous protests of the Republican leaders, and to the universal dissatisfaction of both leaders and people, as was shown by the result of the recent State elections. But, as I had said, we were saddled with Lincoln for two more years, and so, individually, he should be disposed to let the rascally slave-drivers go in peace; for it was morally certain that, during that period, the country would be so ravaged and depopulated as to be scarcely worth saving. But the Republican leaders, — nearly all of whom he had conferred with, — and the Northern people, thought differently; their back was up, and they would fight till doomsday, rather than consent to disunion. This being so, there was no alternative but for the war to go on to the end, and to abide by its consequences. But should the country survive Lincoln's term of office, it would, were he reëlected, of a certainty go to destruction. This was the opinion of every prominent Republican he had conversed with on the subject, and they all thought the only hope of its final salvation lay in defeating a reëlection of Lincoln; and to accomplish that, some suitable candidate should be at once decided upon, and during the succeeding eighteen months be written up by the entire loyal press, so that he might be sure to carry the country. His own first choice would be Robert J. Walker.

With this last remark he looked at me inquiringly, and I promptly replied, "He would not be a candidate. He shares Henry Wilson's opinion that God's hand is in the war, and he believes that Lincoln is his selected leader. Nothing would induce Walker to act against Lincoln."

He answered that he had thought so, and it was marvellous, — Lincoln's power over those who came in close contact with him. Next to Walker, he and those he had consulted were of opinion that General Rosecrans would be the best and most available candidate. He had been uniformly successful in the war, and seemed to be the

"coming man;" and though some might object to him as a Roman Catholic, he deemed that an advantage, inasmuch as it would command the solid Irish vote. Rosecrans was every way an able man, and an ardent patriot, and would be sure to prosecute the war energetically; the only question was, "Is he sound on the goose?" that is, would he refuse to listen to any peace that did not provide for the total extinction of slavery? He and his friends desired an answer to that question, and if I would go to Rosecrans's headquarters, and get an answer to the question, and also take Rosecrans's measure from head to foot, he would equip me with such letters as would carry me through a stone wall. In no other way, he said, could I so effectually serve the country.

I replied that I did not relish the idea of thus going deliberately to work to undermine Mr. Lincoln, — that I had a strong personal liking for him, and should much prefer he would shoulder the task upon some one else.

His answer was that there would be no undermining of Mr. Lincoln, — no harsh criticisms directed against him from any quarter. The aim would be to build a strong man up, not to pull a weak man down. Left to himself, Lincoln would fall of his own weight. And this was not a time for any one to consult his personal likes or dislikes. He had himself a liking for Lincoln personally, but he would sacrifice his best friend, cut off his right arm, if it would serve the country in its great extremity. He had always thought that I would do the same. I had done so, he added, in regard to my lifelong friends of the South.

"Well," I said, "I am not the man for this kind of business, — I am too open, too frank. Rosecrans would detect my purpose before I had been with him a day."

"I don't believe it," he replied. "Your frank, free ways would compel his confidence, and he would open himself to you, unreservedly. You are just the man for the business."

I answered that he was like Lincoln, — there was no resisting him. I would go, but I must not be expected to take sides against Lincoln, either then, or after my return. I was firmly of the opinion that he had done all that he could do. The fault lay with his commanders. He had furnished them with an abundance of men and supplies, but, though fighting two against one, they had failed from sheer incapacity.

All, he replied, except Rosecrans, — he had always won, and always fought with inferior forces. He and his friends asked only for an impartial report, and my kindly impressions of Lincoln would prevent my coloring Rosecrans too highly. He then gave me the names of his principal associates in this movement. The list included Thaddeus Stevens, Senator Wade, Henry Winter Davis, David Dudley Field, Governor Andrew, and, as I remember, about all the more prominent Republican leaders, except Roscoe Conkling, Charles Sumner, and Henry Wilson. Even Chase and Seward had been conferred with; and while they had failed to commit themselves, — owing to their relations to the President, — Mr. Greeley was satisfied they silently sympathized with the movement.

It was to me a fearful revelation. What chance of success had Mr. Lincoln, thus forsaken by his friends, and forced to fight, with incompetent generals, some of the ablest soldiers of the time? From sheer pity my feeling grew warmer towards him; and I went away with a heavy heart, forgetting that "one with God is a majority."

In a few days came tidings of the battle of Chancellorsville, wherein nearly 30,000 men were sacrificed to the incompetence of Hooker. On the afternoon succeeding the last day's fight, I was seated in Mr. Gay's private room at the *Tribune* office, when Mr. Greeley entered it, having in his hand the latest telegram from the front, which he had taken from the despatch-box in the outer editorial room. His face was pallid, his step almost tottering, and his lip trembled as he exclaimed, "My God! it is horrible — horrible; and to think of it, 130,000 magnificent soldiers so cut to pieces by less than 60,000 half-starved ragamuffins!"

No response being made to this remark, he sank into a chair and finished the reading of the telegram. Then, his lip still trembling, he said to me, "I have your letters all ready, — can't you go at once? I will give you my word that if you find Rosecrans the man that is needed, I will go personally to Lincoln and force him to resign. Hamlin will give Rosecrans command of the armies, and there'll be a chance of saving the country."

In looking over the letters which he handed me, I found they were from more than a dozen of the Republican leaders, some of whom did not know me personally; but by all of them I was commended strongly to the courtesy and confidence of General Rosecrans. On the following night I set out for his headquarters at Murfreesborough, Tennessee.

CHAPTER X.

TRAVEL IN WAR TIME.

It was early in May, 1863, and, arriving at Cincinnati, I discovered that I could proceed no farther without a pass from General Burnside, who was then in command of the Department of the Ohio. Calling at his office in the Burnet House to procure the requisite permission, I was introduced by Burnside to Parson Brownlow, with whom I dined and passed the greater part of the afternoon, listening to his very interesting experiences, and his graphic report of the terrific condition of things in the States of Kentucky and Tennessee. I told him that I had set out to reach the headquarters of General Rosecrans, whereupon he assured me that to attempt going to the front just then was a risky undertaking. The railroad below Bowling Green was infested with guerillas, who, on several recent occasions, had assailed the trains, and robbed and maltreated passengers. The cars were insufficiently guarded, and travelling was therefore attended with considerable personal hazard. He advised me to "make haste slowly," by proceeding no farther than Louisville, and lying over there until he came down with Governor Andrew Johnson, in about a week, when they would take me as far as Nashville. They would be attended by a guard strong enough to beat off any roving band that might venture to attack the train. Not being anxious to get a bullet under my waistcoat, or such an inside view of the Confederacy as would not be agreeable, I told him I was inclined to adopt his suggestion, but would look over the ground and decide upon my course when I reached Louisville.

Arrived at Louisville, I stopped over at the Louisville Hotel, and, on going in to dinner, met a tall, squarely built man, wearing the uniform of a lieutenant-colonel. He had a face that seemed to invite conversation, and I said to him, " You are travelling, sir ? "

" Yes, sir," he replied. " I am returning to my regiment, — the 82d Indiana, at Triune."

" Is it entirely safe going down the Nashville road ? "

" Not entirely. When I came up, a week ago Monday, we were fired into by a band of about fifty guerillas; but we beat them off."

He then related to me the circumstances, and I remarked that I had set out to visit Rosecrans, but was undecided whether to go on at once, or to wait for Governor Johnson and his escort.

He answered that it would be safer to go at once. The Governor would doubtless stay in Louisville a day or two, and, as the place was full of Confederates, every guerilla in Tennessee would know when he set out; and if they could muster strong enough they would be sure to attack him. He should go down by the next train and would be glad to have me for a travelling companion.

I thanked him, remarking that his revolver had acquitted itself so effectively that I was disposed to put myself under its protection, and would go with him.

In the hotel office I had noticed a placard which read: " Passengers for the Louisville and Nashville road are notified that the wagon will be in readiness to take baggage to the Examiner's Office at 4 P. M." As this applied to us,

I suggested to the colonel that we should repair to the "Custom House."

We found it on a side street, — a dingy room of about twenty feet square, densely crowded with carpet-bags, portmanteaus, packing trunks, and a score of German Israelites, every one of them soliciting the immediate attention of the single examining officer. Another official was behind the counter affixing to the "passed" packages a strip of white muslin and two mammoth daubs of red sealing-wax. The office was advertised to close at five o'clock, and it soon wanted but ten minutes of that hour. As our luggage could not leave the State unless it had two of those red seals upon it, each duly stamped "U. S.," the prospect for our going by the morning train seemed decidedly dubious; so I said to the coatless official, "Is there any probability of our turn coming this evening, sir?"

Scarcely looking up, he asked, "Are you an Israelite, indeed?"

"No, sir; neither in name nor in deed. I'm a rover at large; this gentleman is a Union officer."

Glancing at the colonel's uniform, he touched his cap, saying, "Ah, colonel, how are you?" and in a moment he was at the bottom of our trunks. In three minutes the ceremony was over, and we left the "receipt of custom," devoutly thankful that we were not of the "wandering tribes of Israel." The whole scene was decidedly suggestive of a landing among the customs officials on the continent of Europe, and to my mind it was a foreshadowing of what would happen in our own free country if the Confederates had their way, and the Union were rent into forty fragments.

On the following morning we set out for Nashville. At the railway station we were again reminded that we might be entering the French or Austrian dominions. At every turn my military passport was called for. I offered to pay my fare, and " Please show your pass, sir," greeted me from the small opening in the ticket-office. I tried to wedge my way through the crowd that blocked the inner gateway, and " Please show your pass, sir," arrested my steps. I applied for a check to my trunk, and " Please show your pass, sir," echoed from the lungs of the luggage department. I attempted to get upon the train, and " Please show your pass, sir," was demanded by a slim young man in shoulder straps ; and finally, when congratulating myself that one-fourth of my perilous journey was over, " Please show your pass, sir," was repeated by a young gentleman in military dress, who halted abreast of me in the aisle of the car. Drawing it forth in decided impatience, I asked, " Is this never to end?"

" Oh, yes, sir. We'll not trouble you again till we reach Nashville. It is annoying, but absolutely necessary."

When we entered the car it was packed with a general assortment of Kentucky jeans, butternut linseys, regulation buttons and shoulder straps, — these last returning to their regiments; but a solitary, timid-looking woman in a corner, and the small sprinkling of civilians among the military, told plainly that none of our fellow travellers were leaving home on a pleasure excursion. We found seats among some agreeable gentlemen, one of them an army surgeon who was decidedly useful to me in recounting the incidents connected with the various interesting localities through which we passed.

We soon entered a beautiful region where the thick blue grass was waving in the meadows, and the early wild flowers were blooming by the roadside; but where the rich red soil lay unturned by the plough, the stalks of last autumn's corn stood rotting on the ground, and desolation and ruin stared at us from every visible thing. Broken fences, wasted fields, deserted plantations, dismantled dwellings, and now and then a burned woods, or a charred chimney, standing a lonely sentinel over a weedy garden or amid a blackened grove, told that the whirlwind of war had passed that way and left only ravage and devastation in its path. A ragged woman, looking out from a wretched hovel; a solitary half-clad man, lingering around a heap of ashes and crumbling bricks that may once have been his home; or a group of naked negro children, gambolling on the porch, or lolling lazily on the lawn of some deserted homestead that still looked down in faded grandeur on the ruin around it, were the only indications of human existence, and the only remnants of a once peaceful and happy population. It was one of the most lovely regions of the earth, — naked, but beautiful in its nakedness. A curse had fallen on those once happy homes, — the "abomination of desolation" sat in those pleasant places.

Suddenly the engine-whistle sounded shrilly through the woods; the train broke up, and every man in the car sprang to his feet, a dozen voices crying out, "The guerillas are on us!"

"Are you armed, sir?" said the colonel to me, as coolly as if we were at his dinner-table.

"No, sir; I am not."

"Take this," he said; "it may be useful."

Cocking the revolver, I seated myself and breathlessly awaited the expected attack. The surgeon, who had been indulging in a short nap, now opened his eyes and asked, "What's to pay?"

"I reckon the bushwhackers are on us," said the colonel.

"That can't be, this side of Bowling Green, — some one had better reconnoitre," said the surgeon, drawing from his pocket a small pistol, and striding towards the car door.

"For God's sake, don't go there; keep inside!" exclaimed half a dozen voices.

Giving no heed to these warnings, the surgeon stepped out upon the platform, saying, "Where's the guard? Well, these fellows are never where they should be."

The single soldier who had been stationed before the door, naturally objecting to standing as a target for an unknown number of rifles, had disappeared into the forward car. The surgeon glanced cautiously around, and apparently seeing nothing to satisfy his curiosity, he made a sudden spring for a huge tree that stood a short distance from the track. By this movement he secured two breastworks, — the tree in his front, and the car in his rear.

"He jumps like a wildcat!" exclaimed the colonel. "But look at our neighbors! Ha! ha!"

Turning about, I beheld nearly all the civilians crouched beneath the windows, and not a few of the military with arms and legs couchant. The surgeon, springing from tree to tree, explored the woods for about a hundred yards. He found numerous tracks of men and horses, but no human being was anywhere visible. A few rails were displaced, and stringpieces torn from their places, showing a design to stop the train; but for some unknown reason the assault had been abandoned. I breathed more freely; for, if the truth must be told, my respiratory apparatus had not performed its functions with its usual composure. Even a brave man — and bravery is not essential to one of my profession — is shaken when confronting an unseen danger; and it surprised me to see the perfect coolness which the surgeon and the colonel had maintained. I said as much to them when, at the end of a half hour, the rails were replaced and the train got under way again.

"Courage," said the colonel, "like almost everything else, is a matter of habit. A man who has for two years daily expected every bush would give him a bullet, gets indifferent to danger; but, after all, I had rather have death come at me face to face than spring at my back from behind a rail fence."

Soon afterward the train arrived at Memphis Junction, and the colonel and the surgeon left the car, and took a train which was on the track for Clarksville.

My travelling companions gone, I stretched my legs upon the seats they had occupied and was soon far away in some corner of the universe where strife and bloody contention have never been known. My slumber was, after awhile, rudely broken by a heavy hand laid on my shoulder, and a gruff voice saying, "Don't want ter 'sturb yer, stranger, but thar hain't nary 'nother sittin'-place in the whole kear."

I drew in my extremities, and he seated himself before me. He was a spare, muscular man of about forty years, a little above the medium height, with thick, sandy hair and beard, and a full, clear gray eye. There was nothing about him to attract particular attention except his clothing, but that was so out of all keeping with the place and the occasion, that I opened my eyes to their fullest extent, and scanned him from head to foot. He wore the gray uniform of a Confederate officer, and in the breast of his coat, right over his heart, was a round hole, scorched at the edges, and darkly stained with blood. Over his shoulder was slung a large army revolver, and at his side, in a leathern sheath, hung a weapon that seemed a sort of cross between a bowie knife and a butcher's cleaver. He styled it a sword, and I afterwards discovered that it had been fashioned from a large horse-file by a back-country blacksmith. On his head, surmounted by a black plume, was a mouse-colored slouch hat, and falling stiffly from beneath it, and tied under his chin, was a white cotton handkerchief saturated with blood. Nine motley-clad " natives," all heavily armed, had entered the car with him and taken the vacant seats around me, and at first view I was inclined to think that in my sleep the train had gone over to the enemy, and left me in the hands of the Philistines. However, I was soon reassured, for, looking about me, I perceived the Union guard and my fellow travellers all in their previous places, and as unconcerned as if no unusual thing had happened. Still, it appeared singular that none of the soldiers had the newcomer in charge, and more singular that any one in the uniform he wore should be allowed to carry arms so freely. After awhile, having gleaned as much knowledge as my eyes could command, I remarked, in a friendly way, " Well, my friend, you seem to take things rather coolly."

" Oh, yes, sir," he answered. " I orter; I've been mighty hard put, but I reckon I'm good for another pull now."

" Where are you from ? " I asked.

" Fentriss County, nigh onter Jimtown " (Jamestown). I'm scoutin' it for Burnside, — runnin' boys inter camp."

" Oh! Then you wear that uniform as a disguise on scouting expeditions ? "

" No, sir, I never hed sech a rig on afore, I allers shows the true flag; an' thar hain't no risk in doin' it, 'case, yer see, the hull district down thar ar' Union folk, an' ary one uv 'em would housen me ef all Buckner's army was at my heels. But this time they run me powerful close, an' I *hed* ter show the Secesh rags." And as he said this, he looked down on his clean, unworn suit of Confederate gray with ineffable contempt.

"How could you manage to live with such a hole there?" I asked, pointing to the bullet-rent in the breast of his coat.

"Oh, I warn't inside uv 'em jist then; but I warrant me he war a likely feller thet war. I ortent ter a done it,— but I hed ter. It war my life or his'n. This war he." And taking from his side pocket a small miniature, he handed it to me.

It was a plain circlet of gold, attached to a piece of blue ribbon. One side of the rim was slightly clipped, as if it had been grazed by the passing ball, and the upper portion of the ivory was darkly stained with blood; but enough of the face was unobscured to show the features of a young man, with dark, flowing hair, and a full, frank, manly face. With a feeling akin to horror I was handing the picture back to the scout when, in low, stammering tones, he said to me, "T'other side, sir. Look at t'other side."

I turned the miniature over, and saw the portrait of a young woman scarcely more than seventeen. She had a clear, transparent skin, regular oval features, full, swimming black eyes, and what must have been wavy brown hair, but changed to a deep auburn by the red stains that tinged the upper part of the portrait. With intense loathing I turned almost fiercely on the scout, and exclaimed, "And you killed that man?"

"Yes, sir; God forgive me,—I done it. I couldn't holp it. He hed me down,—hed cut me thar," turning up his sleeve, and displaying a deep wound on his arm, "an' thar!" removing the bandage and showing a long gash behind his ear. "His arm was riz ter strike agen,—in another minnit he'd hev cluv my brain. I seed it, sir, an' I fired! God forgive me,—I fired. I wouldn't a done it if I'd know'd thet!" and he looked down on the face of the sweet young girl, and the moisture came into his eyes. "I'd hev shot him somewhar but yere,— somewhar but yere." And placing his hand over the rent in his coat, he groaned, as if he felt the wound. Listening, with that blood-stained miniature in my hand, to the broken words of that ignorant scout, I realized something of the horrible barbarity of war.

By this time we had crossed the Cumberland, and were approaching Nashville. Its beautiful suburbs, though covered with the early foliage of spring, wore a most desolate appearance. Stately villas were heaps of ruins; fine plantations and charming gardens were overrun with weeds. At the railway station I ran the gantlet of another set of military officials. Passes were examined and luggage looked into, but after awhile I disengaged myself from the crowd, and was driven off to the Commercial Hotel.

CHAPTER XI.

WITH "OLD ROSEY."

I WAS now in the dominion of "Old Rosey," as General Rosecrans was affectionately styled by every man and woman, white and black, within the limits of his department. To get into it, I had been obliged to have a permit from General Burnside, and on my arrival at Nashville I discovered that to get out to it, or to move forward to my destination at Murfreesborough, I was required to have a similar document from the provost marshal at Rosecrans's headquarters. This involved my remaining over for a day at Nashville, and I whiled away the time by roaming about the town, visiting the military prison and the various Union camps in the neighborhood. About noon, finding myself in the vicinity of the capitol, I called there and left with his private secretary a letter of introduction I had to Andrew Johnson, then military governor of Tennessee. I knew that he was absent in the North, but it occurred to me that I might need to know him before I got out of Secessia. Then, after dinner, I strolled out into the open fields, where a short walk brought me to the city cemetery, — a beautiful spot, with growing grass, and waving trees, and numberless flowers bending over low mounds; and in one corner half a thousand new-made graves, whose simple headstones told that the soldiers of the Union were sleeping beneath them.

One of these graves was open, and an old negro was filling it with earth, — singing as he worked. Seating myself on a low paling, I listened to his song, and these are some of its words as I took them down soon afterwards, from his dictation. I quote them not for their poetic merit, but to show the kind of music which was then popular in that section of the country.

> "Say, darkies, hab yo seed de massa
>   Wid de mufftash on his face,
> Gwo long de road some time dis mornin',
>   Like he gwine ter leab de place?
> He toted 'way a hoss and saddle,
>   An' forgot ter leab de pay;
> So I spec' he'm jined de big skedaddle;
>   I spec' he'm run away.
>   De massa run, ha! ha!
>   De darky stay, ho! ho!
>   It mus' be now de Kingdom comin',
>   An' de year ob jubilo.
>
> "He leff ahind some likely darkies,
>   A-suffrin' sad wid grief,
> Fur dat dar high and mighty massa
>   Hab turned a mean hoss-tief!
> Dey greab as ef dey wuz his chillen,
>   An' I haff suspec' dey ar';
> For dey's his nose, his big base fiddle,
>   An' his reddish wolly ha'r.
>   De massa run, ha! ha!
>   De darky stay, ho! ho!
>   It mus' be now de Kingdom comin',
>   An' de year of jubilo."

"Lamenting for your master, eh, uncle?" I said, approaching him. "It was wrong in him to turn 'hoss-tief.'"

The old man paused at his work, and, turning on me with a look of wounded pride, said, "My massa hain't no hoss-tief, sar. He neber done no sech a ting, — neber, sar!"

"I merely took your word for it, — that's all."

"Dat warn't my massa, sar," he answered, good-naturedly; "dat was some on dem low Secesh. My massa done gone away, sar; but he leab eberyting ahind, eben old Joe."

"And did you want to go with him?"

"No, sar! I hain't no Secesh; an' I was fotched up dis a way ter Nashville. Massa know'd I didn't want ter leab, an' he reckoned I cud shirk fur myseff somehow."

"How do you get on, shirking for yourself? You are very old."

He seemed more than seventy. His hair was white, his body bowed, and scarcely more than a skeleton. His story was illustrative of the fearful experiences of the negro in the war, but I have not space here to tell it; so I will merely say that, saying good-by to him, I strolled about Nashville, leaving, meanwhile, at the State House, a letter I had for Andrew Johnson.

I had invited the old negro to come to me when his work was over that evening, and I was seated with him in the smoke-beclouded hotel office, when the landlord brought to me a tall, fine-looking man, whom he introduced as the Hon. Edward H. East, Secretary of State, and acting-Governor in Governor Johnson's absence. Mr. East said he had seen my letter to the Governor, and had come to offer his services in any manner I might require them. I thanked him, and invited him to a seat, at the same time apologizing for the reception-room in which I had to receive him, — the smoke-begrimed office of a filthy tavern, its every seat occupied by a noisy crowd, and not even a broken-backed chair or a three-legged stool to offer to the second official of the State of Tennessee. I was looking about for a chair, when Mr. East pulled a trunk from a pile in the corner, saying, "Never mind, never mind, this will do." I was near the close of a two-hours' conversation with this gentleman, when a paper was handed me, signed " W. Truesdell," which said that if it were shown upon the cars it would secure me a free passage to Murfreesborough.

I set out on the following morning, and, on alighting from the cars at Murfreesborough, I was told that General Rosecrans was at the front, and not expected to return until the following day; so, not being able to deliver my letters of introduction, and seeing a dilapidated omnibus — some cast-off Northern vehicle — drawn up at the doorway of the station, I applied to the driver to take me to where I could pass the night. "I can take you to jail, sir, — it's the only house here that takes in strangers," was his answer. The town was then a military camp with 40,000 soldier inhabitants, but with not a solitary inn or other accommodation for travellers.

I was questioning with myself what to do in the emergency, when I was accosted by a "native," whom I had met, years before, in the mountains of East Tennessee, who offered to take me to the house of a lady of his acquaintance. "She's Secesh," he said, "way up ter the cars, and her fixin's hain't nothin' ter brag on, but if I ask her, I reckon she'll tuck you in."

I was pursuing knowledge under difficulties, and if Rosecrans did not turn out to be a better President than the common run of those officials, it was certain that I was undergoing a good deal of unprofitable privation. But it was Hobson's choice, — that or nothing, — so I gladly went along with my "native" friend, and was cordially welcomed by the Secesh lady. She had a son and a husband in the Confederate army, and had stayed behind to attack the most vital part of the Yankee enemy, — the stomach; but she did it with such unaffected grace, such genuine, though effusive, kindness, that it gave a relish to coarse corn-pone, and to bacon fried in lard, and tougher than gutta-percha.

After dinner, I sent my letters of introduction by a messenger to the general's headquarters, and on the succeeding morning, being told that he was an early riser, I followed them for a personal interview. I found his quarters in a modest brick building on a side street, and knew it at once from a large Union flag that was flying above its entrance. Entering the open doorway, I inquired of one of his aides if the general received visitors at so early an hour; the answer was that he was accessible at all hours of the day or night, but he was just then at breakfast; however, if my business was pressing, it would be attended to by his chief of staff, General Garfield, who was in the next apartment. I expressed a desire to meet that gentleman, and the aide ushered me at once into an adjoining room, where, seated by a window in a corner, at an unpainted pine desk, — a sort of packing-box, perched on a tall stool, with pigeonholes and a turn-down lid, — was a tall, deep-chested, sinewy built man, with large, regular features, a full, bluish-gray eye, and an expansive forehead, decidedly prominent under the eyebrows. He gave me a hasty glance, and when I mentioned my name rose and, with a warm grasp of the hand, said, "I am glad to meet you. I have seen your handwriting, — Edmund Kirke, his (X) mark," as he spoke, cutting the air in the form of a cross.

"And I have seen yours," I replied; "but you write with a steel pen, — epics in the measure of 'Hail Columbia.'"

I sat down with him, and did not think again of Rosecrans until Garfield reminded me that I had better see him before he was overrun with visitors. He then led me into a larger apartment, which, from the gaudy papering of the walls and its other vestiges of gentility, I concluded had

been the drawing-room of the former tenant of the mansion. At the right of the doorway was a high-post bedstead, and scattered about the bare floor were a dozen hard-bottomed chairs, a pine wash-stand, a wooden water-pail, and an old-fashioned sideboard. Against the wall, by the front window, was a large pine table surmounted by a framework of pigeonholes, and covered with various open maps, Secession newspapers, and official documents. At this table — in a rosewood armchair sadly out at the elbows, a cigar in his mouth, and a paper-cutter in his hand, with which he was rapidly dissecting a large pile of unopened letters that lay before him — sat the man whom the Republican leaders had selected as their next candidate for the presidency.

He took no notice of us until Garfield led me up to his desk, and said, "General, this is Mr. — " He did not complete the sentence, for Rosecrans no sooner looked up than he rose to his feet and, extending his hand in a cordial way, said, "How are you, Gilmore. I am glad to meet you."

As I took his hand, I remarked, "Why, general, have we met before?"

He answered, "No, I think not; but Quincy Gillmore was in my class at West Point, and you are exactly like him, — only he is a better-looking man than you are."

I laughed, saying, "We are often taken for one another; but I think our kinship is very remote. Once we sat down together to see how near we were related, and, after floundering about for a time, I told him we must have come from those two brothers, Cain and Abel, and, as I had no particular preference, he might take his choice. 'Then,' he said, 'if it makes no difference to you, I'll take Cain, for he was the more of a man of the two.'"

Rosecrans laughed, saying, "That sounds exactly like

Quincy, — he is a royal good fellow. I've read your books, and I'll wager a dime you are of the same kidney. But, lest you may think me a closer observer than I am, I'll tell you that I knew you were coming, and was expecting you."

"Expecting me!" I echoed. "On my way down an old darky told me that you knew everything, — I reckon it's so."

"I *reckon* it isn't," he answered, motioning me to a chair, resuming his own, and plunging again into the unopened letters. "But I knew you were coming, for you've been announced." Saying this, he handed me one of the letters he had recently opened. It was from the chaplain of an Indiana regiment who had been my roommate at the dingy hotel in Nashville. He had concocted a plan for educating the negroes in "ten lessons of one hour each," and, not content with keeping me awake with it until two o'clock in the morning, had, without my knowledge or consent, written Rosecrans by the previous mail, referring him to me for " further particulars."

"What do you know of that man?" he asked, going on with his letters.

"Nothing," I answered, "but I think he knows about as much of the Southern negro as I know of the moon."

"I thought so. A mere theorist. Only practical men are fit for the work we have in hand. What do you think we should do with the negro?"

"Let him alone."

"You are right," he answered, dropping his letters for a moment. "Give him the Bible and a spelling-book, freedom, and a chance for something more than six feet of God's earth, — and let him alone."

Saying this, he plunged again into his correspondence, all the while continuing the conversation. It had lasted for perhaps a quarter of an hour, when the door opened, and a tall, erect, rather stoutly built man, with square but regular features, and a somewhat impassive face, entered the apartment. From his uniform, and the portraits of him that I had seen, I recognized him at once as Gen. George H. Thomas. He said "Good morning" to Rosecrans, and then the latter introduced him to me, and he sat down beside us. By this time Rosecrans had gotten through his letters, and had begun to dictate replies to his senior aide, Major Frank S. Bond, who had seated himself on the other side of the pine table; but he continued to discuss the negro question. General Thomas, who had been reared among slaves, soon joined in the conversation, and before long it ranged over the entire field of what, as Rosecrans expressed it, would "prove to be the most difficult and perplexing problem of the nineteenth century." The course that things had so speedily taken chimed in with my desires exactly, for my wish had been to get at the sentiments of Rosecrans without asking him any direct questions.

After a time the conversation was interrupted by the entrance of a throng of visitors, and I adjourned with General Thomas to his quarters, where I dined and passed the remainder of the day till evening, when I went with him again to the private apartment of Rosecrans. There, about midnight, one of the officers present asked of me the question: "What effect would the abolition of slavery have upon the amalgamation of the whites and negroes?" and I was giving him my views upon the subject when Rosecrans came to where we were seated, and, placing his hand upon the back of General Thomas's chair, said, at the first break in the conversation: "Speaking of white-blacks reminds me of two who came within the lines a few weeks ago. They were as white as I am,—a little boy and girl, belonging to a rich planter, and a 'strong Union man,' living some twenty miles from here. He called on me the other day, and feeling it my duty to be courteous to 'our friends,' I asked him to dinner. Every moment I expected he would broach the subject of his slaves, but he left without saying a word about them. However, he came back in a few days. I invited him again to dinner, and he declined, but said, 'Gen'ral, some of my property has come inter yer lines. I knowed they wuz here when I seed ye afore, but I was telled ye'd yered they wuz my children,— ye sees they's as white as I am,— and I felt sort o' delicate like 'bout axing ye fur 'em till I could show fur certain they wasn't. They's my nevy's,— yere's the papers to prove it.'

"'I don't see what difference it makes whether they are your children or your nephew's,' I answered. 'But I suppose you have come to claim them?'

"'That is what I'se come fur, gen'ral,' he replied. 'I s'pose ye'll guv 'em up?'

"'Of course,' I answered, 'we are not negro-stealers. Every man shall have his rights within my lines.'

"'I am obleeged to ye,— much obleeged to ye, gen'ral,' he said, showing strong symptoms of hugging me. 'I was telled ye was a blasted Ab'lishioner, and wouldn't guv 'em up, and I'm right glad ye does, fur it'll do a heap uv good; it'll conciliate the loyal people 'round here mightily. Whar is they, gen'ral?'

"I answered him, 'I don't know,— Major Bond can tell you.'

"'Won't it require an order from ye to git 'em, gen'ral?' he asked.

"'Oh, no,' I answered; 'you only need ask them to go

with you, — slavery is so benign a thing that even white children must love it.'

"'And karn't I hev 'em 'cept they'll go peaceably?' he exclaimed, in consternation.

"'Of course not,' I replied. 'You must use no force. We neither steal negroes nor catch them.'

"With a big flea in his ear the planter left, no doubt cursing me for a blasted 'Ab'lishioner.'"

This was when the Government was pursuing its "conciliatory policy," and nearly every department commander was returning fugitives. There was no mistaking such sentiments, and yet the question remained whether, in his anxiety to save the Union, Rosecrans might not consent to its restoration "as it was," and without the extermination of slavery. To get an answer to this, without putting to him any direct queries, and also to measure him, as Mr. Greeley had suggested, "from head to foot," I remained with him a fortnight, in which time I fully satisfied myself that he was not only " sound on the goose," but was also a man of remarkable executive ability, extensive culture, broad, comprehensive views, and, moreover, a true Christian gentleman, who would do honor to any station within the gift of the American people.

He made me perfectly at home, going out of his way to give me every facility for observing the organization and operation of an army, and introducing me to every one of his general officers, commenting on them as freely as if he had known me for half a century. Of his chief of staff, General Garfield, he said, "He has, you know, been elected to Congress. He will make his mark there, and come out at the top of the heap. He is the best-read man in my army." Of Sheridan, "You wouldn't suppose that quiet, unassuming gentleman was a perfect tornado in battle.

I rode up to him at Stone River when nearly a half of his men were on the ground either dead or disabled, and he was pouring such a volley of oaths into the remainder as made my blood curdle. 'Hold on, Sheridan,' I said to him, 'omit the profanity. Remember, the first bullet may send you into eternity.' 'I can't help it, general,' he answered, 'we must hold this point; and my men won't think I'm in earnest unless I swear at them like hell.' If he lives, and has a chance, Sheridan will rise to the highest rank in the army, for he is not only a born fighter but a great general. Of Arthur C. Ducat, his inspector-general, a young man of thirty, bearing a strong facial resemblance to the first Napoleon, he said: "That is one of the bravest men I ever knew; I saw him once coolly face almost certain death, to perform a duty. Three on the same duty had fallen before his eyes, and he had to run the gantlet of a thousand muskets; but he did it."

I cannot repeat the general's words, but I think I can correctly relate the circumstances. It was at the battle of Iuka, where Rosecrans, with only 2,800 men actually engaged, was fighting a Confederate force of 11,000, holding a chosen and very strong position. Ducat, in riding up to the general, had observed a regiment of General Stanley's division that was about to be enveloped and overwhelmed by a much larger force of the enemy. "Ride on and warn Stanley at once," said Rosecrans. An acre on fire and swept with bullets lay between him and the menaced regiment; Ducat glanced at it and said, "General, I have a wife and children."

"You knew that when you came here," said Rosecrans, coolly.

"I'll go, sir," said Ducat, moving his horse forward after his momentary hesitation.

"Stay a moment. We must make sure of this," said Rosecrans. He thought a thousand lives of more value than four, so, hastily writing some despatches on the pommel of his saddle, he gave one to each of three orderlies, and sent them off, at intervals of about sixty yards, over the bullet-swept battle-field. Then he looked at Ducat, who had seen every one of the orderlies fall lifeless, or desperately wounded. Without a word, Ducat plunged into the fire, and, wonderful to tell, he ran the gantlet in safety, and with his clothes torn by Minie balls, and his horse reeling from a mortal wound, he got to Stanley, and saved the regiment.

On the following morning, I strolled out after breakfast to get a view of Murfreesborough, and was returning to headquarters, about eleven o'clock, when I was met by a young gentleman of Rosecrans's staff, who said: "I have been looking for you everywhere, sir. The general wants me to tell you that General Garfield is holding a camp meeting in his room, and about all the division and brigade commanders are there — he thinks you'd like to meet them."

I knew that Garfield had written those gentlemen the day before, asking their opinions as to the advisability of a forward movement of the army which had been recently ordered by Secretary Stanton; but I supposed their answers were to be given in writing, and not personally. However, I hurried to the meeting, where I found every chair and stool in the room and a low camp cot in the corner filled with sitters, — and "sitters" who would have graced any portrait gallery in the country. Garfield sat at the end of the apartment, and was speaking when I entered, but he paused, and, beckoning me to an unopened camp stool by his side, said: "Gentlemen of the jury, let me remind you that

"'A chiel's amang you taking notes,
And, faith, he'll prent 'em.'

"I beg to make you acquainted with Mr. Gilmore, of the New York *Tribune,* and allow me to suggest that if you don't behave yourselves you may have your portraits drawn in decidedly ragged regimentals."

"I don't believe it," said a voice behind me; "I'd trust any man of that name to write my biography. I knew Quincy Gillmore at West Point, and there's not a better fellow living. I say, Mr. Gilmore, why do you write under an assumed name? Your own is not to be ashamed of."

The speaker was a very tall, slim man of about thirty-five, with long, dark hair, and flowing beard, who sat canted back in a chair, with his long legs perched on the window-sill. A glance satisfied me that he was General Stanley, the chief of Rosecrans's cavalry. I answered, "For the same reason that you prefer to fight behind a stone wall."

"But he never fights in that way; he never was behind a stone wall in his life. His long legs could straddle any wall ever built. Why, sir, if you had seen him at Stone River, standing erect in his stirrups in the hottest fire, you'd have taken him for Trinity Church steeple, belching hot smoke and blue blazes."

This was said by a seamed veteran on my right, with a long white beard, and two thin tufts of gray hair on either side of his head. With his bent form and spectacled nose, he seemed more like some country doctor than a renowned soldier, — the hero of I don't know how many battles. It was General Van Cleve, who had been dangerously wounded at Stone River. He was the oldest man in the room.

"Come, come, my ancient friend," said Stanley, "don't be poking fun at my legs. If they had been yours in that fight, you might have run away and so escaped those half-dozen bullets."

"Silence in the meeting!" now roared a voice from the other end of the room. "The sensible people here want Garfield's exposition of the first chapter of Genesis, or his 'Decline and Fall of the Roman Empire,' — we don't care which."

In a few moments Garfield resumed some remarks he had been making on the character of the Southern Confederacy, which he compared to the conspiracy of Catiline, it having, he said, a like origin and objects, and the most of its leaders being a set of bankrupt scoundrels. I attributed his remarks to his ignorance of the South, and gave my attention to a study of his auditory. They numbered twenty-five or thirty, and every one was of marked character, more or less famous, and some were to become decidedly eminent.

From time to time Garfield told me who they were. The stout, full-faced, blond-complexioned man leaning against the wall by the window was the "old Russian," General Turchin; the handsome officer seated next to him, with wavy brown hair, and face so much like James Russell Lowell's, was St. Clair Morton, chief of the engineers, who might have been a poet, and was a hero. Leaning against the wall, at his back, the dark man with keen, intense eyes, heavy black beard, and coarse, wiry hair starting up into a sort of pyramid on the top of his head, was Jeff C. Davis, who killed General Nelson, and did such great service at Stone River. The plain, farmer-like, plucky-looking man on my right was General Palmer, subsequently commander of the Fourteenth Corps, Governor of Illinois, and United States Senator. The tall man next to him, in rusty uniform and top-boots, with a full, clear eye and an expressive face, was General Negley, and in other parts of the room were General Lytle, who wrote "I am Dying, Egypt, Dying," and was killed at Chickamauga, and Generals Hazen, Reynolds, King, Wood, and Colonels McKibben and Dan McCook. Altogether it was a gathering of men worth going a thousand miles to meet.

At the close of Garfield's remarks a singularly quiet, unassuming man of about thirty years entered the room and took a seat on the window-sill by the side of Stanley. He wore plain trousers, a loose sack coat, and everyday boots, and was below the medium height, compactly built, with closely cut hair and beard, and a dark, sun-browned face. There was nothing about him to attract attention except his eye, but that seemed a ball of black flame. "How are you, Phil?" "Good morning, Sheridan!" greeted him from various parts of the room, and Garfield, turning to me, said: "Mr. Gilmore, this is General Sheridan."

"Do you remember, sir, Pope's thirty thousand muskets, and ten thousand prisoners?" asked a young officer near me.

"Yes, very well," I replied.

"Well, I took the muskets, and Sheridan took the men. How many men were there, Sheridan?"

"I don't remember," answered the quiet general.

"Well, I remember the muskets. They counted nine hundred and thirty, — not one more or less."

"I was with Pope at the second battle of Booneville," said another general, "when Sheridan rode up to him, and reported sixty-five prisoners."

"'Why don't you say five hundred?' asked Pope. 'There ought to be five hundred, — call them five hundred, anyway;' and five hundred they were, but not in Sheridan's report."

A laugh followed; but the quiet general said nothing, and, in all I saw of him afterwards, I never heard him speak disparagingly of any one.

"As we are indulging in personalities," said Garfield, "let me ask if you have heard what Sheridan said when the general rode up to the wreck of his division, which, at the cost of 1,600 men, had held two-thirds of Bragg's army in check, after the rout of McCook, and long enough for Rosecrans to form a new line in face of the enemy. 'General,' he said, pointing to the part of his division that was still fit for duty, 'general, here are all I have left.'"

"The general said to me, only last night," I remarked, "that if General Sheridan lived, and had a chance, he would occupy a large space in our military history."

"Did the general say that?" asked Sheridan.

"He did, sir," I replied. "He said it to me personally."

"It gratifies me exceedingly," he remarked. "I think a good deal of his opinion. He is one of the ablest generals and bravest men I have ever known. In battle I am apt to get a little excited, but he is as serene and calm as a June morning. A little incident will illustrate this. I didn't see it myself, but I have it from one who did see it. The general has a distressing faculty for getting into the hottest places, and in the first day's fight at Stone River, after Garesche's head had been shot off by his side, and several other casualties had occurred among his staff, one of his aides — I think it was Major Bond — rode up to him, and said, 'Do you think it right to expose your life so, sir?' His only reply was to dash into a hotter place, to correct an alignment and regulate a battery that was firing somewhat recklessly. He was suddenly checked by a regiment lying across the field, the men with blood in their eyes. They were firing at the men who were working several rebel batteries that were flinging shot and shell all around them. The general thought this a good time to make a speech. He is not a finished orator, but he can jerk out sentences that can't be misunderstood. 'Men,' he said, 'would you know how to be safe? Then shoot low, — aim at their shins. But I'll tell you how to be safest of all. Give them a blizzard now at short range, right at their shins, and follow it up with the bayonet. Give them the bayonet, I say.'"

"That killing of Garesche was a horrible thing," said Garfield. "Major Bond, who rode by his side, and directly in the rear of Rosecrans, says that his headless body sat upright in the saddle for some twenty paces after it was decapitated, when, with a sudden movement of the horse, it rolled to the ground. The general was greatly attached to Garesche, — they were fellow Catholics, and much together, — and the major was reluctant to tell him of his death; but he did ride up to him, and say only, 'Garesche is dead.' 'I am very sorry,' was the sole response, 'but we cannot help it.' Soon afterwards an officer came to the general with the erroneous report that McCook was killed. 'We cannot help it,' was his cool reply. 'This battle must be won.'"

"Those last words of his," I remarked, "reveal the secret of his wonderful coolness. I asked him yesterday what his sensations were, while so constantly under fire during those two terrible days, and he answered, 'I had no sensations; I was absorbed in planning how to beat them.' The fact is, gentlemen, your general is a natural-born hero. I have studied him closely, and I conclude that while he has the strongest personal attachments, he is, above all things, attached to his duty. He regards his life as not his own, but the property of the country."

"No doubt that's so," said Stanley, "and his coolness is catching. Every member of his staff has the same impassible courage. Not one of them at Stone River so much as flinched when he led them right into a fiery furnace. You have met that youngster of his staff, — a boy of only eighteen, — little Willie Porter. His business in the first day's fight was to carry the general's dinner, and, before he mounted in the morning, he filled the general's haversack with luncheon, and slung it over his shoulder. After Garesche's death, a shell exploded in the midst of the staff, and a fragment struck between Willie's side and the haversack, bruising him severely, and tearing open the haversack. The luncheon tumbled to the ground, and, regarding it with a droll grimace, the boy exclaimed, 'There! the general's dinner is all gone!'"

At this moment a tall man in a rusty uniform entered the room and looked around for a vacant chair or camp stool. None being visible, he said to Garfield, "I say, general, is this the way you receive your visitors, — giving them only the floor to sit on?"

"The fact is, colonel, we are a little crowded," said Garfield, "for the general is closeted with the corps commanders. But we'll find a seat for you on one condition."

"Name the condition; I'll agree to anything if you'll give rest to the weary sole of my foot."

"We only ask you to sit in the middle of the room and give us some of your army experiences. You've been in forty battles and killed in every one of them."

"That's so," said the colonel. "I've had a surfeit of blood and glory; but nothing to compare with the experiences of the bright galaxy of shoulder-straps that is here assembled. Napoleon said that at the end of ten centuries he wouldn't have more than a single page of general history, but I see gentlemen here that will have ten pages, and I think I should be within the truth if I said that some of them will have a hundred. I naturally shall be diffident in addressing so brilliant an assemblage, but if you'll give me a chair I'll try it on, regardless of consequences."

"Come, come!" cried Sheridan, "stop your nonsense and begin. I haven't heard a good story since you told how Private Smapes winged the Confederate picket."

"What! Are you there, my little Phil? My steam-engine in breeches! But where are you? Let me behold the effulgence of your countenance."

"I'm here," said Sheridan, "hidden behind this big buckeye warrior, whose legs fill the entire window."

"Ah, I see!" rejoined the colonel, "the man with the seven-league boots. But here comes my chair, — upon my word, I believe it's the general's. I say, Mr. Orderly, where did you get this?"

"From the general, sir," was the answer. "Every other one has been brought in here."

As the colonel took his seat, Garfield said to me: "He's in the mood, and we shall hear something rich. He is a capital mimic, and the best actor and story-teller in the army."

The colonel now leaned back in his seat, stretched his long legs before him, and, gazing complacently around on his auditory, said: "Friends, countrymen, and lovers, favor me with your attention. When I had finished recruiting for my last regiment, I took my men to Camp Curtin to give the green ones a little drill preparatory to my bringing them out here and feeding them to the Confederate batteries. The camp was crowded with recruits, the most of them fresh from the country, their pockets full of money, and their hearts longing to see the world, and eager for what are styled 'war experiences.' Going in and out among them was one of those peripatetic nuisances who vend razor-strops and patent medicines, and he was intent upon victimizing the verdant young soldiers. He was a hatchet-faced fellow, with an enormous nose, and a wardrobe gotten up regardless of expense in the extreme of fashion. He was an oddity to look at, largely on account of his proboscis, which one of my men said was of the shovel-plough variety.

"For several days in succession he was located in a corner of the camp, where he did a thriving trade, but his business there falling off, he removed to where my regiment was quartered. I found him there one sunshiny August morning, with his hand-trunk perched on a box he had borrowed from the commissary, and another box near by from which he intended to address his auditory. Soon a crowd gathered around him, prepared to listen to his songs, laugh at his jokes, and waste their small currency upon the worthless trash in his hand-trunk."

Now the colonel assumed an attitude, while his voice and manner suddenly changed and became indescribably comic. He acted the peddler to absolute perfection. "Fellow soldiers!" he cried, in a nasal twang that was not unmusical, "yeou, I mean, who air about to go forth to slay the inimy as the angel did the hosts of Sennacherib, I hev a few words tu say tu yeou. I see it in yeour honest faces that yeou air prepared tu peel the Secesh rats wherever and whenever yeou come on ter 'em." (Laughter from the assembled officers.) "There is not won of yeou, I kneow, but will face the meusic.

"Yeou hev a high and holy duty tu perform, and yeou'll do it slick as ile, or I'm no jidge of human natur." (Great laughter.). "When yeou return home, as most on yeou, I hope, will, yeour brows will be beound with victorious wreaths, and the hills and valleys of the old Keystone State will echo and reëcho with songs of welcome, and fair hands will spread yeou repasts tu which milk and honey is nowhere, — nuther is army rayshuns a showin', by a long chalk!" (Renewed laughter and applause.) "Sheould yeou fall on the field of battle, yeou will fall in a glorious cause, and yeour widows and orphans and sweethearts will be entitled tu a pension, — and they'll get it, fur this Republican party is a-goin' tu holt the reins till Gabriel's trump calls it tu gloary." (Uproarious applause, mingled with a few "Not by a d——d sights!")

When the noise had somewhat subsided, the colonel went on, unmoved by the applause, and with a face as grave as a funeral procession. "My friends and fellow citizens," he said, "the life of a soldier is a hard one; all on yeou will find that cout afore yeou're much older. It's hard lodgin's, hardtack, and hard fare ginerally, with a great lack of cretur comforts. But these things must be endured, if we're goin' tu save eour kedentry, and ef it hain't wuth fightin' fur, it hain't wuth a continental dime, nohow."

The colonel's manner then changing entirely, he added: "The peddler then stooped down, opened his hand-trunk, and drew from it a small gallipot and a vial of a reddish fluid. Holding them up, one in each hand, he resumed his speech. 'But yeou see, my friends, there air men in the world who think of the pore soldier, 'way off there on the gory battle-fields, and if Professor Girard, of the anshunt 'Niversarsity of Pennsylvany, ain't one of 'em, I wouldn't tell yeou so. He is the inventor of the great intment that is warranted ter cure cuts, bruises, burns, scalds, wounds, and corns, and is called the great Military Intment. Also the great remedy for rheumatics, neuralgar, teuthache, etcetary, called the Balm of Gilead. Yeou've heard of it. The anshunt poet speaks of it. He asks, "Is there no balm in Gilead? is there no 'pothecary there?" This is that balm, feller citizens, told of three thousand years ago, and come to light in these latter days for the relief of our sick and sufferin' soldiers. This is the genuine article, — yeou hev my word fur it, and it's a fact, by ginger! The medicins air wuth their weight in gold, — when it's not at tu high a premium; but I sell 'em cheap, — twenty-five cents a box for the balm, and a quarter of a dollar for the intment. So walk up, gentlemen; buy one of each and I'll change a dollar bill, — I knowd specie change was scase with yeou, so I've brought the silver along, — or you kin take five for a dollar, and I'll change yeou a five-dollar bill.'

"The crowd by this time had grown to two or three thousand, and it included members from every regiment in the camp, but my men composed the circle directly around the peddler. 'Look here,' said one of them, 'if your medicines are what you say they are, just let me have three of the ointment and two of the balm.'

"' Bully for you, — warrant 'em, or the money returned. Here you air, — cash down.'

"The articles were passed over and a five-dollar bill tendered. 'Pennsylvany money, eh!' exclaimed the peddler. 'Redback, good as wheat. Here's your change; and who is the next customer?' No one replying at once, he opened his batteries again. 'Layin' on the damp ground brings rheumatics;' and then another soldier came forward, took the balm and ointment, and tendered another five-dollar bill. As he gave the change, the peddler held up the bill, saying: 'On the same bank, eh? Wall, I just declare; if I was in the saltin'-deown line I'd as soon pickle this stuff as gold itself.' As he thrust the bill into his side pocket, he gleefully exclaimed: 'Sold ag'in and got the tin, — and who is the next customer? Boys, remember, gov'ment shoes air made of hard leather, and walkin' must bring corns ter feet not used ter 'em.'

"Then another recruit stepped up, bought the wares, and took the change, the peddler once more exclaiming, 'Sold ag'in and got the tin.' He was followed with a perfect rush, until the peddler's stock of silver was exhausted, and still his buyers showed no disposition to cease purchasing. 'By golly, gentlemen,' he said, 'I must gin in till after dinner, when I'll be on hand ag'in, and supply you all, or bust in tryin'.' With this he jumped into a hack, and asked the driver, as a special favor, to 'let 'em rip.'

"He drove direct to the Bank of Harrisburg, where the cashier reported that he threw upon the counter a handful of five-dollar bills, and asked for smaller bills or specie at the current premium of ten per cent.

"'Central Bank of Pennsylvania, at Hollidaysburg!' exclaimed the cashier. 'Why, sir, that bank exploded four years ago, and never was of much account.'

"'Du tell!' cried the peddler, gazing upon the notes spread before him. 'Du tell!' Then, grasping the bills, he rushed from the bank, exclaiming, 'Sold ag'in and got the tin.'

"He must have realized the impossibility of recognizing his victimizers from among several thousand men, all clad alike, for he was not again seen in Camp Curtin."

Soon afterwards the three corps commanders emerged from the inner apartment, and the colonel's auditory scattered, the larger number into the general's room, the others, including the story-telling colonel and myself, to the quarters of General Garfield for dinner.

CHAPTER XII.

ROSECRANS DECLINES THE PRESIDENTIAL NOMINATION.

DURING the fortnight that I was with him, General Rosecrans placed at my disposal one of his three horses, — the big gray that he rode through his campaign in West Virginia, — and he gave me a suitable escort whenever I desired to ride outside of the Union lines. Except on one occasion, he never went himself to the front without asking me to go along with him. What occurred on that one occasion I will here relate, as it has a bearing on the subsequent portion of this narrative.

One morning, as we sat at breakfast together, Rosecrans handed me a letter he had that moment received, saying, " Here is an application from one of my officers for a furlough. It explains itself. I have to be at the front all day, and I wish you would stay and see him. If you think well of it, I will telegraph the Department for the furlough. The colonel was a prominent member of the Western Methodist Church, and, though a clergyman, is one of my best and bravest officers. You will be glad of his acquaintance."

I cheerfully assented, and an orderly was at once despatched to his camp for the colonel. Breakfast over, I read the application. It is too lengthy for full quotation here, but its essential part is in the following paragraph:

A considerable part of the territory occupied by the Methodist Episcopal Church, South, is now in possession of our armies. This has brought a large number of that communion within our lines. . . . From these persons I have learned personally the following facts, viz.: That they consider the rebellion has destroyed the Methodist Church, South; that it has virtually abolished slavery; that they are sincerely desirous of returning to the "Old Church," and that their brethren within the rebel lines are most heartily tired of the rebellion, and most ardently desire peace, and the privilege of returning to their allegiance to Church and State, and will do so whenever they are assured of amnesty for the past. . . . From these considerations . . . I would submit to the proper authorities the following proposition, viz.: *To go into the Southern Confederacy, and return within ninety days with proposal of peace that will be acceptable to our Government.*

About an hour after the departure of the orderly, an erect, spare man, in the undress uniform of a colonel of infantry, entered the inner room at the general's quarters, where I was seated. He seemed somewhat more than forty, and was a little above the medium height, with gray hair and beard, a high, open forehead, and a thin, marked face, expressing great earnestness, strength, and benignity of character. He came directly up to me and, bowing rather stiffly, said, "Is this Mr. Kirke?"

I answered, "That is the name I sometimes go by. You are Colonel Jaquess. I am very glad to meet you," and I took his hand cordially. After some unimportant remarks, he said, "The general has sent me word that he has referred my application to you."

"He has asked me to hear what you have to say," I replied, "and you know he is very busy."

He then made an extended explanation of his hopes and purposes, ending with, "I want to go to them, — to offer

them the olive branch, — to tell them, in the name of God and the country, that they will be welcome back."

To this I answered, "The Methodist element, colonel, is, I know, strong in the South; but I fear the peace part of it is not strong enough to control the politicians. They, if I know them, care little about church or country. They have other views than submission. They mean to establish an independent government at all hazards."

He replied, "I don't know what their views are. It is not my business to ask. I feel that God has laid upon me the duty to go to them, and go I must, unless my superiors forbid it."

"But how will you go?" I asked. "The Government, I feel sure, will give you neither authority nor protection. How, then, will you go?"

"Openly, in my uniform, as the messenger of God."

"I fear that the rebels, like the people of old, will fail to recognize the Lord's messenger. They will shoot or hang you as a spy."

"It is not for me to ask what they will do; I have only to go." This was said with a simple earnestness that showed the faith which casteth out fear.

I answered, "Well, I'll report what you say to the general; but I must be frank with you. If he asks my opinion, I shall advise him not to apply for the furlough. I have heard of you, and your life, in my judgment, is altogether too valuable to be wasted on such an embassy."

"That is not for you to judge," he said, coolly. "But I want more than a furlough; I want an interview with Mr. Lincoln to learn the terms on which he will give amnesty to the rebels. Will you say this to the general?"

"Yes; and, as I have told you, will advise him to do nothing about it."

I kept my word with him,—that is, I reported the interview to General Rosecrans, and recommended that he should do nothing about it.

"Why not?" asked the general.

"Because he could accomplish nothing, and might throw his life away."

"I know," he answered, "if he talks peace to the people the leaders will hang him; but he'll not do that. He'll go to the leaders themselves. The terms he will offer may not be accepted, but it will strengthen our moral position to offer them. It will show the world that we do not seek to subjugate the South. As to his life,—he takes the right view about that. He considers it already given to the country. If you had seen him at Stone River you would think so."

That evening the general sent a telegram to Washington, stating the colonel's objects, and asking for him a four months' furlough, and an interview with the President. Answer came in the morning, declining the requests, but asking a fuller explanation of Colonel Jaquess's purposes by mail. The message was sent out to the colonel, and in a few hours he appeared at headquarters. I happened to be with the general at the time. He was as busy as usual, but, as Jaquess came in, he looked up, and said, "Well, colonel, you've got your sentence."

"I don't think so, general," answered the colonel, "I never give up with one trial."

"That's right; but what's to be done now?"

"Try again," said the colonel. "Mr. Kirke must go to Washington. I've known Mr. Lincoln for years; but I might write him forty letters, and accomplish nothing. Writing won't do it. Mr. Kirke must go to him." This was spoken with such inimitable coolness that I burst into a laugh.

"Yes," said the general, with his peculiar smile, "that is it. You must go. You've been besieging me for a pass for a week; now, I'll give you one if you'll take Washington on your way home. I've some other business, you know, that I want attended to, and you will do it, — to oblige me."

"Well, to oblige you, I will; but allow me to suggest that you write Mr. Lincoln about the colonel's project. One word from you would be more effective than all I might say, even if I believed in it."

He turned about to his desk, and wrote a letter at once, of which the following is a copy:

HEADQUARTERS DEPARTMENT OF THE CUMBERLAND.
MURFREESBOROUGH, TENN., May 21, 1863.

To his Excellency, the President of the United States: — The Rev. Dr. Jaquess, Colonel commanding the 73d Illinois, — a man of character, — has submitted to me a letter proposing a personal mission to the South. After maturely weighing his plan, and considering well his character, I am decidedly of opinion that the public interests will be promoted by permitting him to go as he proposes.

I do not anticipate the results that he seems to expect, but I believe that a moral force will be generated by his mission that will more than compensate us for his temporary absence from his regiment.

His letter is herein enclosed, and the bearer of this, Mr. Gilmore, can fully explain Colonel Jaquess's plans and purposes.

Very respectfully,
W. S. ROSECRANS, *Major-General.*

The "other business" which General Rosecrans desired me to attend to had, in part, relation to a disagreement between himself and Secretary Stanton. Soon after the battle of Stone River, the Secretary had written the general a personal letter, saying that he had made up his mind to offer a major-generalship in the regular army to the brigadier who first won an important victory. The letter aroused the general's intense indignation. Major Bond, in relating to me the incident, said, "I never saw him so angry as when he received that letter. With it in his hand, he cried out, 'Does he seek to bribe me to do my duty? Does he suppose I will sacrifice the lives of my men to serve my personal ambition?'"

It seemed to Rosecrans that Stanton was about to administer the affairs of the army on the plan of a gift enterprise, and Rosecrans, who was frankness itself, said about as much in his response to that letter. Stanton was a good hater. He took mortal offence at the attitude of Rosecrans, and then began to make a series of demands upon him that were impossible of execution; his last being a peremptory order for a forward movement upon Chattanooga. This order Rosecrans had refused to obey, on the ground that it would imperil his army,—a truth demonstrated four months later by the slaughter at Chickamauga,—and now he asked me to lay before Mr. Lincoln his reasons for disobeying the Secretary's demand. This I cheerfully consented to do, for even my unmilitary eye could perceive the extreme hazard of a forward movement.

Another "little matter of business" that the general desired me to lay before the President, was a projected negro insurrection to which he had been invited to give his countenance and support. Early one morning, as I sat alone with him in his private apartment, one of his aides entered the room and handed him a letter, saying that the bearer was waiting for an answer. Rosecrans opened the letter, and became at once absorbed in its contents. He then asked the aide, "What sort of a looking man gave you this?"

"A bright-colored mulatto, decently clad, and, I should judge, of more than ordinary intelligence," was the answer.

"Tell him to wait," said the general. He then re-read the letter, and, handing it to me, said, "Read that; tell me what you think of it."

The outside of the letter was worn and leather-stained, indicating that it had been pressed between the outer and inner soles of a shoe; but the inside startled me. It was written in a round, unpractised hand, which, though badly spelled, showed that its author was accustomed to the hearing of good English. The date was May 18, 1863, and it began thus:

GENERAL: — A plan has been adopted for a simultaneous movement, or rising, to sever the rebel communications throughout the whole South, which is now disclosed to some general in each military department in the Secesh States, in order that they may act in concert, and thus ensure success.

The plan is for the blacks to make a concerted and simultaneous rising, on the night of the 1st of August next, over the whole States in rebellion; to arm themselves with any and every kind of weapon that may come to hand, and commence operations by burning all railway and country bridges, tearing up all railroad tracks, and cutting and destroying telegraph wires; and when this is done, take to the woods, the swamps, or the mountains, whence they may emerge, as occasions may offer, for provisions or for further depredations. No blood is to be shed except in self-defence.

The corn will be in roasting ear about the 1st of August, and upon this, and by foraging on the farms at night, we can subsist. Concerted movement, at the time named, would be successful, and the rebellion be brought suddenly to an end.

The letter went on with some other details, and ended as follows:

The plan will be a simultaneous rising over the whole South, and yet few of all engaged will know of its full extent. Please write "I" and "Approved," and send by the bearer, that we may know you are with us.

Be assured, general, that a copy of this letter has been sent to every military department in the rebel States, that the time of the movement may be general over the entire South.

As I finished the letter, the General asked, "What do you think of it?"

I answered, "It would end the rebellion. Coöperated with by our forces, it would certainly succeed; but the South would run with blood."

"Innocent blood! Women and children!"

"Yes, women and children. If you let the blacks loose, they will rush into carnage like horses into a burning barn. St. Domingo would be multiplied by a million."

"He says no blood is to be shed except in self-defence."

"He says so, and the leaders may mean so, but they could not restrain the rabble. Every slave has some real or fancied wrong, and he would take such a time to revenge it."

"Well, I must talk with Garfield. Come, go with me."

We crossed the street to General Garfield's lodgings, where he was bolstered up in bed, just recovering from a fever. Rosecrans sat down on the foot of the bed and handed him the letter. Garfield read it over carefully, and then, laying it down, said, "It would never do, general. We don't want to whip by such means."

"I knew you would say so," said Rosecrans. "But he speaks of other department commanders, — may they not come into it?"

"Yes, they may, and that should be looked to. Mr. Gilmore tells me that he must soon go home. Send by him this letter to the President, and let him head off the movement. He can do it by restraining the department commanders. Without their support it will soon fall through."

I had before this become fully satisfied that Rosecrans would be a suitable candidate for the presidency; it only remained to ascertain if he would accept of the nomination should it be tendered to him. I was awaiting a favorable occasion to approach him on the subject, when I was informed that General Garfield was dangerously ill at his lodgings. I had missed him from his desk, but had been told that he was not seriously sick, and would be out in a few days; and I went at once to him. I found him in a raging fever, delirious, and attended only by his body-servant, a West India negro. The surgeon, soon coming in, told me that he hoped to "pull him through," but it was all-important that he should have his medicines regularly, and it was next to impossible to get any one, except his body-servant, who would watch faithfully with him at night. In these circumstances I volunteered for the duty. I remained with him several days and nights, — meanwhile meeting Rosecrans only occasionally, — and it was not long before Garfield passed the crisis, and could talk freely and coherently. Then he told me of his early life and campaigns, and I told him what had brought me to Murfreesborough. He was greatly pleased; said that if the country were canvassed from East to West, so fit a man could not be found, and advised my going at once to Rosecrans and opening the subject to him in direct business fashion. I did so.

It was near to midnight before Rosecrans and I were left alone in his private apartment, but, the moment the door closed upon the last visitor, I went into the subject with him. He heard me through with evident surprise and gratification, and then said:

"The good opinion of those gentlemen is exceedingly gratifying to me, and so is yours, and I assure you that

I have not had the remotest suspicion that you were here for any such purpose. I have supposed you were merely gathering literary material; but, my good friend, it cannot be. My place is here. The country gave me my education, and so has a right to my military services; and it educated me for precisely this emergency. So this, and not the presidency, is my post of duty, and I cannot, without violating my conscience, leave it. But let me tell you, and I wish you would tell your friends who are moving in this matter, that you are mistaken about Mr. Lincoln. He is in his right place. I am in a position to know, and if you live you will see that I am right about him."

These were his exact words as near as I could recall them half an hour after they were spoken. For more than twenty-five years I refrained from making them public, principally because I soon saw that I had erred about Mr. Lincoln, and was not anxious to trumpet the fact that I had even temporarily been willing to act in opposition to him. However, the circumstance of my having tendered Rosecrans the nomination on behalf of the Republican leaders, and Rosecrans having declined it, got into print some years ago in A. G. Riddle's "Life of James A. Garfield," the materials for which, the author states, were derived directly from Garfield. But, as is often the case with twice-told tales, the facts are there inaccurately stated. The book attributes the declination of Rosecrans to Garfield's advice, whereas Rosecrans decided upon his own judgment, and without a moment's deliberation, and, as I understood, against the views of Garfield.

It was not thought prudent to entrust the letter in regard to the negro insurrection to the mails, nor, with the railway infested with John Morgan's men and Confederate guerillas, was it a safe document to carry about the person.

If I should be captured and searched, and that found upon me, — with no attending proof to show the use of it that was intended, — a short shrift and a long rope would be my way to glory. So, ripping open the top of my boot, I tucked it snugly away in the lining, and then having a shoemaker-soldier nicely restore the broken stitches, I took it, with the other documents furnished me by General Rosecrans, to Washington.

CHAPTER XIII.

CONFERENCES WITH PRESIDENT LINCOLN.

I ARRIVED in Washington from my visit to Tennessee near the close of May, 1863, and I lost no time in forwarding by a messenger, to the White House, the papers which were intended for the personal inspection of the President. Among these papers were the letter to him from General Rosecrans; another from Colonel Jacquess; the one from the colored man who had asked Rosecrans's aid and countenance to a proposed negro insurrection; and the rest were full notes of conversations I had myself held with no less than sixteen of Rosecrans's general officers, in regard to the forward movement upon Chattanooga which had been ordered by Secretary Stanton. The letter from Colonel Jaquess to the President he had given to me open, asking that I would read it. Having done so, I hesitated about delivering it to Mr. Lincoln, lest what struck me as its half fanatical tone — of which there was not a trace in the colonel's conversation — should prejudice him against the request. However, as frankness seemed to demand that the President should know just exactly of what "manner of spirit" Jaquess was, I despatched his letter with the other papers. It read as follows:

MURFREESBOROUGH, TENN., May 23, 1863.
HON. A. LINCOLN, *President U. S. A.*

My Dear Sir, — This, with other papers, will be handed to you by Mr. Gilmore, who has been introduced to me by General Rosecrans.

Mr. G. will explain to you in full what I propose to do. Meanwhile, should you feel that my proposition is *too strong*, and cannot be realized, I would say, I may not be able to reach the specific object stated in the proposition, but the mission cannot fail to accomplish great good.

It is a fact well known to me and others, perhaps to yourself, that much sympathy exists in the minds of many good people, both in this country and England, for the South, on the ground of their professed piety. They say, "Mr. Davis is a praying man," "Many of his people are devotedly pious," etc., etc. Now, you will admit that, if they hear me, I have gained a point. On the other hand, if Mr. Davis and his associates in rebellion refuse me, coming to them in the name of the Lord on a mission of peace, the question of their piety is settled at once and forever. Should I be treated with violence, and cast into prison, shot, or hanged, — which may be part of my mission, — then the doom of the Southern Confederacy is sealed on earth and in heaven forever. My dear Mr. Lincoln will excuse me when I say that I am ready for any emergency, and though not Samson, I should, like him, slay more at my death than in all my life at the head of my regiment. No, the mission cannot fail. God's hand is in it. I am not seeking a martyr's crown, but simply to meet the duty that has been laid upon me.

I have talked freely with Mr. Gilmore, and he will explain to you more fully, if you desire. To him I would refer you, and with my best wishes and prayers, I am, dear sir,

Your obedient servant,
JAMES F. JAQUESS,
Colonel Com'd'g 73d Illinois Infantry.

I enclosed with the letters a note to Mr. Lincoln, asking at what hour I might have a private interview. The answer, written in pencil on a small card, was, "Come at half past seven this evening, and I'll be glad to see you. A. L."

I had been taught promptness by Robert J. Walker, and at precisely the appointed time I presented myself in the anteroom to the President's apartment. There I was told that Mr. Lincoln was closeted with Reverdy Johnson, and, taking a seat, I waited. In about half an hour Mr. Johnson passed out, and then the homely, humane face that every one is now familiar with appeared in the doorway. Taking me by the hand, he said, " Sorry to have kept you waiting. Come in," adding, as he closed the door behind me, " Do you know, I can't talk with you about that Jaquess matter?"

" Why not, sir?" I asked, in some surprise. He answered, " Because I happen to be President of the United States. We can make no overtures to the rebels. If they want peace, all they have to do is to lay down their arms. But never mind about that; you've been to Tennessee, and I want to see you. So sit down and tell me all you know; it won't take you long."

I laughed, saying, " I am not sure as to that, sir. But you look fatigued; will not a long talk tire you?"

" No, no!" he answered, " never mind if it does. I am obliged to be tired. I have looked over the papers you've sent me, and I've many questions to ask. Now, first about this negro insurrection," taking up the letter; " is not this a hoax?"

I answered that at first I thought it was; however, it bore so many marks of genuineness, — its style, just that of an uneducated negro who had gathered a certain kind of oral culture from intercourse with the whites, but not the ability to express himself correctly in writing, and the leather stains upon the envelope, — these looked so genuine that it seemed to me it would not be safe to treat it as bogus.

" Well," he said, " it does have a genuine look. What do Rosecrans and Garfield think of it?"

I told him.

" And they want me to put my foot upon it?"

"They do, most decidedly; they urge its having immediate attention. They think the country would be seriously compromised if the project were for a moment countenanced."

"They are right, and I will give it immediate attention. You may write them to that effect."

As I shall not again have occasion to refer to this subject, I may as well break into this interview to relate what else I know of it. The interview was near the close of May, and early in June I received a letter from General Garfield, dated the 4th instant, of which the following is an extract:

> I am clearly of opinion that the negro project is every way bad, and should be repudiated and, if possible, thwarted. If the slaves should, of their own accord, rise and assert their original right to themselves, and cut their way through rebeldom, that is their own affair; but the Government could have no complicity with it without outraging the sense of justice of the civilized world. We should create great sympathy for the rebels abroad, and God knows they have too much already. I hope you will ventilate the whole thing in the *Tribune*, and show that the Government and people disavow it.

I submitted this letter to Horace Greeley and Sidney Howard Gay, who both urged the immediate publication of the whole affair. But I said, "The matter is now in the hands of Mr. Lincoln. It might interfere with his plans if it should be prematurely published. However, I will write him at once."

His reply is now in the historical library of the Johns Hopkins University, at Baltimore. It was in a letter from his private secretary, John G. Nicolay, dated June 14, 1863. So much of it as refers to this subject is as follows:

> The President has no objection whatever to your publishing what you propose concerning the negro insurrection, providing you do not in any way connect his name with it.

Before the arrival of this reply from the President, I received another letter from General Garfield, in which he said:

> The negro scheme of which we talked has been pressed upon us again, and the letter asserts that five out of our nine department commanders have approved it. Another letter, received yesterday, says one more department has gone into it, and that the scheme is being rapidly and thoroughly perfected, and the blow will certainly be struck.

This last letter convinced me that no time was to be lost, and, after conferring again with Messrs. Greeley and Gay, I decided to go on to Washington to urge upon Mr. Lincoln the necessity for prompt action, and to gain from him such other facts as would be prudent to make public.

The President read the two letters of Garfield in his quiet, thoughtful way, and then, moving his one leg from where it dangled across the other, he said: "I've been thinking on that subject. I guess you had better say nothing whatever just yet. You see, I have scotched the snake, not actually killed it. When it is dead it will be time enough to preach its funeral sermon."

"And you will let me know when you are ready for the sermon?"

He promised to do so, and soon the interview ended.

I do not assert that this projected insurrection was not what Mr. Lincoln at first surmised it might be,—a hoax. I simply affirm that Generals Rosecrans and Garfield—and soon Mr. Lincoln, also—believed it to be a real danger, which threatened the South with all the horrors of St. Domingo. But whether the danger was real or not, the action of the President, and of the others who had cognizance of this projected insurrection, has the same character of genuine human kindness towards the South.

All know that the insurrection did not take place, and I

have always doubted if the conspiracy was so widespread and universal as it was supposed to be by the subordinate leader who wrote the letters to Rosecrans.

The uprising was fixed for August, and serious outbreaks occurred among the blacks in Georgia and Alabama in September. May not those have been the work of subordinate leaders who, maddened at the miscarriage of the main design, were determined to carry out their part of the programme at all hazards?

Mr. Lincoln was disinclined to talk about the part he took in the affair, and I was too diplomatic to press him with questions. The last he said to me upon the subject was a short time before his death, when, alluding to it, he remarked, " Some time, when I have a little leisure, I will tell you the whole of that story."

The assassin's bullet cut short the story.

I will now return to the interview I began to relate in the opening of this chapter. Mr. Lincoln having thus disposed of the projected negro insurrection, said, " Now tell me what you saw of Rosecrans and his army, and what you think of the general personally."

" Well, sir," I answered, " I was in intimate intercourse with him daily for more than a fortnight, and I say without reservation that he is one of the most all-accomplished men I ever met, with remarkable executive ability, quick, unerring judgment, and views as broad as those of Robert J. Walker. I am not a soldier, and so not competent to give a military estimate of him, but, before I met him, Quincy Gillmore told me that he was the most tenacious fighter and the ablest strategist in our army; and this is the opinion of every one of his general officers. He fills up fully the idea I have of Wellington. Moreover, he is a thorough Christian gentleman."

"But, on occasions, somewhat irascible?" he said, in an inquiring tone.

"Never," I answered, "unless under provocation that would move even you from your equanimity."

"Then you know that he is at loggerheads with Stanton?"

"Yes, I know all about it."

"And what is your opinion of the controversy? Speak freely, no matter who it hits."

"Well, Rosecrans is all right, and Stanton is all wrong. If I were in Rosecrans's place I would resign before another day is over. I think he would have resigned a month ago had he not been restrained by feelings of patriotism. He may do it yet, if you don't hold Stanton in check. You can't afford to lose Rosecrans."

"Then you think him the right man in the right place?"

"No, sir; I think he is the right man in the wrong place."

"Then," he asked, "where would you put him? Tell me; I may not follow your advice, but nevertheless I would like to have it."

"Well, sir, if I were in your place I should put Halleck into the field, retire Stanton to a clerical position, and give Rosecrans full command of all the armies. The old gentleman who gave me my business education used to say there could be but one head to a commercial establishment. I suppose the same principle applies to military matters."

"There is a good deal in that," he remarked. "Now, you have heard the forward movement to Chattanooga discussed,—what is your opinion about that?"

"The same as that of Rosecrans and every one of his general officers, with all of whom I have conversed on the subject. They think that under present circumstances it would be suicidal — would end in the defeat, and perhaps the total destruction, of our army. Have you not read the reports I sent you this morning of my interviews with those gentlemen?"

"Not fully; but I see they are all of one mind, — decidedly opposed to a forward movement."

"They are, sir; and let me add what General Thomas said to me when I was stepping upon the cars to come away. He knew that I was to have a talk with you on this subject, and he said, 'Impress upon Mr. Lincoln that the movement cannot be safely made with less than 100,000 men in the marching army.'"

"Well," he said, "they all think alike; so they must be right. You may say to Rosecrans that the order will be countermanded, and he will not again be ordered forward till he is supplied with men and horses enough to move in safety."

"It will give me great pleasure to do so," I answered. "But, Mr. Lincoln, permit me to suggest that you say the same thing to him yourself — and to-night, by telegraph, so he may get it in the morning. Old Rosey is just the man to appreciate such a courtesy, and it would be a salve to a good many of Mr. Stanton's wounds."

"I'll do it," he said, "very cheerfully, just as soon as I've said a few more words to you. Then I'll let you go, for it's growing late, and I want some sleep. As to Stanton — you know that it is hard to teach old dogs new tricks. He is terribly in earnest; and he does not always use the most conciliatory language. He very sensibly feels the need we have of victories, and he would take almost any means to get them. And the fact is, unless we have them soon the war is likely to be prolonged indefinitely. Say this to Rosecrans, and ask him to have patience with Stanton. His bark is a great deal worse than his bite."

A short desultory conversation followed, and it was half past ten when I rose to take leave of him. As I did so he asked, "When do you return home?"

"In the morning, sir," I replied.

"Can't you stay another day," he said, "and come to see me to-morrow evening? I want to think more of that Jaquess matter."

That night before I slept I mailed a full report of this interview to General Rosecrans.

On the following evening I called again, as he had requested, upon Mr. Lincoln. I found him in a more anxious mood than I had ever seen him. He wore a fagged, dejected look, and for a time indulged in none of his accustomed raillery and jocoseness. His concern was for Grant, who was before Vicksburg with numbers inferior to Pemberton and Johnston. His fear was that Johnston had cut Grant's communications, for he had not heard from him for more than twenty-four hours. As despatch after despatch came in from the War Department, he opened and glanced over it, then laid it down, saying in a weary way, "Nothing from Grant yet! Why don't we hear from Grant?" Had the life of one of his sons been trembling in the balance, he could not have shown greater anxiety. I felt too much sympathy with him to attempt to divert his mind to the business I had come about, and it was a full hour before he alluded to the subject. Then suddenly he said, "Well, I've kept you over to consider about that Jaquess matter. I've about concluded to let him go. My only fear is that he may compromise me; but I don't see how he can if I refuse to see him, and he goes altogether on his own responsibility. But he must understand distinctly that I have nothing to do with his project, either directly or indirectly. If the impression should go abroad that I had, it might complicate matters badly."

"I understand, sir," I remarked. "It might be construed into a quasi-acknowledgment of the rebel Government, and give France and England the pretext they want for recognizing the Confederacy."

"Partly that," he answered, "and partly its effect on the North. The Copperheads would be sure to say I had shown the white feather, and resorted to back-door diplomacy to get out of a bad scrape. This, whether true or not, would discourage loyal people. You see, I don't want to be like the dog that crossed the brook with the piece of meat in his mouth, and dropped it to catch its enlarged shadow in the water. I want peace; I want to stop this terrible waste of life and property; and I know Jaquess well, and see that, working in the way he proposes, he may be able to bring influences to bear upon Davis that he cannot well resist, and thus pave the way for an honorable settlement; but I can't afford to discourage our friends and encourage our enemies, and so, perhaps, make it more difficult to save the Union."

"I appreciate your position, sir," I said, "but what weight will Jaquess have, if he goes without some, at least implied, authority from you?"

"He may have much," he replied, drawing from his side pocket the letter to him from Jaquess, and glancing over it. "He proposes here to speak to them in the name of the Lord, and he says he feels God's hand is in it, and he has laid the duty upon him. Now, if he feels that he has that kind of authority, he can't fail to affect the element on which he expects to operate, and that Methodist element is very powerful at the South."

"Why, sir!" I remarked. "I hesitated about delivering you that letter. I feared you would think Jaquess fanatical."

"If you had not delivered it," he answered, "I would not let him go. Such talk in you or me might sound fanatical; but in Jaquess it is simply natural and sincere. And I am not at all sure he isn't right. God selects his own instruments, and sometimes they are queer ones; for instance, he chose me to steer the ship through a great crisis."

I was glad to see him relapsing into his usual badinage, but, desiring to keep him to the subject, I said: "Then, sir, you decide to give Jaquess the furlough, but refuse to grant him an interview. He will need to know your views about peace. What shall I write him are the terms you will grant the rebels?"

"Don't write him at all, — write to Rosecrans. I've been thinking what had better be said. My views are, peace on any terms consistent with the abolition of slavery and the restoration of the Union. Is not that enough to say to Jaquess? He can do no more than open the door for further negotiations, which would have to be conducted with me here, in a regular way. Let Rosecrans tell him that we shall be liberal on collateral points; that the country will do everything for safety, nothing for revenge."

"Do you mean, sir," I asked, "that as soon as the rebels lay down their arms you will grant a general amnesty?"

"I do; and I will say to *you* that, individually, I should be disposed to make compensation for the slaves; but I doubt if my Cabinet or the country would favor that.

What do you think public opinion would be about it? Nicolay tells me you have recently lectured all over the North; you must have heard people talk."

"I have, sir, almost everywhere; and my opinion is that not one voter in ten would pay the South a dollar. Still, I have observed very little hatred or bitterness in any quarter."

"No," he answered; "the feeling is against slavery, not against the South. The war has educated our people into abolition, and they now deny that slaves can be property. But there are two sides to that question: one is ours, the other the Southern side; and those people are just as honest and conscientious in their opinion as we are in ours. They think they have a moral and legal right to their slaves, and until very recently the North has been of the same opinion; for two hundred years the whole country has admitted it, and regarded and treated the slaves as property. Now, does the mere fact that the North has come suddenly to a contrary opinion give us the right to take the slaves from their owners without compensation? The blacks must be freed. Slavery is the bone we are fighting over. It must be got out of the way, to give us permanent peace; and if we have to fight this war till the South is subjugated, then I think we shall be justified in freeing the slaves without compensation. But in any settlement arrived at before they force things to that extremity, is it not right and fair that we should make payment for the slaves?"

"If I were a slaveholder," I answered, "I should probably say that it was; but you, sir, have to deal with things as they are, and I think that if you were to sound public sentiment at the North you would find it utterly opposed to any compromise with the South. A vast majority would regard compensation as a price paid for peace, and not for the slaves."

"So I think," he said, "and therefore I fear we can come to no adjustment. I fear the war must go on till North and South have both drunk of the cup to the very dregs, — till both have worked out in pain, and grief, and bitter humiliation the sin of two hundred years. It has seemed to me that God so wills it; and the first gleam I have had of a hope to the contrary is in this letter of Jaquess. This thing, irregular as it is, may mean that the higher powers are about to take a hand in this business, and bring about a settlement. I know if I were to say this out loud, nine men in ten would think I had gone crazy. But — you are a thinking man — just consider it. Here is a man, cool, deliberate, God-fearing, of exceptional sagacity and worldly wisdom, who undertakes a project that strikes you and me as utterly chimerical: he attempts to bring about, single-handed, and on his own hook, a peace between two great sections. Moreover, he gets it into his head that God has laid this work upon him, and he is willing to stake his life upon that conviction. The impulse on him is overpowering, as it was upon Luther, when he said, 'God help me. I can do no otherwise.' Now, how do you account for this? What produces this feeling in him?"

"An easy answer would be to say that Jaquess is a fanatic."

"But," he replied, "he is very far from being a fanatic. He is remarkably level-headed; I never knew a man more so. Can you account for it, except on his own supposition, that God is in it? And, if that be so, something will come out of it, perhaps not what Jaquess expects, but what will be of service to the right. So, though there is risk about it, I shall let him go."

"There certainly, sir, is risk to Jaquess. He will go without a safe-conduct, and so will be technically a spy. The rebel leaders may choose to regard him in that light. If they don't like his terms of peace, they may think that the easiest way to be rid of the subject. In that event, couldn't you in some way interfere to protect him?"

"I don't see how I could," he replied, "without appearing to have a hand in the business. And if Jaquess has his duties, I have mine. What you suggest reminds me of a man out West, who was not overpious, but rich, and built a church for the poor people of his neighborhood. When the church was finished, the people took it into their heads that it needed a lightning-rod, and they went to the rich man, and asked him for money to help pay for it. 'Money for a lightning-rod!' he said. 'Not a red cent! If the Lord wants to thunder down his own house, let him thunder it down, and be d——d.'"

"So," I said, laughing, "you propose to let the Lord take care of Jaquess?"

"I do," he answered. "His evident sincerity will protect him. I have no fear for him whatever. But I shall be anxious to hear of him, and I wish you would send me the first word you get. In writing to Rosecrans, omit what I have said about paying for the slaves. The time has not come to talk about that. Let him say what he thinks best to Colonel Jaquess; but the colonel must not understand he has the terms from me. We want peace, but we can make no overtures to the rebels. They already know that the country would welcome them back, and treat them generously and magnanimously."

"To avoid any possibility of misunderstanding, sir," I remarked, "would it not be well for you also to write to Rosecrans?"

"Perhaps it would," he answered. "I think I will."

As I have said, I had never seen Mr. Lincoln so deeply depressed. And now, when I thought of the gigantic combination that had been formed for his overthrow; how the men on whom he most relied, and who were bound by a due regard for their country to give him the most zealous support, were deserting him and leaving him to carry on the tremendous struggle alone, my sympathy went out to him irresistibly, and I resolved to make such amends as I could for having given even a qualified aid to the furtherance of their project. I could not betray the confidence that Mr. Greeley had placed in me, nor so much as hint at the existence of the unfriendly combination; but I might afford him some little comfort by telling him what a lady, whom he knew to be one of the best of her sex, had said to me about him. So, drawing a letter of hers from my pocket, I said, "Mr. Lincoln, I want to read to you a letter which I received at the *Tribune* office here this morning. It is from a young woman whom you know. Long ago she gave herself to the Lord, and that, you know, means the country; so she has a right to be heard."

He nodded, but said nothing, and I went on with the letter, which was as follows:

> You write that you are going to Washington, so I know you'll see "Old Abe." Now don't *you* find any fault with him. I know your impatient disposition, — I know you think he ought to have done a good deal more than he has done. But remember that he has had an untried way, difficulties all about him, conservatives advising one thing, radicals another, and all deceiving him. So don't *you* find fault with him, but bid him "Godspeed." Tell him that all good men and women everywhere are with him, — that they pray for him, and bless him for what he has done, and will yet do. One word from a man he knows has nothing to ask for may cheer him, — cheer him more than you know, — and don't you fail to say it. As

you love truth and God, say it, for it is true and you ought to say it.

His lip trembled slightly, and his voice had a most soft and mellow tone as he asked, " Who is she ? "

I answered, " She is a daughter of Judge John W. Edmonds, of New York. You have met her personally."

"Ah, yes, I remember," he said. "As soon as you see her, tell her that I thank her, — that I hope God will bless her. Be sure to do this as soon as you meet her."

It may not be in strictly good taste, but my feelings constrain me to say that the lady who wrote that letter has been for now many years my wife, and for a longer period — a full third of a century — my good angel.

It was near midnight when I rose to go. As I did so, Mr. Lincoln said, "Don't go yet. I shall stay here until I get something from Grant."

I resumed my seat, and half an hour later the much desired despatch came in. Then the worn, weary man took my hand, saying, " Good-by. God bless you," and I went to my quarters.

I wrote at once to Generals Rosecrans and Garfield, and soon afterwards had a response from Major Frank S. Bond, senior aide to Rosecrans, dated Murfreesborough, June 4, 1863. A portion of it was as follows:

> Your letter to the general and enclosure to Garfield & Company were both duly received, and will probably be acknowledged by the parties to whom they were addressed. A letter has also been received [the one promised by Mr. Lincoln] as to the matter of Doctor J., of similar import to that stated in your letter. On receipt of this letter I sent for Colonel J., and had a talk with him. He says he does not wish to start at once, if the army is to move. He also asks would he be warranted in saying that the Government would, under certain circumstances, be willing to pay a *fair price* to the smaller

slave-owners, — say, to the owners of five slaves and under; also, would they allow the leaders to leave the country without molestation, or would they make it compulsory. Please write me your views on these points.

All letters and most of the conversations which are quoted in the course of these sketches, I copy from the originals, or from minutes made by me at the time, but of my reply to this letter I either did not keep a copy, or have mislaid it. To the best of my recollection, the substance of my answer, addressed to Major Bond, or directed to General Rosecrans, was that Jaquess had better not go into details in his proffers to the rebels; that conceding Union and Emancipation, they would find Mr. Lincoln most liberal on all collateral matters; also that Colonel Jaquess, on his return, had better report to General Rosecrans, and not attempt to communicate direct with Mr. Lincoln, there being strong reasons why the President should have, at the time, no intercourse with him.

The next tidings I had of Colonel Jaquess were in a letter to me from General Garfield, dated Murfreesborough, June 17, 1863. He said:

> Colonel Jaquess has gone on his mission. The President approved it, though, of course, he did not make it an official matter. There are some very curious facts relating to his mission which would particularly interest your friend Judge Edmonds, and which I hope to tell you of some day. It will be sufficient for me to say that enough of the mysterious is in it to give me almost a superstitious feeling of half faith, and certainly a very great interest, in his work. He is most solemnly in earnest, and has great confidence in the result of his mission.

I had no further tidings of Colonel Jaquess until the following November, though I was in frequent correspondence with General Garfield, and would have heard of him had Jaquess reported, as was expected, to General Rosecrans. Nor did Mr. Lincoln hear from him. I was twice in Washington during the summer, and on each occasion saw the President, who at our last interview expressed much concern about Jaquess. He feared some evil had befallen him, and regretted having let him go, for just then such men could be poorly spared by the country. My own opinion was that Jaquess had been detained by the Confederates; but about the middle of November I received a letter from him which showed that he had returned in safety. He subsequently told me that, on leaving Murfreesborough, he went direct to Baltimore, where he reported to General Schenck, who, on learning his purpose, forwarded him on to Fortress Monroe. There he explained to General Dix his object in going into the Confederacy, and he, after some delay (probably to secure instructions from Washington), allowed him to go on board a flag-of-truce boat, which was about to start for the Confederate lines. He was in his uniform, but was courteously treated, and a message from him to General Longstreet was promptly conveyed to that officer. Before the return of the boat General Longstreet came down to meet him, received him cordially, and invited him to his own quarters. There he met many of the Confederate leaders, with all of whom he discussed the situation frankly and freely. To all of them he said, " Lay down your arms, go back to your allegiance, and the country will deal kindly and generously by you." He could not say more, for he was restricted from going into details. From all he had, in effect, the same answer: " We are tired of the war. We are willing to give up slavery. We know it is gone; but so long as our Government holds out, we must stand by it. We cannot betray it and each other." It was this sentiment of loyalty to their Government which made the Southern people follow so blindly the lead of Jefferson Davis, and it throws upon him the responsibility of the two years of carnage that followed. It will also appear, farther on in this volume, that it was altogether owing to the blind obstinacy and insane ambition of that man that the Southern people came out of the war stripped, without payment, of their slaves, and with scarcely more that they could call their own than the ground they trod upon.

Colonel Jaquess failed to gain audience of Mr. Davis, and was told that it would be useless to approach him without having distinct proposals from Mr. Lincoln. But if he brought those, and they were on a liberal basis, they would without doubt be accepted. To obtain more definite proposals, Jaquess, forgetful of my warning, returned to Baltimore, from where he wrote to Mr. Lincoln. He waited a fortnight, but, no answer coming, and thinking that he was needed with his regiment, — it being on the eve of a great battle, that of Chattanooga, — he returned to the army. His subsequent movements I shall relate farther on in this volume.

CHAPTER XIV.

THE TRIBUNE IN THE DRAFT RIOTS.

ON the morning succeeding my last interview with Mr. Lincoln, I went on to New York and reported my various proceedings very fully to Mr. Greeley. He expressed regret that Rosecrans would not act as a presidential candidate, but said at the close, "He will at any rate serve the country; and it is a comfort to have one such man in control of an army."

The report finished, I said to him, "I have thought this thing over, and I have concluded to tell you that I can have no part or lot in your project to unseat Mr. Lincoln. I have the highest regard for you personally, but you must allow me to withdraw from all connection with the *Tribune*."

"Tut, tut," he said; "have I not told you that we shall not say one word against Mr. Lincoln? And did not Gay agree that you should write what you please for the *Tribune*? You are worn out now with your long tramp; but get rested, and then write for us some sketches of what you saw in Tennessee, — omitting, of course, why you went there." This ended my attempt to secede from the *Tribune*.

The sketches I then wrote for it at Mr. Greeley's suggestion have been somewhat drawn upon in the preparation of this volume. Then things went on in their usual way for several weeks and until occurred the draft riots, which seriously threatened the *Tribune* office with destruction. I took part with Mr. James Parton, the widely known biographical writer, in the arming of the building, and with Sidney Howard Gay, the managing editor, in the successful resistance of the mob; and the following account is the combined report of all three of us, — each one describing the portions of which he was an eye-witness. The report being first written out by Mr. Parton and myself, it was submitted to Mr. Gay while he was confined to his bed in his last illness, and he then dictated to his daughter some additions to it which are incorporated in this narrative.

It was July, 1863. General Lee had invaded Pennsylvania, John Morgan was riding roughshod over Ohio, and President Lincoln had called for another half million of men to aid in suppressing the Southern Confederacy; and Congress had passed an injudicious law exempting from the operation of the draft all who should pay into the treasury the sum of three hundred dollars. Discontent was almost universal, and it was systematically fomented, especially in New York City, by a class of "pot-house politicians," who, haranguing in barrooms and on street corners, declared that the draft was unconstitutional, that no allowance had been made for seven thousand men who had recently been sent from New York City to repel Lee's advance into Pennsylvania, and that it bore with peculiar oppressiveness upon the poor man. Blind to the gathering storm, the Government, after denuding New York City of all but three hundred troops, went on with the enrolment; and on Saturday, the 11th of July, began the draft in the Ninth District. Twelve hundred and thirty-six names were drawn, but no trouble occurred. Early in the morning of Sunday, though, throngs of excited men began to crowd the hotels and barrooms in the locality where the draft was to continue on the morrow. Gathering in little knots, they denounced the conscription, and openly talked of attacking the drafting offices. Mingling among them were men in common, and in some instances shabby, clothing, but whose speech indicated cultivation, and whose hands showed them unused to labor. They advised concert of action, and the gathering together of clubs, fence-rails, stones, rusty guns, and every variety of offensive weapon, to be secreted in convenient places, in readiness for a grand outbreak on the morrow. In the evening excited crowds paraded the streets, singing and shouting; but towards midnight they dispersed, leaving New York to its usual quiet.

About three o'clock on the following morning (Monday), Sidney Howard Gay, having finished his work on Monday's paper, left his office in the dingy building then standing on the corner of Spruce and Nassau Streets, and boarded a street-car to go to his up-town lodgings. The driver on the platform said to him: " Stirrin' times, sir. Fa'th, an' ye'll have something to talk about to-morrow."

" How so ? What do you mean ? "

" Nothing ; only a mob will resist the draft to-morrow, and New York will see the biggest riot in history."

Mr. Gay went to his lodgings, and slept quietly until nine o'clock on the following morning. Then he rose, took a hasty breakfast, and went out upon the avenue. The stores were closed, the streets deserted, but excited crowds were gathered on every corner. This recalled to him the words of the car-driver. Evidently a storm was brewing, and, it might be, it was about to break in a torrent of bloody rain on the defenceless city. His post was with the *Tribune*; so he boarded a street-car, and two hours before his usual time entered his office, two miles away, all unconscious of the high havoc already reigning in the upper part of the city.

Soon tidings came in to him that the enrolment offices had been sacked and burned, and all up-town was in the control of an infuriated mob. Meanwhile, an excited crowd had gathered in Printing House Square, that was being harangued by a Virginian named Andrews, who denounced the *Tribune* in violent language, and raised his hands with threatening gestures to those who were looking down from the windows of the editorial rooms. While he did so, there rose every now and then from the crowd a cry of "Down with the *Tribune!*" "Down with the old white coat what thinks a naygar as good as an Irishman."

These ominous storm-gatherings Mr. Gay reported to Mr. Greeley on his arrival, soon afterwards, in the editorial rooms, adding: "The authorities have taken no steps for our defence. The *Evening Post* has armed its building; we must do the same if it is to be saved. This is not a riot, but a revolution."

"It looks like it," said Mr. Greeley; "it is just what I have expected, and I have no doubt they will hang *me;* but I want no arms brought into the building. We must rely upon the authorities, and submit to our fate, if no help comes from them."

Saying this, he put his arm within that of the editor of the *Independent*, who was present, and went away to his dinner. Crowds of excited people were in Printing House Square, but the two editors passed them in safety. An hour or two later, Mr. Gay set out to find Mr. George Opdyke, the mayor, and to demand of him the protection of the authorities; but while he was in pursuit of that official, one of those trifling incidents occurred which now and then save nations and printing-offices.

Two gentlemen, having heard up-town of the danger threatening the *Tribune*, had left their homes to give it warning, and they met in the business office of the great newspaper. There they learned from Mr. Samuel Sinclair, the publisher, that Mr. Greeley had gone away, enjoining that no arms should be provided to defend the premises. Neither of them had any pecuniary interest in the establishment, but both felt that a blow aimed at the *Tribune* was aimed equally at free speech; and one of them said to the other: "The *Tribune* editor is wrong; let us arm the building on our own responsibility."

This proposition was assented to, and the two gentlemen — one of whom was James Parton, the biographer, the other the writer of this sketch — repaired at once to the police and military headquarters.

I will now let Mr. Parton relate what fell under his observation before and after we parted from each other at the headquarters of General Wool.

"On Monday afternoon," writes he, " about four o'clock, my wife and I were strolling down Fourteenth Street, in that languid state of mind which writers know who have spent a long morning at the desk. Near the corner of the Fifth Avenue, we were startled from our state of vacancy by a large stone falling upon the pavement before us, which was followed by a yell of many voices, and the swift galloping past of a horse, with a black man on his back. We saw streaming down the Fifth Avenue a crowd of ill-dressed and ill-favored men and boys, each carrying a long stick or piece of board, and one or two of them a rusty musket. They were walking rapidly, and without order, on the sidewalk and in the street, and extended perhaps a quarter of a mile; in all, there may have been two hundred of them. The stone which had recalled our attention to sublunary things was aimed by one of these scoundrels at the negro, who owed his escape from instant death to his being on horseback.

"Having heard nothing of the riots of that morning, we were puzzled to account for the presence of this motley crew in a region usually so serene, until one of them cried out, as he passed, 'There's a three-hundred-dollar fellow.' When the main body had gone by, I asked one of the stragglers where they were going. The reply was, 'To the *Tribune* office.'

"It was a strange-looking gang of ruffians. I had lived in New York from childhood, and supposed myself acquainted with the various classes of its inhabitants. But I did not recognize that crowd. I know not to this day whence they came, nor whither they vanished. Three-fourths of them were under twenty-one years of age, and many were not more than fourteen. The clubs with which they were armed were all extempore, evidently seized, as they passed, from some old pile of boards and timber. Their clothes were not of any kind of shabbiness that I have ever seen in our streets. They were not the garments of laborers or mechanics, nor of any other class usually seen here. I should say they might be dock-thieves, plunderers of shipyards, and stealers of old iron and copper.

"It occurred to me that, by taking an omnibus, I could get ahead of the gang, and give warning at the office threatened,— about a mile and a half distant. So we hurried to Broadway; but the omnibuses being full, I strode on at a great pace down-town, and thus had the exquisite satisfaction of seeing that crew of villains put to flight near the corner of Tenth Street. It so happened that, just as the head of the gang turned into Broadway, a body of policemen was passing on towards the scene of the riots up-town. The police instantly formed into two lines, extending from curbstone to curbstone, and rushed upon the mob. 'Strike hard, and take no prisoners,' was the word. There was a rattling of clubs for a moment, a dozen knock-down blows given, and the ruffians fled by every street, leaving their wounded in the mud. The police re-formed in marching order, and continued their course, making no arrests. It was all over in about a minute. All the wounded were able to get away, except one, who staggered into a drug store as I got into an omnibus. He was evidently in a damaged condition about the head, and his face was covered with blood. Only one of the police was hit, and he was able to go on with his company.

"At the *Tribune* office, everything wore an aspect so little unusual that I felt rather ashamed to tell my story. The windows and doors were all open, and the business office was nearly empty, the editorial rooms quite so, and there was no crowd around the building. The reporters and editors were absent, collecting details of the riot.

"While I was suggesting the propriety of shutting up the office, as a precautionary measure, Mr. Gilmore came in, to whom I stated what I had seen and heard. He was fully alive to the situation, and proposed that we should go to the Chief of Police and to General Wool, and see what was prepared for the protection of the office during the night. We went. At police headquarters we found a squad of more than a hundred men drawn up on the sidewalk, who, we were assured, would march to the office, and remain on guard there. This seemed sufficient; but to make assurance doubly sure, Mr. Gilmore insisted on our going to General Wool. We found the general at the St. Nicholas Hotel, with the mayor and a staff. Mr. Gilmore procured from him an order on the ordnance officer at Governor's Island, for one hundred muskets and the requisite ammunition. He started immediately for the island; and I, satisfied that the *Tribune* was safe, walked leisurely to the office to report progress.

"It was about seven in the evening when I reached it. The appearance of the neighborhood had changed. The office was closed, and the shutters were up. A large number of people were in the open space in front of it, talking in groups, but not in a loud or excited manner. Not a policeman was to be seen. Upon getting into the office I found only two or three persons there, neither of whom knew anything about the body of police detailed to guard the premises, nor had they heard of any measures taken to defend them. Their official position made it their duty to stand by the ship; and there they were, helpless and alone. Crossing over to the police-station, in the City Hall, in search of the promised squad, I found one policeman in charge, who said that a hundred and ten men had, indeed, come down to that station; but that, upon a rumor of a riot in the First Ward, they had immediately marched away again. As Mr. Gilmore could not possibly get back with the arms under two hours, the office was no safer than before.

"I went among the crowd in front of the *Tribune* office, to learn the tone of the conversation going on there. There was nothing remarkable in the appearance of the people, most of whom seemed to be merely attracted by curiosity, and detained by the impulse there is at such times for people to gather in knots, and talk. One good-natured-looking bull of a man was declaiming a little, 'What's the use of killing the niggers?' said he. 'The niggers haven't done nothing. They didn't bring themselves here, did they? They are peaceable enough! They don't interfere with nobody!' Then, pointing to the editorial rooms of the *Tribune*, he exclaimed, ' *Them* are the niggers up there.' Others were holding forth in a similar strain.

"Little by little, the crowd gathered more closely about the office, and became more compact. The sidewalk was kept pretty clear; but from the curbstone back to the middle of the square there was a mass of people, who stood looking at the building, which loomed up in the dusk of the evening, unlighted, and apparently unoccupied. The crowd was still very quiet. At length a small gang of such fellows as I had seen demolished by the police in the afternoon came along from Chatham Street, and mingled with the crowd, which from that time began to be a little noisy. A voice would utter something, and the rest of the people would laugh, or cheer, or both. It was the laughter and the cheers which appeared to work the mob up to the point of committing violence. Gradually the shouts became louder and much more frequent. At last, a stone was thrown, which hit one of the shutters, and fell upon the pavement close to the building. This was greeted by a perfect yell of applause; and then, for the first time, I felt the office was in danger. Before that, the crowd had laughed too much to suggest mischief. Besides, the fringe of the crowd nearest the building was composed of boys, — newsboys, apparently, — some of whom were not more than twelve years old.

"I ran over to the police-station in the City Hall. A few policemen were there, to whom I said, 'The mob are beginning to throw stones at the *Tribune* office. Five men can stop the mischief now; in ten minutes, a hundred cannot.' It happened that the number of men present was six, five of whom very promptly drew their clubs, and repaired to the scene. By the time they arrived, stones were flying fast, and little boys would run forward, under the shower of missiles, pick up a stone or two, and run back. Occasionally, a window would be broken, eliciting a yell of triumph from the mob. The five men went boldly along the sidewalk, and gained a position between the office and the crowd. The firing totally ceased for a minute or two, and the mob slunk away from the police, as if fearing, possibly, revolvers. Very soon, however, the smallness of the force became apparent; no revolvers were shown; and the stones again began to batter against the shutters and smash the windows. The mob surged forward, those in front being pushed upon the clubs of the policemen, who were soon overpowered and thrust aside. Then the mob rushed at the lower shutters and doors. There was a loud banging and thumping of clubs, and in an exceedingly short time, amid the most frantic yells of the multitude, the main door was forced, and the mob poured into the building. I supposed then that the *Tribune* was gone. But at that moment the report of a pistol was heard, fired somewhere in front of the building, whether from one of the windows, or from a policeman below, I know not. Instantly, the whole crew of assailants on the sidewalk crowded back into the street, and the gates of the opposite Park seemed choked with fugitives. Before the dastards had time to rally, a whole army of blue uniforms came up Nassau Street on the double-quick, and the office was saved. These men, I suppose, were the original one hundred and ten detailed for the purpose; but in the dim light of the evening it seemed as if Nassau Street was a rushing torrent of dark blue cloth and brass buttons.

"The men that saved the office from destruction were the five who rushed in between the building and the mob. They caused the suspension of the efforts of the rioters for about five minutes, which gave time for the large body to arrive before the fire had begun to spread."

Unquestionably the considerate action of Mr. Parton was the means of saving, for the time being, the *Tribune* building. The proceedings of the police are graphically described by a member of the one hundred and ten who had been ordered to Printing House Square by Commissioner Acton. "A false report," he writes, "whether designed or not, of the gathering of a mob in Wall Street, started us down Broadway to Beaver Street, and so through to Broad Street, when we found that the disturbance, a slight one, had been suppressed. After a brief delay, we resumed our return march up Broad and Nassau Streets. On reaching the corner of Beekman and Nassau Streets, we could distinctly hear the crashing of wood and glass in the *Tribune* building; the work of riot and devastation had commenced; but, with the earnestness and thoroughness which marked the conduct of the outbreak from the start, there was no shouting or profane clamor. *It was a storming party, under competent and effective leadership.* So earnest were they in their work, so absorbed, in fact, that the low, stern order, 'Keep together, men; steady; now, then, Forward! Charge!' was unheard, save by a few spectators on the *Times* corner. With a shout from a hundred and ten throats, we struck the rioters like a thunderbolt, cleaving and scattering them in utter rout, confusion, and dismay. A few of us entered the office. They had only gone as far as the ground floor; and the few foolhardy rebels who were there were mercilessly clubbed into the street, or into insensibility, and hurriedly dragged off by friends to die in unknown homes, or linger, with maimed and shattered heads and limbs, for months and years of pain and disfigurement. Printing House Square — a minute previous crowded by a surging mass, five thousand strong — was in five minutes cleared to a point below French's Hotel (the site of the present *World* building), save where the dead and wounded were being dragged off by terrified friends. We did not try to take prisoners."

He adds: "The importance of our action can hardly be overestimated. The suddenness and vigor of the blow disconcerted the murdering thieves, and demoralized for the time whatever of organization they had in the lower part of the city. The *Tribune*, *Times*, and *Post* buildings would inevitably have gone as a consequence of even their partial success; and speculation stops aghast when reflecting on the possible havoc and destruction of the massed and hoarded wealth collected below Canal Street."

Sidney Howard Gay, meanwhile, was closeted with the mayor and General Wool, at the St. Nicholas Hotel. A secretary, in a captain's uniform, was writing orders at a tall desk perched against the wall, and a score or more of army officers and civilians were talking together in low tones in various parts of the room. Anxiety and irresolution were depicted on every countenance; and even the scarred veteran who had ridden unmoved through a score of battles, seemed, for the moment, mastered by the occasion. And well he might be. With only three hundred men, he had to make headway against an infuriated mob of thirty thousand. The occasion demanded a hero, and heroes are scattered only here and there through the centuries.

Mr. Gay explained the defenceless condition of Printing House Square, and asked for men or muskets, but was met with a courteous refusal. Of men, the general had not a corporal's guard; and muskets! those he might furnish; but, if he did, they would be seized by the mob before they could possibly reach the *Tribune* office. He had just given a requisition for a hundred to some importunate gentlemen who insisted on themselves arming the *Herald* building; but he could give orders for no more; they would surely be seized by the mob, and used against the Government. The muskets he alluded to were the ones secured by myself and Mr. Parton; but the confusion in the street had got into the head of the old general, and he had mistaken — what no one else ever did — the *Tribune* for the *Herald*.

As he went down Broadway, the managing editor heard that the *Tribune* building had been sacked and burned; but he kept on, and in half an hour reached the office, just as the police were driving off the rear-guard of the rioters. Entering the lower story, he came upon a scene which beggared description. In the two minutes they had held possession the mob had accomplished the most thorough and complete destruction. Gas-burners were twisted off, counters and desks were overturned, and, in the centre of the room, two charred spots, littered over with paper cinders, showed where fire had been kindled to reduce the building to ashes.

Ascending to the upper stories, he found the editorial rooms silent and deserted by all save one of the corps, — the brave George W. Smalley, who, a year before, had ridden through the fire of Antietam by the side of Hooker. The composing-rooms had only four tenants, — Amos J. Cummings, then a practical printer, now a member of Congress for New York City, his brother, and two other printers. In the pressroom were only Patrick O'Rouke, the senior pressman, and Thomas N. Rooker, the veteran foreman of the *Tribune* establishment. Out of a force of about one hundred and fifty men, only seven were at their posts. But if the whole number had stood their ground, what could they, unarmed, have done against an infuriated mob of five thousand?

But Mr. Gay did not waste time on the subject, for it was already eight o'clock at night; and before daybreak forty thousand copies of his journal had to be in press, and borne on the four winds to every quarter of the country. Looking down on the street, he saw that the mob had fully dispersed, and, quietly sallying out, he rallied a dozen of his printers. With this small force he began work. But soon, one by one, the others fell in, and in half an hour the types were clicking, and the monstrous press was rumbling, as if only quiet reigned over the great city.

But the handful of police who had so opportunely scattered the rioters were unable to long keep the mob out of Printing House Square, and soon again the sinister-looking ruffians began to gather in front of the *Tribune* building. They were evidently bent on reducing it to ashes before morning; but the managing editor determined to stand his ground, and die game, if need were, right there among his editorials.

Nine o'clock came, and still the mob kept increasing. All Nassau Street and Spruce Street and Printing House Square, and the skirts of the Park, and Chatham Street as far up as French's Hotel, had become one swaying sea of battered hats, lit by the flaring glare of the street lamps, and flecked with the foam of perhaps ten thousand human faces. At half past nine a reporter named Bowerman bounded up the long stairway, and, out of breath, entered the office of the managing editor. He had mixed with the mob, he said, and eleven o'clock was the hour fixed upon for the final assault upon the *Tribune* building. He reported that a considerable portion of the rioters were armed and drilled, and the police could no more make head against them than a feather can withstand a whirlwind. Mr. Gay put his pen over his ear, looked down at the fast-gathering mob, and then went on with his writing.

The situation seemed desperate. But at that very moment the writer of this sketch, who three hours before had set out to get the muskets from Governor's Island, entered the apartment. My greeting of the managing editor was somewhat laconic. "I have a hundred muskets," I said, "to arm this building. They are a few blocks off. Have as many police as you can muster ready to guard the dray when it comes up Spruce Street from Franklin Square." This was all I said, and then, turning about, I went two steps at a time down the stairways, and soon the huge boxes were hoisted into the building.

Parting from Mr. Parton at the headquarters of General Wool, I had mounted to the top of an omnibus, and made my way with all possible speed to the Battery. The route was obstructed with vehicles, and it was past seven o'clock before I reached the South Ferry. There, to my consternation, I was told that not a boat could be procured to convey me to Governor's Island. Every boatman had knocked off work two hours before, and disappeared from the locality, probably to reinforce the mob which was then raising high havoc in the upper part of the city.

I must, however, cross to the island; and, going rapidly along the docks, I at last came upon an old longshoreman, in a ragged tarpaulin and greasy trousers, quietly smoking a pipe on the taffrail of a low fore-and-aft schooner, from whose stern a small boat was dangling. "Old man," I said to him, "I have a ten-dollar greenback in my pocket that is yours, if you will jump into that boat and row me at once to Governor's Island."

"Can't do it, sir," answered the man; "the captain is away. Couldn't do it for ten times the money; but you can get a boat at the Battery."

"Well, come along and show me where. I'll pay you well for your trouble."

The old fellow sprang upon the dock, and led the way at a pace I was troubled to keep up with, and soon we were at the signal-station at the head of the Battery. Here, moored to the stairs, were a half dozen boats, but not a human being was anywhere visible. My only course was to confiscate one of these craft, and I proceeded to do it without ceremony. In a very few minutes I was seated in the stern of a boat, with my feet ankle-deep in water, and the old man was pushing the leaky craft out into the river. "Now, old fellow," I said, "an extra dollar if you're there in a quarter of an hour."

"Ay, ay, sir," answered the old man, stretching himself to the oars, and shooting the boat out into the current.

It was already dark, and the tide was running swiftly; but within a quarter of an hour we were at Governor's Island. Springing ashore, I counted out the hire of the confiscated boat by the lamp of a small steamer which was moored at the landing, and then hurried off to the office of the commandant. No light was burning in the office; in fact, the whole island seemed deserted. I shouted several times, but no one answered, and at last I went back towards the landing. There I found a young officer with his arm in a sling, and to him I explained my business. The young man set off at once, at the top of his speed, for the commandant's house, and soon that gentleman appeared at the landing. The whole island, with its immense store of arms and ammunition, was defended only by him, twelve privates, and the wounded lieutenant, the remainder of the garrison having gone to the city to reinforce the troops engaged with the rioters.

Ordering the small steamer that was moored to the dock to "up with the steam," the commandant directed his men to get out the arms and ammunition; and in less than an hour the enormous boxes were trundled on board, and the steamer was on its way to the Battery. The moon was down, and a thick veil of clouds muffled the stars; but a deep glow lit up the whole northern horizon. Here and there great banks of lurid light were rising on the night, — the reflection of half a hundred conflagrations. Evidently the upper part of the city was in a blaze; and perhaps the commandant was right, — the cargo of muskets might only serve to arm the rioters.

As the boat touched the pier I sprang ashore, and was accosted by the old man who had ferried me over to the island. "I saw the boat a-coming," he said, "and come down to warn you. The *Trybune* is burned to the ground, and a mob of ten thousand is emptin' all the banks in Wall Street. If ye go up, every musket'll be taken."

The captain of the steamer coincided in this opinion, and for a moment I hesitated. Then, looking at the sky, and seeing no fire in the region of the Park, I turned to the old sailor and asked: "Can you get me a trusty man and a wagon? I'll pay you well for your trouble."

"I've had pay enough," said the old man. "I'm at your orders the rest of to-night free gratis;" and at once he set off to find a drayman. In about ten minutes he returned with a dray and an Irishman, who expressed a readiness, for a consideration, to drive his dray, freighted with firebrands, into the hottest part of the infernal regions; and in a quarter of an hour the vehicle was loaded, and he had taken the reins of his animal. Then I took the old sailor aside, and said to him:

"Old man, I can trust you, or I'm no judge of faces. These are muskets to arm the *Tribune* building. I must go ahead to see that the coast is clear, and I want you to take this revolver and ride along with the drayman. See that he goes directly up Pearl Street, and stops at the corner of Franklin Square, and does not exchange a word with any one."

"Ay, ay, sir," answered the old man, his eyes glowing like coals in the gaslight; "I'll stand by ye, sir, if you *are* a black Republican."

Then I mounted to the top of an omnibus to go up Broadway, and, looking back, saw the heavily loaded dray creeping slowly around the south side of Bowling Green on the way to its destination.

It was now nearly ten o'clock, and I was still uncertain whether the *Tribune* building were not already a heap of ashes. My way was slow, for the street was a turbulent river of men and wagons; but at last I came abreast of the Park, and saw the well-known sign and a flame of gaslight streaming down from the upper windows. A dense mass of men, hooting, shouting, and yelling, filled every open space around the building.

The Spruce Street entrance was bolted and barred, but I made myself heard, and, entering the building, announced the reinforcement. This done, I made my way to Franklin Square, where the dray was just pulling up at the street corner. Requesting the Irishman to get down, I took the reins, and started the jaded horse towards Printing House Square. Soon after we turned into Spruce Street, some thirty policemen emerged from the shadow of the opposite warehouses, and quietly formed a cordon around the slow-paced vehicle. Not a word was said, but it was evident that they knew their business. As they went on, brandishing their clubs, the crowd parted, and in ten minutes, amid the jeers, groans, and yells of the mob, the huge boxes were hoisted into the second story of the *Tribune* building.

The fortress was now armed, but the peril was not over. About a score of gentlemen, hearing that the building was in danger, had come in with revolvers, rifles, or the first weapon they could lay hands on; and the garrison then numbered, all told, perhaps a hundred and twenty-five men, every one of them determined to sell his life at its highest market value. But could they resist an attack from the fierce, tumultuous mob that was then surging in black waves all around the building? This question was in my mind as I turned to ascend to the fourth story, thinking, as I did so, of being roasted like a live eel upon a gridiron. Close behind me was the old longshoreman, and I said to him : " Old man, you have done enough for to-night. You had better go home. Every man that stays in this building may be in eternity before morning."

"I know, sir; but I told you I was at your orders for the rest of to-night. I never go back on my word."

Little more was said, and the old man followed me up the stairway.

The view from the upper windows would have made the most incorrigible free-thinker a convert to the orthodox theology. There was no need of texts or arguments; for the doctrines were all there,— total depravity, and the devil and his angels, shouting, and hooting, and yelling, in living reality on the pavement. A hundred muskets discharged among the rioters would have no more effect than a bundle of firecrackers let off among so many boys on a Fourth-of-July morning. The discharge would only inflame their blood and rouse them to greater fury.

I had come to this conclusion, when my arm was touched lightly by a reporter, who asked me to step into the room of the managing editor. The arms had been unboxed, and the hundred guns and ammunition had been ranged on the long table in the library. The reporter, a keen, inquisitive Yankee from Connecticut, had assisted in the operation, and, taking it into his head to load one of the muskets, had discovered that the cartridge was not adapted to the barrel. He tried several and found them all misfits. The armorer at Governor's Island, in the haste of getting the arms ready, had put up the wrong ammunition, and the muskets were absolutely useless. With admirable discretion the young man had mentioned the mischief to no one but the managing editor.

Evidently the building was completely at the mercy of the rioters; but what force cannot do, strategy can sometimes accomplish. The mob had seen the huge cases hoisted into the building; and a hundred muskets boxed up, each gun with forty rounds of ammunition, look, to any but a military eye, like a complete arsenal. "You can get out safely," said I to the old longshoreman. "They'll not think you belong to the *Tribune*. Go over to the police office in the Park, give my compliments to Inspector Carpenter, and tell him that the mob intend to attack the building at eleven o'clock; and suggest to him to let some of his men mix with the crowd and talk together of how we are loaded up to the muzzle. That may keep them off over night. And, old fellow, when you get out, stay out."

The old man wedged his way safely through the throng, and in fifteen minutes the mob seemed to sway to and fro, as if moved by some invisible force, and soon little knots of the more savage-looking were seen, here and there, to talk earnestly together.

So the night wore away until the City Hall clock told that the hour fixed upon for the attack was closely approaching. Outside all again had become noise and tumult, but inside everything was as staid as a Quaker meeting. The volunteers were standing idly at their guns; the printers were clicking busily away at their types; the reporters were writing rapidly at their desks, each one stripped to his shirt-sleeves, and with here and there a loaded revolver beside him; and Mr. Gay, with his spectacles on his nose, was perched on a tall stool in his *sanctum*, inditing an editorial that branded the mob as the rear-guard of Lee's army as coolly as if those muskets were loaded, or the riot had gone into history, and he were scoring it at the safe distance of half a century.

But suddenly this quiet was broken, — as suddenly as the air is rent by the first rush of a hurricane. Coming up as if from the very bowels of the earth, a long yell echoed through every corner of the building. It was the signal of attack, — so, at least, it sounded to the hearers. Every man on the fourth floor caught up his rifle or revolver, and took his appointed station by the windows, and a moment of intense suspense followed.

Streaming from Broadway into the Park was a gang of about three hundred ruffians, mostly in red shirts, shouting and yelling like fiends. In the flaring light of the Park lamps it could be seen that every one of them was armed, and that, though they moved on the double-quick, their step had the precision of trained soldiers. They were the fiery nucleus of the entire riot, which, wheresoever it had moved, had spread devastation. Fresh from the sack and burning of the Shakespeare Hotel, they had come to crown their night's work with the spoil and destruction of the *Tribune*. It was for them that the mob below had waited, and the long yell they had sent up was a shout of welcome. On they came like the rushing wind, straight across the Park, direct for the *Tribune* building. As they came nearer their pace increased, and clear and loud their tread sounded, like blow after blow upon the cover of a coffin. They were within a hundred feet of the nearest Park gate when suddenly a tall man sprang from the shadow of the high iron fence which then encircled the Park and, waving his club, shouted: " Up, boys, and at them!"

There have been beautiful sights in the heavens above, and on the earth beneath; but to none of that small garrison, watching there with bated breath, was anything ever more beautiful than that charge of Inspector Carpenter and his glorious squad of only one hundred and ten. They fell on the rioters like a thunderbolt, and, surprised and panic-stricken, the ruffians went down before them as dry leaves go down before a November tornado. In precisely three minutes by a chronometer watch the thing was done, and those of the three hundred who were not on the ground dead or helpless, were fleeing wildly in all directions. Accounts differ, and the number killed cannot be accurately stated; but the police had orders to " Hit their temples, strike hard, and take no prisoners," and they followed their instructions.

This work was no sooner over than we heard the Inspector's voice again: " About face, men! Form outside!" and in less time than it takes to tell it, the hundred and ten bluecoats seemed to grow together into a solid body,

— about twenty men front and five or six deep, — on the hither side of the Park fence. Then once more rang out the voice of the "metropolitan war-horse," Dan Carpenter: "Keep together, men, — steady, now forward, double-quick, and give them fury!"

Then — one hundred and ten welded, as it were, into one — they moved on, mowing a broad swath through the dense mass of rioters as far down Nassau Street as Beekman, then up Beekman to Park Row, at the point of starting, scattering the crowd of probably ten thousand like frightened deer, — all but those they left on the ground killed or badly wounded. Twenty-two were borne away dead; the wounded were never counted, but they must have been many, for not less than a thousand blows were dealt by that compact squad on its deadly journey.

Not long after this the clouds, which had been gathering all the evening and night, broke over our heads, and the rain came down from the merciful heavens, driving the ruffians to their holes, and leaving Printing House Square to its wonted quiet till the sun shone down upon it on the morrow.

Thus did the *Tribune* weather the first day of the storm that shook the great city. The police did their work nobly; the unloaded muskets were not without their influence, but more effective than either was the downpouring rain from heaven.

It was about four o'clock on Tuesday morning when Mr. Gay and I stretched ourselves upon a couple of hard-bottom settees in the editorial rooms, for some much-needed sleep. How it was with the others in the building I do not know; but I am very sure that I myself felt no concern about anything underneath the moon, until some one shook me by the shoulder on the following day, and announced that my breakfast had come in from the Astor House.

Over our morning coffee Mr. Gay and I discussed the situation. We had the whole field in view, for the brave reporters, at the risk of their lives, had mingled with the rioters, witnessed their atrocities, and ascertained that it was their fixed intention to raze the *Tribune* building to the ground. It followed, as an obvious corollary, that if the *Tribune* would preserve its existence, it must set up as an independent nationality, with war-making powers. In other words, it must arm itself to the very teeth, and, looking for no outside aid, resist the rioters to the last extremity.

This decided upon, Mr. Gay returned to his post, and I took a cab and with all possible speed made my way to the Brooklyn Navy Yard. There I found the venerable Admiral Paulding, and, making known to him the situation, I asked for such arms as would do the most effective execution upon the rioters.

There was a pleasurable gleam in the old veteran's eyes, as he said: "It's bombshells, young man,— bombshells and hand-grenades,— and I'll give you enough of both to send ten thousand of those rascals to the devil to-night."

Soon two heavy wagons were loaded with hand-grenades, and then about fifty forty-pound shells were brought out, and the Admiral with his own hands adjusted the fuses so that the shells would explode when they struck the pavement. Then he instructed me how to handle the death-dealing missiles. I had watched, with a kind of amused admiration, the belligerent zeal of the white-haired admiral, and when the vehicles were ready to set out I said to him: "I thank you very much for these arms; but I hope to return them all to you when this trouble is over."

"Don't you do it, young man," said the old admiral; "don't return one of them. Plant every one of them in Printing House Square to-night. If you do there never will be another riot in New York."

At the *Tribune* office, on my return, I found affairs in a state of astonishing activity. Col. Julius W. Adams, of the Eighth Long Island Regiment, had taken command, and was proving himself to be, like the rain of the previous night, "a special providence" for the protection of the old building. Cool, brave, determined, and of remarkable skill and resources, he saw exactly what to do, and before noon of that Tuesday had done it.

As has been said, the lower story lay all exposed, with broken doors and battered windows. Soon every opening upon it was densely barricaded with bales of printing-paper, thoroughly saturated with water, and a hose was attached to the huge boiler below, so that the whole floor could be deluged with scalding steam in an instant. Had the paper rampart been carried, not a man who entered there would have lived to get out. The second story had at one of the windows a howitzer, heavily charged with grape and canister, and at the others huge piles of hand-grenades. The third story was armed in a similar manner; and in the larger editorial rooms were ranged, in a grim semicircle, near one of the front windows, Admiral Paulding's bombshells, of which I was in special command.[1] These, with a

---

[1] In a letter to the writer of this sketch Mr. Cummings refers as follows to this event:

HOUSE OF REPRESENTATIVES,
WASHINGTON, D. C., April 6, 1893.

MY DEAR GILMORE:— I had forgotten about our fighting, bleeding, and dying together in the *Tribune* office during the draft riot; but true it is, as you say. It all comes back to me as vividly as though it were yesterday. One thing there I shall never forget. It was the big, round shells that you brought over from the Navy Yard, and the wooden troughs that were to run out from the windows to roll the shells out on the heads of those who should again attack the office.

brace or two of muskets, now capped and loaded, at every window, a hundred and fifty determined men, and Henry Ward Beecher's Sharp's revolving rifle — sent by him, with his "compliments to the rioters" — completed the armament of the building; while across the way, in the second story of the *Times* building, was a rifle battery of twenty-five barrels, manned by sailors sent from the Navy Yard by Admiral Paulding.

A long trough had been provided to throw the bomb-shells into the middle of the street, and away from the *Tribune* building, and the letting off of one of these shells was to be the signal for a general fusillade from both the *Times* and *Tribune* buildings. Every man had his appointed station, and each floor its designated commander, the second floor being under Midshipman Adams, — a son of the colonel, — who had been trained to load and fire cannon with great rapidity.

When every arrangement had been made, I sat down to a light lunch in the room of the managing editor, and over it related to him the details of my interview with Admiral Paulding. "That is too good to be lost," said Mr. Gay. "Suppose you put it into a short editorial for to-morrow's *Tribune*, and add an invitation to the mob to come on, if they want what Garfield calls 'Hail Columbia;'" and this I did.

Into this arsenal Mr. Greeley came a little after noon on

If one of those shells had dropped upon the pavement I think it would have blown out the front of the building. I wish you would mention the fact that I was not the only compositor, but one of four, who remained in the composing-room. The other three were my brother, Sylvester Bailey, and Peter Hackett. I took command. We barricaded the doorway with "turtles," — of course you know what a "turtle" is. We piled the composing-stones with lead and "shooting-sticks," — you know what a "shooting-stick" is, — and if that gang had ever come up that circular iron stairway, there would have been enough lead spilt to have furnished a regiment with bullets for a month. Yours truly,

AMOS J. CUMMINGS.

the second day of the riots, and, entering the larger editorial room, he gazed around at the loaded muskets ranged at each one of the windows, and at the crowd of strange gentlemen stripped to their shirt-sleeves and "ready for the fray;" and then his eye fell upon the semicircle of bombshells near the front window. "What are these, Mr. Gilmore?" he asked of me, as I sat near by, smoking my after-lunch cigar.

"Brimstone pills for those red ragamuffins down there on the sidewalk."

"But I wanted no arms brought into the building," said the philosopher, with a grieved expression.

"Oh, yes; but that was yesterday. Now this building is under martial law, and in full possession of these linen-shirted gentlemen, Colonel Adams commanding."

Without further remark Mr. Greeley went to his room, and all the rest of the day was deep in his editorials. Before he had finished his last leader, friends had repeatedly gone to him to urge his leaving the building, and shortly before dark General Busteed came in, and reported to him that the crowd, which was rapidly augmenting, evidently meant business, and that it would be absolute madness for him to stay longer; but he quietly replied, "I am not quite through; I will go in a few minutes."

At last, when eight o'clock had arrived, Colonel Adams came to Mr. Gay and myself, saying: "Mr. Greeley ought to go. The mob knows he is here, and if he stays it is likely they will attack us. The consequence will be a good deal of useless slaughter."

"Order a close carriage, and insist upon his leaving," said Mr. Gay, scarcely turning about from his writing.

The carriage being ordered, Colonel Adams and I approached Mr. Greeley, who an hour or two before had removed from his own to the large editorial room, as if to make his presence as conspicuous as possible.

Throughout these riots Mr. Greeley showed a very high order of bravery. Strictly defined, it may not have been either physical or moral courage, for neither of these qualities is destitute of prudence; but it certainly was an intellectual courage which mounted to the heroic. He knew that he was marked out as a special victim by at least ten thousand ruthless ruffians, who, had they laid hands on him, would have given him a short shrift and a short rope from the nearest lamp-post; and yet he came and went as usual, and with no regard whatever for his personal safety. He evidently felt that the trial day of his life had come, and had made up his mind to meet it like a man.

Approaching him now, I said: "Mr. Greeley, a carriage will be here instantly. We want you to leave the office."

"I'm not quite ready; I'll go in a few minutes," was his quiet answer.

"But, sir, we insist upon your going *now*. A hundred and fifty of us are risking our lives to defend this building, and you have no right to add to our danger."

At this he rose slowly to his feet, and, with his peculiar smile, said: "But why order a carriage, Mr. Gilmore? I can go just as well in a street-car."

"Nonsense, sir," I replied; "you couldn't get to a car. Look down there and see the kind of crowd that surrounds the building."

He looked down, and saw what might have made a man of iron nerve feel disinclined for any nearer acquaintance.

"Well, they *are* a hard-looking set," he said, drawing on his coat. "Where could those fellows have come from?"

He was smuggled into the carriage, the door was closed, and he was well on his way down Spruce Street before the crowd appeared to notice that the Spruce Street door had been opened. As I was about to reënter the building I felt a light touch on my arm, and, turning around, saw the old longshoreman who had rowed me over to Governor's Island. "Well, are you alive yet, old gentleman?" I asked, jocosely.

"Yes, yer honor," was the answer, "and I want ye to let me into the building. I told ye I'd see the dance out, and ye'll have warm work before morning."

The old man had done essential service the night before, and at once it occurred to me to employ him again in a similar manner. So I drew him inside, and, closing the door, told him that it was Mr. Greeley he had just seen driving away in a carriage, that he was by that time beyond the reach of the mob, and that the building was then so thoroughly armed that the first discharge from it would slay a thousand of the rioters. It would be a Christian deed if he would mix with the mob and tell them this, for he might thus stave off an attack and save many human lives.

All night long the mob surged and howled around the building, but they forbore an assault upon it. On Wednesday morning the *Tribune* announced editorially that it was prepared for an encounter with the mob, and warned the rioters of the terrible slaughter that would follow an attack upon the building. This, no doubt, held the ruffians at bay; but for two days longer they had control of the blood-deluged city, and during the whole of that time there was no telling at what hour some insane freak might hurl them in tremendous force against the *Tribune* building. So the garrison stood to its guns, prepared for an encounter at any moment. For four days and nights Mr. Gay and I never left the *Tribune* editorial apartments, except for my brief visit to Admiral Paulding; therefore we had full opportunity to observe the elements of which the mob was composed. We did not observe a single native-born workingman among the rioters. The mob consisted in about equal proportions of the more ignorant of our foreign-born population, and of the criminal class that lives by plunder, and has a hand against every man's person and property.

These two classes exist to-day in greater strength in every one of our large cities than they did in 1863, when for four days and nights they held a population of more than a million souls, and the untold wealth of a great city, almost completely at their mercy. All honor to the brave police, and to the intrepid soldiery who, after a four days' struggle with desperate odds, put them down, and restored peace to the war-shaken city. But it took four days to put them down, and it could have been done in four hours, had the authorities been prepared for the emergency.

Therefore the lesson of the riot of 1863 is, that every large municipality should be in constant readiness to suppress the lawless elements that ever and always await only a convenient occasion to break out into murderous disorder. The speediest and most vigorous suppression is the most merciful, and is sure to be attended with the least loss of human life. On ordinary occasions water will suffice, — Croton or Cochituate, applied plentifully by the steam fire-engines. If this does not avail, let the locust be resorted to, in the shape of the clubs so effectually wielded by Commissioner Acton's noble army to the saving of New York City; and both of these failing, and the mob, as it did in 1863, riding triumphant over all law and order, then give them cold iron, — in shells and hand-grenades from every beleaguered building, and in grape and canister from the mouths of cannon, which shall clear the streets till they are as empty as on an early Sunday morning. These are the lessons of the New York riots as they were learned by four days' and nights' observation from the upper windows of the old *Tribune* building.

A prominent Copperhead politician to whom Mr. Gay had done some service came to him on the first day of the riots, warning him to leave the city, and saying that the riot was not merely a riot, but a revolution intended to further the cause of Southern independence. Either the mob had gone beyond the control of its leaders, or their designs from the outset had been more bloody than had been disclosed to this gentleman. At any rate, he was appalled and horrified by the havoc and carnage that were reigning; and daily he came and unbosomed himself of his distress of mind to his friend, the managing editor. He was guarded in his reference to persons, but soon Mr. Gay was in possession of enough to identify and single out the secret leaders of the riots from among the prominent men of the Copperhead party. Daily, as the politician made these disclosures, Mr. Gay communicated them to me, and I wrote them out and forwarded them to the President through Samuel Wilkinson, then the Washington editor of the *Tribune*, to be by him personally handed to Mr. Lincoln. When quiet was finally restored, it occurred to Mr. Gay and myself that if it were generally known that men high in the confidence of the Copperhead party had been the secret instigators and directors of the riots, the honest rank and file of the Democratic party would recoil from such treason, and rally more firmly to the support of the Union. Mr. Gay could not use the name of his informant; but he could make such disclosures as would lead to all the facts coming out on a searching judicial investigation. But who among the United States civil officials in New York had the ability, the loyalty, and the courage to conduct such an investigation? Not one, so far as we knew. The only man known to us who possessed all the qualities for the work was my father-in-law, Judge John W. Edmonds. The judge was then at his country-seat at Lake George, and could not be at once consulted; but entertaining no question that he would accept the position, we addressed a joint letter to Mr. Lincoln, recommending his appointment as special commissioner to investigate the origin of the riots, and giving our views of the results that would follow. Then I took the cars and proceeded to Lake George to apprise Judge Edmonds of the appointment that had been asked for. The judge listened to me attentively, and when I had concluded, said, quietly: "Do you know, my dear boy, what you are asking for me? If I should undertake that work my life wouldn't be worth a bad half-dollar. There's not a rough in New York who wouldn't shoot me on sight; but my time is about up, and it may serve the country. You can tell Mr. Lincoln that I will accept the appointment."

After a few days' rest with the judge I returned to New York, and lost no time in asking Mr. Gay what reply had come from Mr. Lincoln. "Not one word," was the answer. Then he at once telegraphed Mr. Wilkinson to call on the President and ask for a reply to our communication. Answer came in about an hour, to this purport: "I have no answer to make," says Mr. Lincoln. "I never before had anything asked of me that I couldn't say yes or no to; but to this I can't make any reply."

Having to be in Washington soon afterwards to lay before the President an important letter I had just received from my former business partner, Mr. Frederic Kidder, of Boston, I called upon Mr. Lincoln, and about my first remark to him was, "Mr. Lincoln, pray tell me why you couldn't say yes or no to our recommendation of a special commissioner?"

He hesitated for a moment, then in his peculiar, half-bantering manner he said, "Well, you see if I had said no, I should have admitted that I dare not enforce the laws, and consequently have no business to be President of the United States. If I had said yes, and had appointed the judge, I should — as he would have done his duty — have simply touched a match to a barrel of gunpowder. You have heard of sitting on a volcano. We are sitting upon two; one is blazing away already, and the other will blaze away the moment we scrape a little loose dirt from the top of the crater. Better let the dirt alone, — at least for the present. One rebellion at a time is about as much as we can conveniently handle."

That Mr. Lincoln was right was subsequently shown when the wide Western conspiracy was so opportunely strangled at Chicago. He was often accused of being too slow; but if he had, on several occasions, moved any faster than he did move, the war might have had a different termination. Subsequently, soon after the disclosure of the abortive plan to capture Camp Douglas at Chicago, he told me that he was fully informed of the Western conspiracy when he omitted to appoint Judge Edmonds to investigate the origin of the New York riots.

Mr. Greeley always regarded these New York riots as the turning-point in the war for the Union. He once said to me, "It was a tidal wave which struck first at Vicksburg, Gettysburg, Helena, and Port Hudson, and dealt its last and worst blow here in the *Tribune* building, and this city of New York, where the ideas and vital aims of the Rebellion are more generally prevalent than even in South Carolina. If it had not been successfully resisted here, it would have swept over the North, and broken the Union into fragments."

Having been so long in close relations with Mr. Greeley, it may be expected that I shall attempt some analysis of his character and account of his characteristics; but this would seem to be unnecessary, for he is already as widely and truthfully known as any public man of this century. What impressed me most in him was the breadth and clearness of his intellect; his ardent and disinterested patriotism; his inborn honesty, that made him recoil from every shadow of deceit and double-dealing; his tenacious adherence to what he thought was right, in the face of pecuniary loss and public censure; the patience with which he bore reproof when it had truth as its basis, and his single-minded devotion to the interests of the bread-winning class to which he belonged. His highest aim in life was to uplift the working classes, — his chief thought to elevate them in "body, mind, and estate." I well remember the gleam of joy that overspread his face, when, early in the riots, I told him that I had not observed a single American workingman among the lawless rabble that beleaguered the *Tribune* building.

But he had faults, or rather decided weaknesses, which the honest chronicler cannot pass over in silence, however much he may admire his many great qualities. He was erratic. While aiming solely at all central truth, he was ever liable to fly off upon tangents. The least disturbing force would swerve him from his course, and it required a firm and steady hand to keep him in the right direction. I think that only two men — Charles A. Dana and Sidney Howard Gay — were ever able to absolutely control him. They harnessed his great powers, directed where the lightning should strike, and so gave the *Tribune* the tremendous influence it wielded during the war period. He was open to flattery, and so the easy dupe of worthless parasites. He had an inordinate love of notoriety, which led him, in the earlier part of his career, into eccentricities of dress and manner; but this foible he had outgrown when I knew him, and his dress and manners were much like those of other men.

I might fill this chapter with incidents exhibiting his characteristics, but I have space for but two, one illustrating his sympathy with the working classes, the other, his patience under the reproof of even a subordinate.

I was reading proofsheets in Mr. Gay's room one winter night, when two poorly clad women entered, and asked if they could have a brief interview with Mr. Greeley. I answered that he was very busy, and a half-dozen gentlemen were waiting to see him, but if they could wait, he would probably give them an audience. They were willing to wait, so I ushered them into Mr. Greeley's apartment, and seated them where they could not fail to attract his attention. He was at his desk, with his back to the door, absorbed in an editorial, and wholly unmindful of his waiting visitors, every one of whom was a prominent man of his party. The women were meanly clad in straw bonnets, calico gowns, and faded worsted shawls, too thin to be much protection against the inclement weather. Curious to see what kind of a reception he would give the women, I lingered near the doorway till he had finished his editorial. This done, he turned about and glanced at his visitors. The gentlemen were all known to him, and had been in waiting half an hour, but giving them only casual attention, he rose, and said courteously to the women, "Ladies, what can I do for you?"

The younger of the two, who, even in her wretched garb, was decidedly good-looking, stepped timidly forward, and explained their errand. They were employees in a hoop-skirt factory, where the workwomen had the day before suspended work, and demanded an increase of wages.

"What pay do you get?" asked Mr. Greeley.

"Three dollars and a half a week," was the timid answer.

"And how much of that goes for your board?"

"Three dollars."

"Do you mean to say that you have only fifty cents a week for your clothes and other necessaries?"

"That is all," answered the woman, in a faltering voice, a deep blush overspreading her features.

Her look and tone, more than her words, revealed the woman's history. Mr. Greeley read it, and in a quick way said, "It's a shame, — a burning shame! You want me to expose these men. I will do it. They shall have a column in to-morrow's *Tribune*." Then speaking to me, he said, "Sub Rosa, be kind enough to show these ladies to the stairway, and (drawing my ear down to him, and speaking in a lower tone) look at their thin clothes, — give them ten or twenty dollars; I'll pay it."

I said to the younger woman, as we reached the door of the outer editorial room, "Did you hear what Mr. Greeley said to me?"

"Yes, sir," she answered, "but we do not want alms, — we ask for justice, not charity."

"He does not consider it charity. His principle is to divide his larger earnings with those who are underpaid. He thinks it a duty; and he will be pained, perhaps offended, if you refuse the money."

"We wouldn't offend him for the world," said the

woman; "but if we take it, you'll let us go back and thank him?"

"Oh, no!" I answered, "not while those gentlemen are with him. Some other time, if you catch him alone, you may say what you please to him."

As she took the bank-note that I tendered her, she said, "I shall pray God to bless both him and you, sir;" and when they went away I felt that "it is more blessed to give than to receive," even when one gives another man's money.

Soon after I returned to my seat his visitors left him, and I heard Mr. Greeley call, "Sub Rosa!" On my appearing in the doorway, he asked, "Did those women take the money?"

"Yes," I answered. "A twenty-dollar bill, — I had nothing smaller; but I'll compromise with you for ten."

"No, you won't," he said, fumbling in his pockets for the money. "But I haven't a dollar. You'll have to get it of Sinclair; and mind, if you don't collect the whole we'll have a row."

The other incident I shall relate shows another phase of his character. It was told to me by the Hon. Amos J. Cummings, who was one of the printers present at the occurrence. Mr. Greeley wrote a wretched hand, hard for the printers to decipher, but he exacted from them a rigid observance of copy, and any departure from his text was sure to bring upon the offending typesetter a hurricane of vituperation. The least departure he was sure to discover, for each morning he scanned the *Tribune*, from initial letter to finis, as regularly as he took his breakfast. On the occasion referred to, the rascally types had made him say precisely what he did not intend to say, — that which was, in fact, in direct opposition to the oft-expressed sentiments of his newspaper and his party; and flaming with wrath he entered his office on the following day, and, ascending to the composing-rooms with the *Tribune* in his hand, he demanded to know, in the highest key of which his voice was capable, " What d—d fool set up this editorial? Let me look at him."

The printers had discovered the blunder the night before, and a general consultation had been held over it, at which they had decided to obey their standing instructions, which were: " Follow Copy Always." Knowing very well what was coming, they now gathered around the great editor, the offending typesetter among them with the manuscript of the article in his pocket.

" Who set up this editorial ? " again demanded Mr. Greeley.

" I did, sir," answered the guilty compositor, coming forward with an assumed air of trembling timidity. Thereupon the winds broke loose, and there descended upon the offending printer a storm of thunder, lightning, and blue blazes. When it had partially subsided the printer meekly remarked, " But I followed copy, sir."

This Mr. Greeley denied, and another storm of unprintable adjectives followed. At a break in the storm the typesetter drew the manuscript from his pocket, and, with his finger upon the offending paragraph, handed it to the editor, saying, " Be good enough to look at your copy, Mr. Greeley."

As the great man did so his face fell, and he let the manuscript drop to the floor. Then glancing around upon the score of assembled printers, all of whom were of less stature than himself, he said, in a tone of abject imbecility, " Is there nobody here big enough to kick me downstairs ? "

But, with all his eccentricities and shortcomings, Horace Greeley was a great man, — undisciplined, ill-regulated, but great, — and measured by his influence upon his time, and on the upward progress of the American people, it may be questioned if this country has produced any greater, excepting only Benjamin Franklin.

CHAPTER XV.

THE PROPOSED RECESSION OF NORTH CAROLINA.

NOT long ago a Yale professor inquired of me at what college I had been graduated. I answered that I took my degree from a Boston counting-room, where I had as preceptors two excellent gentlemen, the senior of whom was for seven successive terms a member of the council of Governor Briggs, of Massachusetts, and a political writer of rare ability; the junior, a historian of some reputation among readers of early New England history, and enough of a Latin scholar to translate "*Necessitas non habet legem*" as "Root, pig, or perish."

But, if somewhat eccentric as a Latin scholar, and only known as a historian by those who dig about the roots of New England history, this younger preceptor of mine, Mr. Frederic Kidder, was a first-class man of business, with broad views, unerring judgment, and a Pauline suavity of manner that made him all things to all men, — to all at least who had a bale of cotton that might be consigned to the house of J. R. Gilmore & Co. Moreover, he knew the Southern country and the Southern people far better than he knew the Latin grammar. He was for several years my business partner, and, though twenty years my elder, and as unlike me as chalk is unlike cheese, we never had a single disagreement. We were often styled the "Siamese twins;" but we might better have been compared to a span of horses that Judge Edmonds once owned, and which he used to say were perfectly matched, for one was willing to go and the other was willing to let him.

Mr. Kidder retired from our New York firm in 1856, and then returned to Boston, where he devoted himself to church-building and doing good generally; but he kept up his intimacy with me by a frequent correspondence and an occasional visit to my home in New York. One of his visits was about the time of Mr. Lincoln's first election to the presidency; and he then expressed the opinion that the consequences of that event would be the secession of the Slave States, and actual war, if the new President should attempt to enforce the Constitution.

To my inquiry if the result would be disunion, his answer was, "No, not if the Government should adopt the British plan for subduing the revolted colonies, which was to separate the New England from the middle colonies; the middle colonies from the more southern, and beat them all in detail." This plan, he thought, would have inevitably succeeded but for the interposition of the Captain of the Lord's Host, who brought about the surrender of Burgoyne and the battle of King's Mountain, — the two events which he considered the turning-points of the war of the Revolution.

When I asked how he would apply this plan to the Southern States, Mr. Kidder said that he would first capture Charleston, and then separate the Cotton from the Border States, by a series of army posts running from Charleston westward to the Mississippi. That done, he would patrol the Mississippi River with gunboats, and closely blockade every port on the Atlantic and the Gulf of Mexico. Thus shut off from the Border States and hermetically sealed up, the Cotton States would soon, he thought, come to their senses and beg to be readmitted to the Union. If the Tobacco States should also secede, he would subject them to a similar treatment, keeping them so separated from the Cotton States that it would be impossible for one to support the other.

Mr. Kidder was not again at my home until the summer of 1862, and then I related to him my first interview with Mr. Lincoln, and mentioned that his plan for subduing the revolted States had seemed to strike the President forcibly.

He said at once, " And now is just the time to put the plan in operation. Ned writes me that there is strong dissatisfaction with the Confederacy throughout North Carolina, and I think that through Governor Vance the State might be brought back into the Union. That done, the Confederacy would be cut in two, and the two ends might be easily handled. I will write to Ned about it."

" Ned" was his brother, Mr. Edward Kidder, a prominent citizen of North Carolina, who, though a resident of Wilmington throughout the war, and an intimate friend of Governor Vance, was a zealous supporter of the Union. By means of the blockade-runners that plied between Wilmington and Nassau, New Providence, the two brothers had corresponded with considerable regularity, and now Frederic wrote to Edward asking if measures could not be taken to bring about the recession of North Carolina. To this Edward replied that he thought the project to be feasible, and that, if the attempt were properly supported by our Government, Governor Vance could, he thought, be induced to coöperate with it, which would make it successful, because Vance was all-powerful with the State Legislature. The recession of North Carolina, Edward Kidder said, would cut the Confederacy in two, and would doubtless result in its destruction. He suggested that Wilmington should be made the point of attack. That city captured, a death-blow would be given to blockade-running, and, the supply of foreign arms and ammunition once cut off, not only would the Confederate armies be crippled, but North Carolina would be fully restored to the Union; for the loyal sentiment there was strong, and it only needed a rallying-point and the support of a strong body of United States troops to make it overwhelming.

This letter Frederic Kidder forwarded to me, suggesting that I should lay it before Mr. Lincoln. I did not at once do this, as I desired before doing so to be more fully informed in regard to the strength of the Union sentiment in North Carolina. Accordingly, I wrote Frederic Kidder to ask his brother to give us, if he could do so with safety to himself, the exact state of public feeling in North Carolina, the names of the prominent men who could be relied on to support a Union movement, and the real sentiments of Governor Vance, who, I was told, was decidedly inimical to the Jeff Davis government; and I added that if his reply showed the plan to be feasible, I would lay it promptly before Mr. Lincoln, through Robert J. Walker, whose influence was very strong with the President. This was in February, 1863, some weeks before I knew of Mr. Walker's intention to go very soon to Europe to negotiate the 5-20 loan.

Frederic Kidder replied to me that he had forwarded my letter to his brother, with whom he could communicate with absolute safety, through a captain who had sailed for Edward Kidder in the European trade for twenty years, and was then in the service of a blockade-runner plying at pretty regular intervals between Nassau, New Providence, and Wilmington, N. C.

Answer came from Edward Kidder in April, — a brief letter saying that he could not then send a reply to his brother's communication. He had written one, but as the letter might be deemed treasonable, and get the captain into trouble if it were found in his possession, he had felt bound to read it to him. He had done so, and the captain had bluntly refused to be the bearer of such a missive. The officer in charge of the Confederate mails, he said, might at any moment demand to see his papers, and that letter found among them would inevitably consign Edward Kidder to the gallows and his property to confiscation. The captain would not be a party to his benefactor's ruin; he would, however, conceal *this* letter in the lining of his coat and mail it at Nassau. A postscript to the letter, written in pencil, said, " Examine closely whatever you receive from me."

This postscript, which probably had not been seen by the captain, led Frederic Kidder to inspect carefully a bag of peanuts that he received from his brother, through the captain, early in the July following. The bag contained a long letter from Edward Kidder, and a diagram of the fortifications around Wilmington, both on tissue-paper. The letter answered fully the questions I had asked, and stated that Mr. Kidder had sounded Governor Vance on the subject of peace with the Confederacy; but he had not deemed it prudent to as yet refer to any separate action by North Carolina. That subject he reserved to bring up in case of the failure of a general negotiation. Vance was anxious for any peace compatible with honor. He regarded slavery as already dead, and the establishment of the Confederacy as hopeless, and he should exert all his influence to bring about any reunion that would admit the South on terms of perfect equality with the North. Mr. Davis and the fire-eaters would insist on a separate government. But they were a minority; a majority of the governors, and a large majority of the people of the South, would be in favor of reunion on any equitable basis.

"Now," continued Mr. Kidder, "have Jim" (a title he had applied to me since our first acquaintance) "get from Mr. Lincoln at once the most liberal terms he will grant the Confederacy; also the terms on which he will receive North Carolina back separately. Then have him come direct to Nassau, and find the captain, or any one of the Wilmington commanders, — he knows them all, — and take passage here, where at my house he can have an interview with Vance. Say to him that he will be perfectly safe, and, moreover, will be able to collect his claims against a dozen of the Union men whose names are on the list in this letter. They have told me they would like to pay their debts to Gilmore & Co. in cotton, which, as soon as our port is open, will be better than specie.

"However," he added, "frankness obliges me to say that I think Vance cannot effect a general peace on the basis of reunion. The Richmond leaders are resolved on separation, and they will fight for it so long as they have an ounce of powder. Therefore, Jim had better suggest to Mr. Lincoln that it would be well to follow up his overtures by a military expedition. Ten thousand Union troops in possession of Wilmington would be a powerful argument with Vance and the Legislature. To this end, I enclose you a map of our fortifications. I need not tell you how Fort Fisher can be flanked, for we have discussed that already. I know you are growing old and are infirm, but can't you come along with the expedition? The sight of you would gladden the soul of your affectionate brother, E. K."

This letter of Mr. Kidder was without date, but it could not have been written later than July 10, 1863, while

Grant and Sherman were still before Vicksburg, and nearly sixteen months (see " Sherman's Memoirs," Vol. II., p. 166) before they had decided upon " Sherman's March across Georgia," which simply accomplished the result aimed at by Mr. Kidder's plan for swinging North Carolina out of the Confederacy.

After conferring with Sidney Howard Gay, I set out that night with Mr. Kidder's letter in my pocket, for Washington. Arriving there on the following morning, I went early to the White House and had an interview with Mr. Lincoln. I first inquired about the appointment of Judge Edmonds, that I have told of in the previous chapter, and then handed him Edward Kidder's letter, saying, " Here is something you ought to see, — it came from Wilmington, N. C., to Boston, in a bag of peanuts."

" Peanuts! " he exclaimed, smiling broadly. " Then you've gone into the fruit business."

" Not yet, sir; it depends on you whether I go into it or not. Please to read the letter."

He leaned back in his chair, stretched one of his long legs upon the corner of his table, and began to read it. Before he had reached the foot of the first page he turned to the last sheet to look at the signature, saying, " E. K.? What does that stand for?"

" Edward Kidder, one of the most prominent men in North Carolina."

" A Southern man?"

" No; he was born in New Hampshire, but went to Wilmington in 1826, when he was a young man of twenty-one. He has lived there ever since, accumulating a vast fortune, and having larger business transactions than any other man in the State."

" Then he must be a man of wide influence."

"He is,— none of wider, and very few so wide. A stanch Union man, he has openly avowed his principles, and the veriest fire-eaters have not dared to molest him because of the hold he has upon all classes of the people."

"Well, let me read the rest of his letter,— this is important."

Having read it through very attentively, he asked, "These other men that Mr. Kidder names,— do you know them?"

"I do, personally, all but two out of the more than thirty that he mentions. They represent every section of the State, and are the best men in it."

"And Vance,— what do you think of him?"

"I don't know him personally," I answered, "but I would sooner trust Mr. Kidder than Vance,— one is a merchant, the other a politician."

"Then you don't think much of the politicians?"

"Not unless they are, like you, also statesmen."

"Well," he said, with his peculiar smile, "jesting aside, don't you think this thing worth serious consideration?"

"I do," I answered, "but I don't believe Vance could bring about a general peace. When I was at Murfreesborough, General Thomas invited to his quarters, to meet me, a half dozen of the best men from a hundred miles around, that I might get from them the real sentiment of that region. They all prayed for the Union, but were unanimously of opinion that no peace could be made with the Richmond leaders without separation. I think Mr. Kidder is right,— Jeff Davis will fight till he has expended his last ounce of powder."

"And is not that idea confirmed by your not having heard from Jaquess? I fear some evil has befallen him."

"I hope not, sir. I prefer to think they are holding on to him, fearing it would hurt them and help us if it were known that they had refused liberal overtures. I do not believe that they would go to the length of doing him personal violence."

"Well," he said, "I sincerely trust they have not. But about Mr. Kidder's project of swinging North Carolina out of the Confederacy, — is not that precisely in line with what you suggested to me some two years ago; what you said was the plan of the British Cabinet in the Revolution? It struck me at the time, and I have not forgotten it."

"It is, sir, precisely the same plan, with the simple change of Wilmington for Charleston. And I think it would be sure to succeed. With the Mississippi now in your control, and Wilmington captured, you would close the Cotton States up tighter than a drum, and soon have them praying to come back into the Union."

"Yes, with Mobile also closed up, — but we could attend to that at the same time. It seems to me important that Vance should be seen and conciliated, for he doubtless could control the Legislature and have everything done regularly and in order. Now, if I were to tell you that if you brought this about you would do a greater service to the country than any you have yet done, would you undertake it? It would give a death-blow to the Confederacy."

"No doubt it would; but I should be risking my life for an uncertainty. If you could not give a safe-conduct to Jaquess, you cannot to me."

"That is true. I could not in any way protect you; but Mr. Kidder says there would be no danger."

"There is none for him, as he is regarded as a North Carolinian. I would be looked upon as a Yankee. Some of those Wilmington fire-eaters owe me considerable sums of money, and they might choose to wipe out their scores by denouncing me to the Confederacy."

He said, "You are right in looking before you leap. But would not a safe-conduct from Vance, as Governor, give you full protection?"

"No doubt it would," I answered; "at any rate I would trust it. But I question if he would give such a paper to Mr. Kidder. He would fear it might get him into trouble with the Davis government."

"Very likely," he said; "but I guess he will give it to me." Then taking an erect position, he reached me several sheets of presidential note-paper, and continued, having Mr. Kidder's letter in his hand, "Now let us see if between us we can't concoct something that will bring Vance — you write and I'll dictate, but alter my phraseology when you can better it. But this letter has no address, — who was it sent to?"

"To Frederic Kidder, of Boston, my former business partner, and the brother of Edward Kidder," and I added some complimentary remarks about him.

"Well, now go on, first writing directly over the word Washington, 'President's Room, White House;' now the address, 'His Excellency Zebulon B. Vance, Governor of North Carolina.'"

MY DEAR SIR: — My former business partner, Mr. Frederic Kidder, of Boston, has forwarded to me a letter he has recently received from his brother, Edward Kidder, of Wilmington, in which he (Edward Kidder) says that he has had an interview with you in which you expressed an anxiety for any peace compatible with honor; that you regard slavery as already dead, and the establishment of the Confederacy as hopeless; and that you should exert all your influence to bring about any reunion that would admit the South on terms of perfect equality with the North.

On receipt of this letter I lost no time in laying it before the

President of the United States, who expressed great gratification at hearing such sentiments from you, one of the most influential and honored of the Southern governors, and he desires me to say that he fully shares your anxiety for the restoration of peace between the States, and for a reunion of all the States on the basis of the abolition of slavery, — the bone we are fighting over, — and the full reinstatement of every Confederate citizen in all the rights of citizenship in our common country. These points conceded, the President authorizes me to say that he will be glad to receive overtures from any man, or body of men, who have authority to control the armies of the Confederacy; and that he and the United States Congress will be found very liberal on all collateral points that may come up in the settlement.

His views on the collateral points that may naturally arise, the President desires me to say he will communicate to you through me if you should suggest the personal interview that Mr. Edward Kidder recommends in his letter to his brother. In that case you will please forward to me, through Mr. Kidder, your official permit, as Governor of North Carolina, to enter and leave the State, and to remain in it in safety during the pendency of these negotiations, which, I suppose, should be conducted in entire secrecy until they assume an official character. With high consideration, I am,

Sincerely yours,

JAMES R. GILMORE.

After reading the above over carefully, Mr. Lincoln took a pen, and added the following:

P. S. This letter has been written in my presence, has been read by me, and has my entire approval. A. L.

At Mr. Lincoln's suggestion, I then enclosed the letter in an envelope, and addressed it to Governor Vance at Raleigh, N. C. On my arrival in New York on the following morning, I made the copy from which the foregoing is transcribed, and then forwarded the letter, open, to Frederic Kidder, at Boston, with a request that he would send it at once to his brother at Wilmington, N. C. This was in July, 1863, and no answer came from Governor

Vance, or Edward Kidder, until near the close of October in that year. Then Frederic Kidder came to me in New York, bringing with him a letter from his brother that enclosed a safe-conduct from Governor Vance, which gave me liberty to enter and leave North Carolina at such times as suited my convenience.

The letter explained that an answer to my communication had been delayed by the two months' illness of the previous messenger to New Providence, which had kept him from duty. From my suggestion that the negotiation should be "conducted in entire secrecy," both Governor Vance and Edward Kidder had inferred that President Lincoln did not desire the correspondence to pass through the Confederate mail; and, except the captain, there was no messenger on whom they could rely in entire confidence.

In the interval, Governor Vance had twice visited Mr. Kidder at Wilmington, to confer with him about the opening of peace negotiations; and he had written Jeff Davis, through Senator Dortch, urging him to listen to any reasonable proposals that might come from the Federal Government. No answer to his letter had yet been received from Mr. Davis, and Mr. Kidder anticipated that when one came, it would be a flat refusal to negotiate upon any basis but that of the independence of the Confederate States. If such were the answer, it would exasperate Vance, and pave the way for Edward Kidder to propose to him the separate action of North Carolina. This, doubtless, Vance would at first refuse, and hence the importance that a strong military force should follow close upon the heels of my appearance in North Carolina. To induce Vance to act, it would be necessary to show him that he would be energetically supported by our Government; and nothing would so thoroughly convince him of that as the presence of a large army already in possession of Wilmington.

With this letter, and all other letters that Mr. Frederic Kidder had received from his brother on this subject, we went on together to Washington. We arrived there late in the afternoon, and I sent the papers at once to Mr. Lincoln, with a note saying that we were waiting his leisure for an interview. Answer came by the same messenger, "Come at once, as soon as you've had your supper." We entered his room a little after seven o'clock, and were received by him very cordially. I had no sooner mentioned Mr. Kidder's name than he grasped his hand warmly, saying, "I have heard of you and your brother, and I am very glad to meet you." Then to me he said, "I felt sure your letter to Vance would bring him if he was in earnest."

"*My* letter, sir!" I exclaimed. "It was yours, — every word of it! And it was just the thing for the purpose."

"Come, gentlemen, be seated," said Mr. Lincoln. As he said this, he leaned his long form against the mantelpiece, — an attitude common with him in conversation. Knowing this, I at once took a chair, but Mr. Kidder continued standing, his eyes fixed upon Mr. Lincoln's face, as if he would read him through and through. Mr. Lincoln returned his look, his gaze having the same inquiring character; and thus they stood for a few moments, neither of them speaking.

His peculiar smile had been gradually overspreading the face of Mr. Lincoln, and soon he said to Mr. Kidder, "Won't you be seated, sir?"

"Pardon me, Mr. Lincoln," said Mr. Kidder, "I want to make an impression on you; but I am a short man, and you a long one, and I fear my ideas would not rise to your level if I were sitting, and you standing."

The situation was so ludicrous that I could not restrain my laughter. In a moment I said, "Pardon me, Mr. President, you don't know this gentleman as I do. I verily believe if he were to call on Queen Victoria in her own palace he would ask her to take a seat, and make herself entirely at home."

At this Mr. Lincoln also laughed, and, sinking into a near-by chair, he said, "I see you have been taking my measure, — what do you think of me?"

"That this young man is about right," said Mr. Kidder. "He generally is, but occasionally he gets upon a high horse, — is somewhat too enthusiastic."

"And what does he think of me? He has never told me," said Mr. Lincoln.

Mr. Kidder replied, "That you are a providential man, specially commissioned to guide the ship through the present storm."

"Then you think," said Mr. Lincoln, gravely, "that I can count upon the help of the Almighty? I need it, sir, badly."

"And you will have it," answered Mr. Kidder. "I feel as sure of that as of my own existence."

"I am glad to hear you say so," said Mr. Lincoln, "for while you have been taking my measure, I have been taking yours. You are an honest man, sir, and you never say one thing, and mean another. I know I can trust you to keep confidential whatever may pass between us. So I shall speak to you freely. I regard your project for the swinging of North Carolina out of the Confederacy as most important. It seems to me that with Wilmington in our hands we can, with or without the coöperation of Vance, strike a vital blow at the Rebellion. Mr. Gilmore tells me that you are entirely familiar with the country around

Wilmington, and have a plan for flanking Fort Fisher and taking the city with small loss of life. Will you tell me what it is?"

Mr. Kidder then drew from his pocket a map which he had prepared of the approaches to Wilmington, showing the mouths of the Cape Fear River at New Inlet and the sea, together with the entire coast as far north as Beaufort, N. C., the whole being marked with the Confederate fortifications as they were indicated by the map and letters of Edward Kidder. Glancing over it, Mr. Lincoln said, "This is of great value. But how do you propose to approach Wilmington?"

Mr. Kidder[1] then went on to explain that by the way of the Cape Fear, Wilmington is all of thirty miles from the sea. At its New Inlet mouth was Fort Fisher; and along its course were several forts and other obstructions that would make the passage of the river extremely hazardous. Mr. Kidder proposed to flank all these obstacles by collecting a body of troops at Beaufort, N. C., and transporting them on flat-bottomed steamers, through an inlet having seven feet of water at high tide, into Masonboro Sound, whose western shore is only twelve miles from Wilmington. Thence along the Wrightsville road the troops would find no defences till within two miles of the city, and those were not of a formidable character. The attacking force he would wish to have coöperated with by a strong body of cavalry from Newbern, which should tear up the railway connecting Wilmington with the North, and also destroy a bridge which was located ten miles from the city.

"It strikes me as a feasible plan," said Mr. Lincoln; "but how many men would you employ in the operation?"

---

[1] In his "Civil War in America" (Vol. III., p. 474), Benson J. Lossing gives, direct from Mr. Kidder, his plan for the capture of Wilmington.

Mr. Kidder answered, "Ten or twelve thousand under an energetic commander; for the Confederates would perceive the dangerous consequences of the movement and would make a desperate effort to recapture the place. Besides, Vance could not be expected to desert the Confederacy unless he saw that he was to be strongly supported."

"What would you do with Fort Fisher?" asked Mr. Lincoln.

Mr. Kidder's answer was that he would let it alone until our force was impregnably entrenched at Wilmington. Then he would surround it with three or four thousand men, cut off its water-supply, and thus, without loss of life, force it to a speedy surrender. He also expressed the opinion that, as the possession of Wilmington was of vital importance to the Confederates, they would make North Carolina the future battle-ground, concentrating their forces in that State, in a desperate attempt to hold it, and to recapture the city. This would be of advantage to us, for then our superior strength would not be neutralized by having to guard long lines of communication.

Mr. Lincoln remarked, "There is a good deal in what you say; and I shall give the subject careful consideration. The difficulty now is a want of men, — we can't spare a man from where he is, and it seems to me that in any move against Wilmington we should have at least twenty thousand. What do you think of Burnside as leader of the expedition?"

The answer was that he was just the man. His operations at Roanoke Island had shown that.

Mr. Lincoln then said that Burnside could not at the moment be withdrawn from East Tennessee; but as soon as he could be he would set him to enlisting a force of

20,000 men for this special service. It would take time to do that; and, meanwhile, what excuse could I give Governor Vance for not at once meeting him at Wilmington?

I answered that I might write him — what would be true — that, owing to the long delay in hearing from Edward Kidder, I had felt at liberty to accept nearly a hundred invitations to lecture before literary associations throughout the North; that these invitations would occupy me for some months to come, and that, meanwhile, I would be glad to have from Vance his views as to a basis of settlement, which — if he should send them — I would forward at once to the President.

"Which," he said, "had better be by private hand; for all this matter, both the peace negotiation and the military movement, must be conducted with absolute secrecy. Now that Governor Walker is away, who is there, Mr. Gilmore, who would be a safe go-between in this matter?"

I suggested General Garfield, with whom I had become well acquainted at Murfreesborough, and who would be in Washington to take his seat in the House on the assembling of Congress in December.

He answered, "Garfield will do. He is a safe man. Now, when did you hear from Governor Walker?"

I replied, "By the last steamer;" and I drew from my pocket his letter to show to him.

"No, no," he said, "tell me what he says. It will save time."

I then said that Mr. Walker wrote that he felt confident of negotiating three hundred millions of the 5-20 loan, and hoped to defeat the loan the Confederates were attempting to secure on the pledge of the cotton-crop. I added, "And, Mr. Lincoln, would it not kill the Confederate loan deader than a door-nail if I were to write the Governor that you have decided upon this Wilmington expedition and the capture of Mobile?"

"No, no!" he almost shouted. "Have you lost your senses? If Walker so much as whispered that, it would be telegraphed here within an hour, and defeat all our plans by giving the Confederates warning. I am surprised you don't see that."

Decidedly nettled by his tone, I answered, promptly, "Well, sir, I *don't* see it. If the Governor were here you would tell him the whole of this, ask his advice, and trust to his discretion. He conducts his negotiations through some one of the great bankers, — the Browns, Barings, or Rothschilds, whichever it is; they are interested in bolstering our credit and depressing that of the Confederacy. Could he not whisper this to them in confidence, and thus strike a secret but fatal blow at the Confederate negotiations? You have yourself told me that the Governor is the ablest financier and diplomatist this country has produced. Can he not be trusted to use this fact to our advantage, or not at all?"

"Yes, yes," he answered, "you are right; and I ask your pardon for my hasty speaking. Write him whatever you like; and don't be impatient with me."

"Impatient with you, Mr. Lincoln!" I exclaimed. "I couldn't be if I tried, — that is, not for many minutes. Shall I tell you what Horace Greeley said of you the other day?"

He smiled and nodded, and I went on, "He was complaining to me that you did not travel with the speed of light, — 186,000 miles a second, — and I suggested that he should come on here and have a talk with you. He said it would be of no use, — that your smile would wilt him in half a minute. It has much the same effect upon me."

Mr. Lincoln laughed, and after a few moments said, "Now, Mr. Kidder, is there anything more for us to say on this subject?"

"Only one word," he answered. "Where will Burnside recruit for the expedition?"

"My idea would be New York and New England," said Mr. Lincoln.

"Then would you object to my opening this matter to my friend, Governor Andrew? He might help Burnside's operations."

"That is so; do it. But talk to no one else without first consulting me; and write me always under cover to General Garfield. Mr. Gilmore will arrange for that. Burnside, of course, you may be perfectly free with."

After some desultory conversation we took our leave, Mr. Kidder thoroughly convinced that the Union would be saved, and that Abraham Lincoln would save it.

Soon after this interview with President Lincoln I wrote to Governor Vance, Edward Kidder, and General Garfield, as was called for by the circumstances. To General Garfield I said that he had been selected by President Lincoln as the intermediary for an important correspondence, which he desired to be kept from the knowledge of all but himself, so that it might by no possibility get to the public; and I briefly stated the purpose of the projected expedition. From him I received a reply, just as I was about to set out on my lecturing tour, in which he thanked me for thus thinking of him, and said he gladly accepted the trust; not only because he strongly approved of the expedition, but also for the reason that it would bring him into close contact with President Lincoln; — a privilege he highly valued. Then I went off on my lecturing tour, first arranging for the prompt forwarding of all letters that might be received for me at my home or at the *Tribune* office. My lecture engagements ran on until April, 1864; but I heard frequently from Frederic Kidder and General Garfield in relation to all things having any bearing upon the Wilmington expedition, — the information through Garfield coming direct from President Lincoln.

Early in December Mr. Lincoln recalled General Burnside from Tennessee, and reinstated him in command of the Ninth Army Corps, with orders to recruit it to the full strength of 20,000 men. This Burnside proceeded to do with satisfactory success, making his headquarters at Annapolis. Early in January, 1864, Mr. Lincoln requested Mr. Kidder, through General Garfield, to come on to Washington to explain his plan for the capture of Wilmington fully to General Burnside and the War Department. Mr. Kidder went, again met the President, and had prolonged conferences with both General Burnside and Secretary Stanton, after which he wrote to me that all things were understood and agreed upon; and that he had given to Burnside all his maps, and full written instructions how to approach Wilmington; and also had agreed — should his health permit — to go along with the expedition.

Soon after Mr. Kidder's return to Boston he forwarded to me a letter from his brother at Wilmington, dated January 23, 1864, in which he said that Vance had written direct to Jeff Davis, strongly urging upon him the opening of peace negotiations with President Lincoln;[1] and that the Governor greatly regretted the circumstances that delayed my meeting him at Wilmington. Edward Kidder desired me to throw my lectures to the winds and come

---

[1] This letter of Governor Vance, and the reply of Jefferson Davis, may be found in Appleton's " Annual Cyclopedia " for 1864, pp. 197 and 198.

there at once. The pear, he said, was ripe, and ready to fall into our hands. And he added that Governor Vance was strongly incensed with the answer he had received from Jeff Davis, and was ready for the separate action of North Carolina. If merely a moderate compensation were offered by Mr. Lincoln for the slaves, he felt sure the Legislature could be carried by an overwhelming majority.

The Southern pear was ripe, but the Northern gatherers were not ready to pluck it, for Burnside's force was not yet recruited to the required 20,000.

Late in February General Garfield wrote me that it had been decided to make Grant lieutenant-general, and to give him control of all the army operations; and therefore, while Burnside's force had reached the necessary strength of 20,000, Mr. Lincoln desired to confer with General Grant before actually setting on foot the expedition. He had no question that Grant would approve of the plan; and as soon as he did he would like to have me come to Washington, to talk over with him the terms to be offered to Governor Vance. On March 11th, Garfield wrote me another letter, saying that Grant had been appointed lieutenant-general; had been in Washington to receive investment of his command; and had that day returned to Nashville. President Lincoln had talked over the Wilmington expedition with him, and Grant had fully approved of it; therefore the sooner I set out to meet Governor Vance the better. Garfield added: "The President says, 'Let Gilmore show me the light of his countenance as early as convenient.'" I had only half a dozen lecture engagements to fill, and, waiting till this was done, I telegraphed to Mr. Kidder to meet me at Washington, being desirous that he should be present at my interview with Mr. Lincoln in order to suggest any points that he might deem of

importance. We met at Washington, and together called upon the President.

He was in unusually good spirits, seeming to be relieved of a load of care by the mere prospect of Grant's assuming control of the army operations. On my remarking upon his improved appearance, he said, "Oh, yes! I feel better, for now I'm like the man who was blown up on a steamboat and said, on coming down, 'It makes no difference to me, — I'm only a passenger.'"

He went very fully into the topics likely to come up in my intercourse with Governor Vance. But the terms need not be here repeated, as they were substantially the same as those which, four months later, I was authorized to offer to Jefferson Davis, — except that I was not to tender compensation for the slaves, unless in case of a negotiation for a separate recession of North Carolina. This was the substance of the interview, and I returned home to prepare for my proposed trip into North Carolina. I was there, just about to set out on a journey to Nassau, New Providence, when I received a despatch signed simply "A. L.," which read, "You can't go. Satisfactory explanation will be made personally."

Without loss of time I went on to Washington and met President Lincoln. His explanation was that Grant, having had time to fully mature his plans for the whole field of operations in both Virginia and Georgia, had concluded that he must have Burnside's 20,000 men — raised expressly for the Wilmington expedition — to successfully meet Lee in Virginia. However, Mr. Lincoln hoped Grant might soon be able to dispense with the Ninth Corps, and allow it to carry out the original plan of operations.

It never did carry it out, and never could; for in little more than a month a large portion of its men left their bones on the disastrous battle-fields of the Wilderness; and, before the campaign was over, all of one-half of them had lain down to their last sleep on the bloody soil of Virginia.

But Mr. Lincoln kept the Wilmington expedition in mind, and subsequently, while Grant was encamped at City Point, he requested me to have Mr. Kidder visit him there, and press upon him the importance and feasibility of the expedition. Mr. Kidder went to General Grant, accompanied by Governor Andrew, of Massachusetts, and both left him with the impression that the expedition would soon be undertaken. But it never was undertaken. General Grant preferred to capture Fort Fisher eight months later at a vastly greater expenditure of life and money. He distrusted all interference of civilians in military affairs, and had no sympathy with a system of warfare which carries the lash of coercion in one hand, and the white flag of conciliation in the other. But it was not so with President Lincoln. He sought to gain his ends by the least sacrifice of life and property, and he always regretted the failure to carry out this Wilmington expedition; and yet, when I once ventured to ask if he were not placing military control too fully in the hands of General Grant, he said, "Do you hire a man to do your work and then do it yourself?" A similar sentiment he is said to have expressed to a delegation of gentlemen who asked the removal of Grant on the ground that he drank brandy. "Find out for me," Mr. Lincoln is reported to have said, "the brand he uses,—I want to furnish it to some of my other generals."

I believe that from the outset Mr. Lincoln held the opinion that was once expressed by the Honorable Henry Wilson: "This is God's war; he is managing it to suit himself;" and that, further on, as the conflict continued and he beheld the loss of six hundred thousand lives, and of five thousand millions of property, it came to be his settled conviction that God willed " the war to continue until all the wealth piled by the bondsman's two hundred and fifty years of unrequited toil should be sunk, and until every drop of blood drawn with the lash should be paid by another drawn with the sword." This was the woe entailed upon our country by human slavery, and thus was it to be purified by fire, and fitted to achieve its destiny as the standard-bearer of the nations. And thus it always is. All history shows that without the shedding of blood there is no national progress; that all nations, as well as individual men, must pass through the Red Sea of struggle before they come to the promised land flowing with milk and honey.

This was Mr. Lincoln's view as he expressed it to me not long before his death; and now, seeing things as he saw them, I have ceased to regret the hundred thousand lives, and eight hundred millions of money that were sacrificed in the last year of the war, or to longer feel that

> " Of all sad words of tongue or pen
> The saddest are these: it might have been."

CHAPTER XVI.

THE PRELIMINARIES TO THE PEACE MISSION OF 1864.

ALL who have a vivid recollection of the war period must remember the Peace Simoon that swept over the country, throwing dust into the eyes of loyal people, during the early months of the year 1864. The struggle had then continued for more than three years with alternate success and disaster, until the national debt had reached the astounding sum of two thousand millions of dollars, with a daily war expenditure of three millions, and a loss of life — counting the deaths on both sides — of fully half a million, including very much of the best blood of the country. No great battle occurred without a loss, on the two sides, of 20,000 to 30,000, — a number of men equal to the males in a community of from one hundred to one hundred and fifty thousand; and this is saying nothing of the deaths incurred by hardship and disease, which were doubtless equal to the losses in battle. How long could this frightful waste go on, in a total population of only thirty-three millions, without sapping the very life-blood of the country? and how long could this immense destruction of property be continued without involving the nation in hopeless bankruptcy, and spreading universal poverty and distress among all classes of the people, both North and South? These were the questions that pressed upon the minds of thinking men in all parts of the North, and, the passions which had brought on the war having subsided, they said to one another, "Cannot an end be put to this terrific waste of life and property? The Southerners are a Christian people, we have the same God, we believe in the same Christ, we hope for a common hereafter; moreover, we are of one blood; our fathers stood together at King's Mountain and Eutaw, at Saratoga and Yorktown, and shall we, their sons, spend the remainder of our lives in destroying one another, and whelming our common country in destruction? There must be some way to end this wretched business. Tell us what it is, and be it armistice, concession, compromise, anything whatever, we will welcome it, so long as it terminates this suicidal war." This was the almost unanimous feeling of the Northern people — of radical Republicans as well as honest Democrats — during the winter of 1863 and the spring of 1864.

But the Northern people were under a delusion. There could be no peace without the utter extermination of slavery, and the total overthrow of the men who were in control of the Southern armies. Those men could reach their end only by disunion. Their end was a great Southern empire, having for its corner-stone human slavery. This they had openly announced; and it had been fully stated to me by one of their most influential leaders, ex-Governor Allston, of South Carolina, while their cannon were levelled against Fort Sumter, but before they had fired a single shot, or taken one human life. One of his declarations to me was, "Mexico and Cuba are ready, now, to fall into our hands, and before two years have passed, with or without the Border States, we shall count twenty millions. . . . Our territory will extend from the Atlantic to the Pacific, and as far south as the Isthmus. We are founding, sir, an empire that will be able to defy all Europe, — one grander than the world has seen since the age of Pericles!"[1]

These being the views of the Southern leaders, there was an irreconcilable difference between them and the North. The North would not consent to disunion; the South would accept nothing short of it. This was fully understood by the leaders on both sides, and hence no peace overtures were made — even after three years of most bloody and disastrous war — by either the Union or Confederate Governments.

But the Northern people fully believed that some terms consistent with honor, and the preservation of the Union, might be arrived at, and this belief had spread with such amazing rapidity that by the spring of 1864 it was undoubtedly entertained by much the larger number of the free-state population, as is clearly shown by the fact that even in November of that year, when every man, woman, and child in the country had heard the declaration of Jefferson Davis made through me, that the Confederacy would make peace only on the basis of the Southern independence, General McClellan, the Peace candidate for the presidency, failed of a popular majority by only 213,672 votes in a total vote of over 4,000,000.

In this delusion there was great danger to the Union, — a danger greater than any it had yet encountered; for a Peace candidate was sure to be nominated in 1864 in opposition to Mr. Lincoln, and on this tide of popular frenzy he might be floated into the presidency; and then the deluded people would learn, too late, that peace meant only disunion. They would learn it too late, because power would then be in the hands of a Peace Congress

---

[1] A full report of this interview I gave in my book, "Among the Pines," which was published early in 1862.

and a Peace President, and it needed no gift of prophecy to predict what *they* would do. They would make peace on the best terms they could get; and the only terms they could get were disunion and Southern independence. Hence, it was of the utmost importance to secure from the Confederate Government a distinct declaration of the terms on which it would make peace; for if these terms were according to the expectation of those best informed, they would dispel the delusion of the Northern people, reëlect Mr. Lincoln, and end the war with the abolition of slavery and the permanent restoration of the Union.

Holding these views, I gladly availed myself of an opportunity to further a second attempt of Colonel Jaquess to gain an interview with the Confederative authorities on the subject of peace. He had written me in November, 1863, recounting his experiences on his previous visit within the Confederate lines; and this letter is now subjoined in order to give a full history of this transaction. It was as follows:

CHATTANOOGA, TENN., November 4, 1863.
J. R. GILMORE, ESQ.

My Very Dear Sir:— I entered upon my mission, passed into the Confederate lines, met a most cordial reception, was received by those to whom my mission was directed as a visitant from the other world, and was strongly urged not to cease my efforts till the end was accomplished. I obtained some very valuable information, which appears more so to me now, since events have transpired to which I need not now refer.

I returned to Baltimore, with a view to communicating with President Lincoln. I wrote him — without stating that I had been within the enemy's lines — "that I had valuable information. Can I have permission to communicate it? If so, how, — by telegraph, mail, or in person? I await an answer at Barnum's Hotel, Baltimore, Md."

I waited there two weeks; no answer came. General Schenck,

to whom I had made known my business when outward bound, was absent. I did not feel at liberty to report to any one else.

At this time I learned from parties here that a battle, at or near this place, would be fought soon, and that my regiment very much desired me to be with them. I hastened to join them, which I did just in time to be in the most desperate and bloody battle of the war. I lost over two hundred of my men, nineteen commissioned officers in killed and wounded, and I had two horses shot under me. I was not touched.

I cannot perceive why President L. should decline any communication with me. I can give him some *most valuable* information; no one else need know it, and he be uncommitted.

Generals Rosecrans and Garfield are gone, and there are no others here with whom I feel free to communicate. I would be most thankful for the privilege of prosecuting this work further,—feel that I ought to do it, that great good would result from it. I find my way perfectly clear on the other side of the line. My only trouble is on this side. I can do our cause more good in one month, in my own way, than I can here in *twelve*. More anon.

Yours truly, J. F. JAQUESS,
Colonel 73d Reg. Ill. Vols.

This letter I received when I was soon to set out on the lecturing tour of which I have spoken, and would not have three consecutive days at my disposal until the following April. Consequently, I could not go to Washington; and writing to Mr. Lincoln seemed to be useless, for if he had not answered Jaquess, it was to be presumed he would not correspond with any one on that subject. Besides, I could tell him nothing till I had seen the colonel. This I wrote to Jaquess, suggesting that he should apply to General Thomas, under whom he was serving, who knew and approved of his first visit, and would, no doubt, depute some trusty person to go to Mr. Lincoln, report what Jaquess had to communicate, and obtain a new furlough. I suggested also that he should not again attempt direct access to Mr.

Lincoln, unless he could bring to him definite proposals of surrender from the rebel leaders.

To this letter Jaquess replied that he would wait until I could go to Washington, as it was necessary he should know more definitely Mr. Lincoln's views before he went again into the Confederacy; and the extreme caution the President had shown convinced him that he would not talk to any stranger as freely as he had talked, and probably would again talk, with me.

I was not able to visit Washington till I went there with Mr. Frederic Kidder near the 1st of April, 1864. Then I asked of Mr. Lincoln why he had not replied to Colonel Jaquess's letter.

"I never received his letter," was the unexpected answer. The person to whom it had come had not thought it of sufficient importance to bring it to the notice of the President. I then handed him Jaquess's letter to me of Nov. 4, 1863. He read it carefully, and then said, "He's got something worth hearing. What a pity it is they didn't give me that letter!"

"It's not too late, sir," I remarked. "Those people," he says, "are ripe for peace. Let him go again. There is no telling what he may accomplish."

Without a word, he turned about on his chair, and on a small card wrote as follows:

To whom it may concern:
The bearer, Colonel James F. Jaquess, 73d Illinois, has leave of absence until further orders.
A. Lincoln.

When he handed this card to me I said, "I will send this at once to General Thomas, and write to Jaquess to report to me at my home. Then I will send to you, through

General Garfield, a full report of his doings within the rebel lines."

"All right," he answered. "Garfield will be discreet. Have you seen him?"

"Not yet, sir; but he is here, and I can see him to-day. However, it seems to me it would be vastly better for you to talk with Jaquess. Would it not do for him to come here in citizen's clothes? It could be managed with absolute secrecy."

"No doubt," he answered, "but the fact would exist; and I couldn't deny it, if it should prove inconvenient."

"Do you desire I should name any more definite terms to Jaquess?"

"What did you tell me, some time ago, that Rosecrans wrote to you about pay to the small slave-owners?"

"His aide, Major Bond, wrote to me that Jaquess asked if you would pay the owners of five slaves and under, and if the leaders would be allowed to leave the country without molestation."

"Let him tell them all to stay at home; and I think I could manage the five slaves, — perhaps more. You see Chickamauga has taught the country something. People don't talk so much about the Confederacy being a shell; perhaps it is, but it's an awful hard shell to crack. You can say to Jaquess that you are satisfied we will grant such terms, but don't say I distinctly offer them. He might construe that into some sort of authority."

It was not till the 13th of June that I heard again from Colonel Jaquess. Then I received a torn sheet, written by him in pencil on the 10th of the same month, from one of the battle-fields about Kenesaw Mountain, in which he said that he was ready to go again, and would see me at my home about the first of July. I at once wrote to

Mr. Lincoln, apprising him of this, and adding that the more I thought of it, the more it seemed to me important that Jaquess should have fuller and more definite instructions. I hoped also that he would change his mind about giving him a personal interview. Should I not bring Jaquess on to Washington, and he then decide what to do in the premises?

This letter I sent open to General Garfield, with a note requesting him to read it and urge my views upon the President. Answer came from Garfield in an appendix to a letter of five pages, which he had written me on other subjects. The appendix was as follows:

I have delayed sending this till I could see the President in reference to Jaquess; and, after two ineffectual attempts, I saw him and talked with him. There were other persons in the room, and we could not talk freely, so he summed it all up by saying, " Tell Gilmore to bring Jaquess here, and I will see him. Of course it should be done very quietly."

My next communication on this subject was a telegram from Colonel Jaquess, dated " Barnum's Hotel, Baltimore, June 30th," which was, " Can you come to Baltimore and Washington? It is important."

As soon thereafter as possible I went to Baltimore, and met Colonel Jaquess. He informed me that he had brought despatches from General Sherman to Washington, and, being there, had sent in his name to Mr. Lincoln, who had declined to see him, but advised his seeing me in Boston. He had telegraphed to me to come on, he said, because he was fearful that some unforeseen difficulty had arisen in the way of his return into the Confederacy. This apprehension I quieted by assuring him that Mr. Lincoln was more anxious for peace than any one in the country.

He then said that while waiting for me at Baltimore he had met a distinguished clergyman of the Methodist Church, South, who, on the 16th of June, had a lengthy interview with Jefferson Davis, at Richmond. The clergyman stated that Mr. Davis had said that his government would make peace on no other terms than a recognition of Southern independence. However, he, personally, would be disposed to agree to two governments, bound together by a league offensive and defensive, — for all external purposes *one*, for all internal purposes *two;* but he would agree to no closer connection.

It at once occurred to me that if this declaration could be got in such a manner that it could be given to the public, it would, if scattered broadcast over the North, destroy the Peace party, and reëlect Mr. Lincoln to the presidency, to which he had been again nominated. It could not be given out as coming from the Southern divine, for in that form it would not have much weight, and, moreover, it might get him into personal difficulty; but coming through Jaquess it would be attended to and believed, and would doubtless deal a death-blow to the Confederacy. This thought in my mind, I suggested to Colonel Jaquess to call at once upon his clerical friend and inform him that he was then on his way to Richmond, for the purpose of having an interview with Mr. Davis on the subject of peace; that he intended to pass through our lines from General Grant's headquarters at City Point, Va. I added that the clergyman would greatly facilitate the work of Jaquess if he would at once return to Richmond by the way he came, — the Maryland back door, — see Mr. Davis, inform him that Jaquess was coming, and request that some one should be sent to the Union lines to meet him. This Colonel Jaquess did, and the clergyman agreed to set out on the following day for Richmond.

Then we took the next train for Washington, and I called at once upon Mr. Lincoln. About his first remark was that on the very day he had told Garfield to write me that he would see Jaquess, General Schenck had called upon him with some volunteer advice as to the terms he should offer the rebels through Colonel Jaquess. On subsequent inquiry the President had learned that Schenck had spoken of the subject freely and everywhere. "This," he said, "may greatly embarrass me. I therefore refused to see Jaquess, and shall countermand his furlough, and send him back to his regiment."

"I am very sure, sir," I said, "that Jaquess has never disclosed his business, except, perhaps, when it was necessary in order to get through the lines."

"No doubt," he answered. "I don't question his discretion; but the fact that he has had to mention it at all shows the thing should not go any further. The whole business is irregular, and had better not be proceeded with."

"That is, of course, for you to determine, sir; but will you allow me five minutes by a slow watch?"

"Yes," he answered, "ten; and if you are very entertaining, I'll give you twenty."

Then, as briefly as I could, I spoke of the universal impression existing at the North that some honorable peace could be made with the South; and I said that if liberal terms were offered to the Confederacy, and were refused, it would remove that impression, kill the Peace party, and secure his reëlection to the presidency. The country was so thoroughly tired of the war that it would welcome any peace that would preserve the Union. The Democrats would promise such a peace, and the result would be that their candidate would be elected and the Union would go to pieces. On the other hand, if Jaquess went, and Davis should refuse to negotiate, — as he probably would, except on the basis of Southern independence, — that fact alone would unite the North, reëlect him, and thus save the Union.

"Then," he said, "you would fight the devil with fire? You would get that declaration from Davis, and use it against him?"

"I would, sir," I answered. "I would spread it wherever the English language is spoken; and in thirty days there would not be a Peace man at the North, except in the Copperhead party. But I would deal squarely with Davis. I would offer him terms so liberal that, if he rejected them, he would stand condemned before the civilized world."

Until this time Mr. Lincoln had sat with one of his long legs upon the corner of the table, but now he drew the leg down, and leaned slightly forward, looking directly into my eyes, but with an absent, far-away gaze, as if unconscious of my presence. Thus he sat, for fully a couple of minutes, in absolute silence. Then, relapsing into his usual manner, he said, "There is something in what you say. But Jaquess couldn't do it, — he couldn't draw Davis's fire; he is too honest. You are the man for that business."

Not stopping to be amused by his equivocal compliment, I replied, "Excuse me, sir, if I differ from you. His very honesty and sincerity exactly fit him for the business. Davis is astute and wary, but the colonel's transparent honesty would disarm him completely."

"Have you suggested this to Jaquess?"

"No, sir."

"Well," he said, "if you propose it to him, he will tell you he won't have anything to do with the business. He feels that he is acting as God's servant and messenger, and he would recoil from anything like political finesse. But if Davis should make such a declaration, the country should know of it; and I can see that, coming from him now, when everybody is tired of the war, and so many think some honorable settlement can be made, it might be of vital importance to us. But I tell you that not Jaquess, but *you*, are the man for that business."

"Ah! I see, sir," I remarked. "You propose that I shall go upon this mission."

"No, I do not," he answered. "I do not propose anything. I can't propose anything about such a business. I can only say that I will give you a pass into the rebel lines, and then — ask Jaquess to pray for you."

"When I might be past praying for!" I rejoined. "This is a new and unexpected thought to me, Mr. Lincoln. Will you allow me to consider it, and talk it over with Mr. Chase and General Garfield?"

"Certainly," he answered. "Talk with them, and bring them both here with you this evening. I should like to confer with them myself, — with Chase particularly. Tell him so."

After explaining the position of things to Colonel Jaquess, I went in pursuit of General Garfield, but found that he was away on a trip to the West. His opinion upon the project he, however, soon afterwards wrote me. "I never had much faith in the power of the 'Methodist Church, South' to control Davis; but I tell you, you've got the idea now that will dethrone him. After that declaration of his there will not be an honest Peace man in the North."

With Mr. Chase I went over the whole ground, and he expressed the decided opinion that, in view of the state of feeling in the North, it was of the first importance that liberal terms should be at once offered to Davis, and, if he should decline them, that the country should know the fact. After I had dined with Mr. Chase, he went with me to the White House. This he did without hesitation, though only a few days before he had, at Mr. Lincoln's suggestion, resigned from the Treasury Department, and it was currently reported that relations between him and Mr. Lincoln were somewhat strained. I judged, however, that if any feeling existed, it was entirely on the part of Mr. Chase, for Mr. Lincoln's manner to him was most cordial, — had the frank trustfulness that he showed only to those who had his entire confidence. Before we were seated, he said, "Ah, Chase, I am glad you've come; but where is Garfield?"

"He is away on a trip to the West," answered Mr. Chase.

"Well, I wanted *you* particularly," said Mr. Lincoln. "This is a delicate and important business, and I don't want to stir in it without your advice."

"I know you are sincere in that expression, Mr. Lincoln," said Mr. Chase, "and I feel honored by it."

"Well, sit down, both of you," said Mr. Lincoln, "and let us get to business. Now, Mr. Gilmore, have you decided to ask me for a pass into the rebel lines?"

"I have, sir," I answered, "on the condition that you allow me to make such overtures to Davis as will put him entirely in the wrong if he should reject them."

"Well," said Mr. Lincoln, "Mr. Chase and I will talk about that in a moment. But, first, another question: Do you understand that I neither suggest, nor request, nor direct you to take this journey?"

"I do."

"And will you say so, if it should seem to me to be necessary?"

"I will, whether you should ask it of me or not."

"And if those people should hold on to you, — should give you free lodgings till our election is over, or in any other manner treat you unlike gentlemen, — do you understand that I shall be absolutely powerless to help you?"

"I understand that, sir, fully."

"And you are willing to go entirely upon your own muscle?"

"No, sir, not upon my muscle. I suspect it will be more a matter of nerve than of muscle."

"Do you hear that, Mr. Chase?" said Mr. Lincoln, with an indescribable look of comic gravity. "He criticises my English at the very moment I am giving him an office. Well, now that we have arranged the preliminaries, Mr. Chase, what terms shall we offer the rebels? Draw your chair up to the table, Mr. Gilmore, and take down what Mr. Chase may say."

"You had better name the terms, Mr. Lincoln," answered Mr. Chase. "I will make any suggestions that may seem necessary."

"Well, either way," replied Mr. Lincoln.

He then went on to dictate to me, without interruption from Mr. Chase, the following:

"First. The immediate dissolution of the Southern Government, and disbandment of its armies; and the acknowledgment by all the States in rebellion of the supremacy of the Union.

"Second. The total and absolute abolition of slavery in every one of the late Slave States and throughout the Union. This to be perpetual.

"Third. Full amnesty to all who have been in any way engaged in the rebellion, and their restoration to all the rights of citizenship.

"Fourth. All acts of secession to be regarded as nullities; and the late rebellious States to be, and be regarded, as if they had never attempted to secede from the Union. Representation in the House from the recent Slave States to be on the basis of their voting population."

Here Mr. Chase remarked, "About that I may want to say something, Mr. Lincoln; but please to go on now, and I will suggest some points afterwards."

"Very well," said Mr. Lincoln.

"Fifth. The sum of five hundred millions, in United States stock, to be issued and divided between the late Slave States, to be used by them in payment to slave-owners, loyal and disloyal, for the slaves emancipated by my proclamation. This sum to be divided among the late slave-owners, equally and equitably, at the rate of one-half the value of the slaves in the year 1860; and if any surplus should remain, it to be returned to the United States Treasury.

"Sixth. A national convention to be convened as soon as practicable, to ratify this settlement, and make such changes in the Constitution as may be in accord with the new order of things.

"Seventh. The intent and meaning of all the foregoing is that the Union shall be fully restored, as it was before the Rebellion, with the exception that all slaves within its borders are, and shall forever be, freemen."

As he finished the dictation, Mr. Lincoln turned to Mr. Chase, saying, "All which, Mr. Chase, is respectfully submitted; and now I am open to amendments."

A two hours' discussion followed upon the fourth and fifth clauses. The fourth clause Mr. Chase desired should be modified, so as to provide expressly for negro suffrage. Mr. Lincoln replied that it did, in effect, secure it, because it based representation upon the *voting* population. It would be unadvisable to embarrass a negotiation like this with such a question.

To the fifth clause Mr. Chase objected altogether, contending that it would be regarded as " buying a peace," and in its present mood the North would not submit to such a measure. Mr. Lincoln must bear in mind that no peace could be lasting that was not based upon principles of eternal justice; and by those principles the black was entitled to both freedom and suffrage, without payment or thanks to any one. To this Mr. Lincoln replied that the sum named was less than would be the cost of another year of war, to say nothing of the bloodshed; and it was also right to pay for property we had destroyed, — repeating much the same arguments he had used to me fully a year previously. The clause was finally modified by restricting payment to owners of fifty slaves and under, and reducing the amount named to an absolute sum of four hundred millions. To this Mr. Chase finally assented, with the remark, " I conceive that it makes but very little difference. Mr. Davis is not likely to accept the offer. Mr. Gilmore is confident that he will not accept of peace without separation. To get his declaration to that effect is why you send Mr. Gilmore."

" True," said Mr. Lincoln, " but peace may possibly come out of this; and I don't want to say a word that is not in good faith. We want to draw Davis's fire; but we must do it fairly. What I think of most is the risk Mr. Gilmore will run. The case is not the same with him as with Jaquess. There is something about that man, a kind of ' thus saith the Lord,' that would protect him anywhere. But Gilmore is not Jaquess. He will go in with my pass, and the rebels won't talk with him five minutes before they ascertain that he is fully possessed of my views. He will say he doesn't represent me; but they will think they know better. Now, as the thing they want most is our recognition of them, may they not hold on to him, to force me to some step for his protection that shall recognize them? And if they decline the overtures, as they probably will, is it not likely they will refuse to let him out before our election, because of the damage he may do their friends by publishing the facts to the country? Now, Mr. Chase, can you see any way by which I can protect him?"

"I cannot," replied Mr. Chase, "unless you should copy the proposals into a letter addressed to Mr. Gilmore, sign it, and in it request him to read it to Mr. Davis. That would give him a semi-official character, and they would not dare to molest him."

"That I can't do," said Mr. Lincoln. "It would be making direct overtures. I don't see, Gilmore, but you will have to trust in the Lord; only be sure to keep your powder dry, for they are wily and unscrupulous fellows."

I then informed him that Colonel Jaquess had agreed to go with me, and I should hesitate to go without him, as I should need the help of his cool courage to give me the backbone requisite for the occasion. To this he assented, and, turning to his table, he wrote a couple of passes. They were on small cards, one of which said, simply:

Will General Grant allow J. R. Gilmore and friend to pass our lines, with ordinary baggage, and go South?
A. LINCOLN.

July 6, 1864.

This I delivered to General Grant; the other I was able to retain. It read as follows, and is now in the Historical Library of the Johns Hopkins University:

Allow J. R. Gilmore and friend to pass, with ordinary baggage, to General Grant, at his headquarters.

A. LINCOLN.

July 6, 1864.

As I glanced at the cards, he remarked, " Tell Colonel Jaquess that I omit his name on account of the talk about his previous trip; and I wish you would explain to him my refusal to see him. I want him to feel kindly to me."

As Mr. Chase and I rose to go, he rose also, and, bidding " Good night " to Mr. Chase, he took me by the hand, and said, " God bless and prosper you. My best wishes will be with you. Good-by." Then he added, still holding my hand, " Have you looked squarely in the face that if you get into trouble I can in no way help you, that I shall be obliged to say that, while I have given you the terms on which I am personally willing to settle this thing, I have not authorized you to offer these, or any terms whatever ? "

I answered, " I think the object, sir, is worth the risk. I shall tell Davis distinctly that I have no authority, and only desire to open the door for official negotiations."

" Well, you had better go to General Butler; tell him the whole story, and that I say *I* cannot protect you, but will shut my eyes to anything he may do. Say this to Butler, but nothing to Grant or to any one else, for if the feeling in Richmond is as hostile to us as it is said to be, you'll need to keep as much in the dark as possible. Now, good-by. I hope to see you again soon."

CHAPTER XVII.

OUR VISIT TO RICHMOND.

IT was after midnight when I recounted this interview with President Lincoln to Colonel Jaquess, and told him that we would take the City Point boat on the following afternoon.

It wanted several hours of sunset the second day following, when the boat rounded to under the abrupt promontory which bears the name of City Point, Va. A large flag was flying among the trees which crown the higher part of the headland, and, making our way to it, we asked for the headquarters of General Grant.

"Yonder in that tent. He is sitting there, you see," replied an adjutant. Without more ceremony we passed down the grassy avenue and presented ourselves before him. He was seated on a camp-stool, smoking a cigar, and listening to the reading of a newspaper by General Rawlins. A few other officers sat near, and something which had just been read appeared to amuse them greatly. The general looked up as we approached, and as he espied my companion he rose rather hastily. "Ah, colonel," he said, extending his hand, "I am glad to see you. It's a long time since we met."

"Not since Pittsburg Landing, I believe, general. I think we met there," returned my companion.

"Yes, I remember; I remember the work you did there for the wounded. When did you leave Sherman?"

"About ten days ago. I brought despatches from him to the War Department."

"I have heard from him later than that. He is doing splendidly; handling his army magnificently."

Then the colonel introduced me to the general, and at this break in the conversation I said to him: "We want your ear, sir, privately, for a few moments."

"Certainly; walk in this way," and, rising, he led us into his sleeping apartment, a square tent, with a single strip of carpet on the ground, a low camp-cot in one corner, and a portable desk, covered with open papers, in the other.

Handing him then a note of introduction I had with me, I briefly explained our wishes.

"I don't believe the rebels will receive you," he answered. "They have not answered a flag for a month. However, I will send one. I shall have to address General Lee. Shall I say you want to meet Judge Ould?" he asked, drawing his stool to the desk.

"If you please; and if he declines to pass us, please ask him to refer our request to President Davis."

While he was writing it I noted more particularly his appearance. He was of about the medium height, with a large head, a compact frame, and deep, broad chest and shoulders. His hair was brown, his eyes were a clear, deep gray, and his features were regular and of a cast that might be called "massive, Grecian." Though his first meeting with the colonel was decidedly cordial, his usual manner was cool and undemonstrative; but with this coolness was a certain earnest simplicity that impressed one very favorably. In his face was the unyielding persistency which had won for him so many battles, but there was nothing else remarkable about him. He did not at once magnetize a stranger with a sense of his genius, as did Rosecrans.

The note finished, the conversation then took a general turn, and in a clear, simple way he explained the military situation, expressing the opinion that the fall of Richmond and the defeat of Lee, though they might be delayed, were inevitable events.

As we passed back towards the wharf we met a number of officers just landed from a small steamer. One of them, though I had never seen him, I knew at once to be General Butler. Obeying a sudden impulse, I halted as he came abreast of us and said to him:

"I want to take you by the hand; I am, myself, a live Yankee," and I mentioned my name.

Giving me a cordial grasp, he replied: "I'm delighted to meet you. Come up and see me. Take the *Gazelle* to Point of Rocks — don't go to Bermuda. Come to-morrow."

I then introduced the colonel, and the general again urging us to visit him, we promised to do so.

Reporting our intended absence to General Grant, and requesting him to forward Lee's answer to us by telegraph, we set out on the following morning for the headquarters of "our Massachusetts general." We found them about a mile distant from the Appomattox River, in a worn-out tobacco field, flanked on two sides by dense woods, and hemmed in on the others by "moving" banks of Virginia sand. It was a dreary spot, but we forgot that the moment we entered the general's tent, and he accosted us with:

"I'm glad you've come. There are two cots in the corner. They are yours. I sent your flag this morning. It may not be back for some days. In the meantime make yourselves at home. Go and come when you like, and do exactly as you please."

When we were seated, he said: "I want to tell you of a smart thing that was done this morning by one of my aides,

— Lieutenant-Colonel Greene, a son of Nathaniel Greene, the veteran editor of the Boston *Post*. On account of our disagreements as to the exchange of prisoners, the rebels have, for several weeks, refused to hold any communication with us; but, on receiving Grant's despatch to Lee about you, I sent Greene down to the lines armed with a flask of brandy and a box of cigars, telling him to get it through, somehow. He sat his horse there for half an hour, the rebels not deigning to notice him; but finally a major on Lee's staff, whom Greene had met before, rode over to meet him. He declined to receive the despatch, but smoked Greene's cigars and drank his brandy, and finally agreed that, if Greene would open and read the despatch to him, he would give the contents to Lee orally. Then Greene brought back the despatch to me. I opened it, and sent him back with it and another flask of brandy. So, with a little Yankee cuteness, we got the despatch to Lee, who forwarded it to Jeff Davis."

We remained with the general nearly three days. Then one morning the flag of truce came into camp with a despatch from the War Department, dated Richmond, Va., July 12, 1864, which announced that Colonel Robert Ould, agent of exchange, would meet us at a point near Deep Bottom, — Mrs. Grover's house, — on Thursday, the 14th of July, to receive any communication we had to make. The despatch had been forwarded to us by General Grant, with a request that we would report to him, at our early convenience, at his headquarters.

It was a seven-mile ride on a couple of hard-trotting horses, but in a little more than an hour we were seated with General Grant in his private tent at City Point. About his first remark was, "I did not expect the Confederates would pay any attention to my letter, but it appears they have. Now, allow me to ask why you want to go to Richmond?"

"We would be glad to tell you, general," I answered, "but we are not at liberty to do so."

"Then you can't go," he replied, curtly.

"But, sir," I said, much surprised, "have you not Mr. Lincoln's order to pass us through?"

"Yes," he answered, "but Mr. Lincoln does not understand the situation. You have been here nearly a week, and have thoroughly inspected everything about my army. No doubt you are both loyal men, but what you have seen would be of great interest to the rebels; and, while you are entirely honest, you may not be altogether discreet. Therefore, I cannot let you go. I couldn't do it if you were my own brothers."

My first thought was that our journey was over, but then it flashed upon me that there was a telegraph between City Point and Washington, and I said, "Your caution, general, is perhaps called for by the circumstances; but you have telegraphic communication with Mr. Lincoln, — will you not kindly put to him, personally, whatever questions you want answered?"

"I will," he answered, promptly, as if relieved from an unpleasant duty. "Meanwhile, make yourselves at home here."

Breakfast was nearly over on the following morning before General Grant so much as alluded to passing us through the lines; then he said, "I will have the flag-of-truce boat at Point of Rocks, ready to take you to your appointment early to-morrow morning, but, meanwhile, I think you had better return to General Butler, and tell him that I wish he would send with you, to meet Commissioner Ould, as many of his general officers as he can spare, —

not less than half a dozen. I will send as many to you with the boat."

" But, is it necessary, general," I asked, " that there should be so much fuss and feathers ? A couple of horses and an orderly will be all we shall need."

He answered, " Mr. Lincoln has specially requested it. He can give you no credentials, and so you have to go without a safeguard; therefore it is important, both for your safety and the success of your business, that those people should understand that you come direct from the President, and do, in fact, represent the Government. And another thing, Mr. Lincoln is fearful that Davis will find some pretext for holding on to you till after the presidential election, and he hopes you will not fail to tell the whole story to General Butler, and to assure him that he will be sustained in whatever course he may take for your protection."

The programme was carried out, and about one o'clock on the following day we met the Confederate officials. Colonel Mulford, the Union exchange commissioner, was with us, and after he had introduced us and our escort to Colonel Ould, the latter turned to Mulford, and said, " It is a long time since we have met, colonel. What can I do for you ? "

" Oh, nothing," answered Mulford. " We have merely come along to escort these gentlemen."

The mingled surprise and deference that came into Ould's face and manner was a living witness to the remarkable shrewdness of Mr. Lincoln. The interview was very brief, for though sent down to meet us by Mr. Davis, Colonel Ould had not seen him, nor had he any authority to take us up to Richmond. We parted to meet again two days later, when Ould would conduct us into the august presence of the grand mogul of the Southern Confederacy.

On the morning of Saturday, the 16th of July, just as the "Yankee" clocks in that part of the country were striking nine, taking General Butler by the hand, I said to him:

"Good-by. If you do not see us within ten days, you will know that we have 'gone up.'"

"If I do not see you in less than that time," he replied, "I'll demand you, and if they don't produce you, body and soul, I'll take two for one, — better men than you are, — and hang them higher than Haman. My hand on that. Good-by."

Our boat ran into the fire of a Confederate battery that was shelling some of our gunboats lying under a high bluff on the river; but at three o'clock that afternoon, mounted on two raw-boned relics of Sheridan's great raid, and armed with a white handkerchief tied to a short stick, we rode up to the Confederate lines. A ragged, yellow-faced boy, with a carbine in one hand, and another white handkerchief tied to another short stick in the other, came out to meet us.

To him we said, "Can you tell us, my man, where to find Judge Ould, the exchange commissioner?"

"Yas. Him and t'other 'change officers is over ter the plantation beyont Miss Grover's. Ye'll know it by its hevin' nary door nur winder" — the mansion, he meant. "They're all busted in. Foller the bridle-path through the timber, and keep your rag a-flyin', fur our boys are thicker'n huckleberries in them woods, and they mought pop ye, ef they didn't seed it."

Thanking him, we turned our horses into the "timber," and, galloping rapidly on, soon came in sight of the deserted plantation. Lolling on the grass, in the shade of the windowless mansion, we found the Confederate officials. They rose as we approached, and I said to the judge:

"We are late, but it's your fault. Your people fired at us down the river, and we had to turn back and come overland."

"You don't suppose they saw your flag?"

"No. It was hidden by the trees; but a shot came uncomfortably near us. It struck the shore, and ricocheted not three yards off. A little nearer, and it would have shortened me by a head, and the colonel by two feet."

"That would have been a sad thing for you; but a miss, you know, is as good as a mile," said the judge, evidently enjoying the "joke."

In addition to two very gentlemanly aides, there were with Commissioner Ould some other officials, whose appearance indicated that we were to be welcomed in Richmond.

One of them was a stoutly built man of medium height, with a short, thick neck, and arms and shoulders denoting great strength. He looked a natural-born jailer, and much such a character as a timid man would not care to encounter, except in range of a rifle warranted to fire twenty shots a minute, and to hit every time. This was Mr. Charles Javins, of the Richmond Provost-Guard, and he was our shadow in Dixie. Another was a "likely cullud gemman," named Jack, who told us he was almost the sole survivor of "Massa Allen's" twelve hundred slaves, — "De res' all stole, massa, — stole by you Yankees;" and the others were two mules hitched to an ambulance, which, over ruts, stumps, and an awful sandy road, bore us safely to the rebel capital.

To give us a *moonlight view* of the fortifications, Judge

Ould proposed to start after sundown; and as it wanted some hours of that time, we seated ourselves on the ground, and entered into a conversation which lasted until the sun had gone down, when he ordered up the vehicles for our fourteen-mile journey. He led the way, with his aides, in an open wagon, and we followed in the covered ambulance, our shadow, Mr. Javins, sitting between us and the twilight. As we went on, we encountered at each picket-station a strong body of men, — strong enough in all to picket an army of thirty thousand, — and half way on the route we espied, on a hill at the right of the road, a collection of Sibley tents, numerous enough to house a thousand men. The tents were lighted up, but, looking closely at them, I observed that the lights were not stationary, but moving from one tent to another. Telling Jack to call to Colonel Ould to halt, as I desired to speak with him, I said, when we caught up with his wagon, "Colonel, how many men have you in those tents yonder?"

"I don't know," he answered; "how many do you suppose?"

"Probably a dozen," I replied, "certainly not more than twenty. Now, colonel, you have taken a great deal of trouble to pull the wool over our eyes, but we can see through a plank when there's a hole in it. We have been three days with General Butler, and he has your entire army mapped, to the smallest company. We know from him that you have less than 2,400 men opposite Deep Bottom, and we have seen at least two-thirds of that number already on your picket-stations. Hurry them back to where they belong, for if Grant should discover this, he might attack you on this line before morning, and your people would think we had something to do with it."

Ould laughed, and asked me to pass to him a flask of Butler's brandy that I had in my pocket, — he had already exhausted one that I had brought for him from the general.

Then we rode on as before, until at about nine o'clock that night we halted at the private entrance of the Spotswood Hotel, in Richmond. As we alighted from the ambulance, Ould said to Colonel Jaquess, "Button your duster up closely, — your uniform must not be seen here."

The colonel did as he was bidden; and, without stopping to register our names at the office, we entered the private doorway of the hotel, and followed the judge and his aide up-stairs to room No. 60. It was a large, square apartment in the fourth story, with a ragged, unswept carpet, and bare white walls, smeared with soot and tobacco juice. Several chairs, a marble-top table, and a pine wash-stand and clothes-press straggled about the floor, and in the corners were three beds garnished with tattered pillow-shams and covered with white counterpanes, grown gray with longing for soap-suds and a wash-tub. The plainer and humbler of these beds was designed for our guard, the burly Mr. Javins; the others had been made ready for the two individuals who, in defiance of all precedent, had just "taken Richmond."

We had eaten nothing since setting out early in the morning from General Butler's headquarters, but now, on our entering the room, the judge said, "You want supper. What shall we order?"

I answered, "A slice of hot corn bread would make me the happiest man in Richmond."

The judge's aide thereupon left the room, and shortly returning remarked, "The landlord swears you're from Georgia. He says none but a Georgian would call for corn bread at this time of night."

Upon this the judge remarked, "It is not entirely safe

for you to pass here as Yankees, — it would be far better if you were supposed to be Georgians, — emissaries from Governor Brown, sent here to arrange his differences with the Confederate Government."[1] On this hint we acted, and when our sooty attendant came in with the supper things we discussed Georgia mines, Georgia banks, and Georgia mosquitoes in a way that showed we had been bitten by all of them. The false news was soon noised abroad, and on the following morning the Richmond papers announced that the two gentlemen the Confederacy had under guard at the Spotswood Hotel were commissioners from Governor Brown, of Georgia.

We invited Judge Ould and his aide to sup with us, and, the meal being over, the judge said, "In the morning you had better address a note to Mr. Benjamin, asking an interview with the President. I will call at ten o'clock, and take it to him."

"Very well," I replied. "But will Mr. Davis see us on Sunday?"

"Oh, that will make no difference."

On the following morning we indited a note, of which the one below is a verbatim copy, to the Confederate Secretary of State.

Spotswood House, Richmond, Va.,
July 17, 1864.

Hon. J. P. Benjamin, Secretary of State, etc.

Dear Sir: — The undersigned respectfully solicit an interview with President Davis.

They visit Richmond only as private citizens, and have no official character or authority; but they are acquainted with the views of the United States Government, and with the sentiments of the Northern

---

[1] Some years after the Civil War I related this incident to ex-Governor (then U. S. Senator) Joseph E. Brown, who, laughing heartily, said that he was glad that he had, though unwittingly, contributed to my safety when in Richmond.

people, relative to an adjustment of the differences existing between the North and the South, and earnestly hope that a free interchange of views between President Davis and themselves may open the way to such official negotiations as will result in restoring PEACE to the two sections of our distracted country.

They therefore ask an interview with the President, and, awaiting your reply, are

Truly and respectfully yours.

This was signed by both of us; and when the judge called as he had appointed, we sent it, together with a commendatory letter I had received on setting out from Washington, from a near relative of Mr. Davis, to the Confederate Secretary. In half an hour Judge Ould returned, saying, "Mr. Benjamin sends you his compliments, and will be happy to see you at the State Department."

Leaving our vacant room under guard of Mr. Javins, we set out, escorted by Judge Ould, for the interview. We found Secretary Benjamin — a short, plump, oily little man in black, with a keen black eye, a Jewish face, a yellow skin, curly black hair, closely trimmed black whiskers, and a ponderous gold watch-chain — in the northwest room of the old United States Custom-house. Over the door of this room were the words "State Department," and about its walls were hung a few maps and battle-plans. In one corner was a tier of shelves filled with books, — among which I afterwards noticed Pollard's "History," Lossing's "Pictorial," Parton's "Butler in New Orleans," Greeley's "American Conflict," my own "Among the Pines," a complete set of the "Rebellion Record," and a dozen numbers and several bound volumes of the *Atlantic* and *Continental* monthlies. In the centre of the apartment was a black walnut table, covered with green cloth, and filled with a multitude of papers. At this table sat the Secretary. He rose as we entered and, as Judge Ould introduced us, took our hands, and said, "I am glad, very glad, to meet you, gentlemen. I have read your note, and" — bowing to me — "the letter you bring from ———. Your errand commands my respect and sympathy. Pray be seated."

The colonel, drawing off his duster, and displaying his uniform, said, "We thank you for this cordial reception, Mr. Benjamin. We trust you will be as glad to hear us as you are to see us."

"No doubt I shall be, for you come to talk of peace. Peace is what we all want."

"It is, indeed; and for that reason we have come to see Mr. Davis. Can we see him, sir?"

"Do you bring any overtures to him from your Government?"

"No, sir," answered the colonel. "We bring no overtures, and have no authority from our Government. We stated that in our note. We would be glad, however, to know what terms will be acceptable to Mr. Davis. If they at all harmonize with Mr. Lincoln's views, we will report them to him, and so open the door for official negotiations."

"Are you acquainted with Mr. Lincoln's views?"

"One of us is, fully," answered Colonel Jaquess.

"Did Mr. Lincoln in any way authorize you to come here?"

"No, sir," said the colonel. "We come with his pass, but not by his request. We say, distinctly, we have no official or unofficial authority. We come as men and Christians, not as diplomatists, hoping, in a frank talk with Mr. Davis, to discover some way by which this war may be stopped."

"Well, gentlemen," said Mr. Benjamin, "I will repeat what you say to the President, and if he follows my advice,

and I think he will, he will meet you. He will be at church this evening; so suppose you call here at nine to-night. If anything should occur in the meantime to prevent his seeing you, I will let you know through Judge Ould."

This gentleman became, after the fall of the Confederacy, one of the most eminent members of the London bar, with an income, as is stated, of a hundred thousand dollars a year; but I saw in him at this time no indication of extraordinary ability. He appeared to have a keen, shrewd, ready intellect, but not the mind to originate, or even to execute, any great good or great wickedness.

After a day spent in our room at the Spotswood Hotel in company with Judge Ould, who did us the honor to dine with us upon the only turkey, as I jocosely insisted, then to be found in Richmond, we called again, at nine o'clock, at the State Department.

Mr. Benjamin occupied his previous position at the long table, and at his right sat a spare, thin-featured man, with iron-gray hair and beard, and a clear gray eye, full of life and vigor. He had a broad forehead, and a mouth and chin denoting great energy and strength of will. His face was emaciated and much wrinkled, but his features were good, especially his eyes, though one of them bore a scar, which, I understood, had lost him its sight. He wore a suit of grayish brown, evidently of foreign manufacture, and, as he rose, I saw that he was about five feet ten inches high, with a slight stoop in the shoulders. His manner was simple, easy, and most agreeable, and there was a peculiar charm in his voice, as he extended his hand to us and said: "I am glad to see you, gentlemen. You are very welcome to Richmond."

This was the man who was President of the United

States under Franklin Pierce, and at that time was the brains and soul of the Southern Confederacy.

I answered, "We thank you, Mr. Davis. It is not often that you meet men of our clothes and our principles in Richmond."

"Not often," he answered; "not so often as I could wish; and I trust that your coming may lead to a more frequent and a more friendly intercourse between the North and the South."

"We sincerely hope it may," was the reply.

"Mr. Benjamin tells me that you have asked to see me to —" he paused, as if desiring that we should finish the sentence. Colonel Jaquess replied, "Yes, sir; we have asked this interview in the hope that you may suggest some way by which this war may be stopped. Our people want peace, your people do, and your Congress has recently said that *you* do. We have come to ask how it can be brought about."

"In a very simple way," said Mr. Davis. "Withdraw your armies from our territory, and peace will come of itself. We do not seek to subjugate you. We are not waging an offensive war, except so far as it is offensive-defensive, — that is, so far as we are forced to invade you, to prevent your invading us. Let us alone, and peace will come at once."

"But we cannot let you alone so long as you repudiate the Union; that is the one thing the Northern people will not surrender."

"I know. You would deny to us what you exact for yourselves, — the right of self-government."

"No, sir," I remarked. "We would deny you no natural right. But we think union essential to peace; and, Mr. Davis, could two people, with the same language, separated by only an imaginary line, live at peace with each other? Would not disputes continually arise, and cause almost constant war between them?"

" Undoubtedly, — with this generation. You have sown such bitterness at the South; you have put such an ocean of blood between the two countries, that I despair of seeing any harmony in my time. Our children may forget this war, but *we* cannot."

"I think the bitterness you speak of, sir," said the colonel, " does not really exist. We meet and talk here as friends; our soldiers meet and fraternize with each other; and I feel sure that if the Union were restored, a more friendly feeling would arise between us than has ever existed. The war has made us know and respect each other better than before. This is the view of very many Southern men; I have had it from many of them, — your leading citizens."

" They are mistaken," replied Mr. Davis. " They do not understand Southern sentiment. How can we feel anything but bitterness towards men who deny us our rights? If you enter my house and drive me out of it, am I not your natural enemy?"

" You put the case too strongly," said the colonel, " but we cannot fight forever; the war must end at some time; we must finally agree upon something; can we not agree now, and stop this frightful carnage? We are both Christian men, Mr. Davis. Can you, as a Christian man, leave untried any means that may lead to peace?"

" No, I cannot," rejoined Mr. Davis. " I desire peace as much as you do; I deplore bloodshed as much as you do; but I feel that not one drop of this blood is on my hands — I can look up to my God and say this. I tried all in my power to avert this war. I saw it coming, and for twelve years I worked night and day to prevent it; but I could not. The North was mad and blind; it would not let us govern ourselves, and so the war came, and now it must go on till the last man of this generation falls in his tracks, and his children seize his musket and fight our battle, *unless you acknowledge our right to self-government.* We are not fighting for slavery. We are fighting for independence, and that, or extermination, we *will* have."

"And there are, at least, four and a half millions of us left; so you see you have a work before you," said Mr. Benjamin, with a decided sneer.

"We have no wish to exterminate you," answered the colonel. "I believe what I have said, — that there is no bitterness between the Northern and Southern people. The North, I know, loves the South. When peace comes, it will pour money and means into your hands to repair the waste caused by the war; and it would now welcome you back, and forgive you all the loss and bloodshed you have caused. But we must crush your armies, and exterminate your Government. And is not that already nearly done? You are wholly without money, and at the end of your resources. Grant has shut you up in Richmond, Sherman is before Atlanta. Had you not then better accept honorable terms while you can retain your prestige, and save the pride of the Southern people?"

Mr. Davis smiled, and said, "I respect your earnestness, colonel, but you do not seem to understand the situation. We are not exactly shut up in Richmond. If your papers tell the truth, it is your capital that is in danger, not ours. Some weeks ago, Grant crossed the Rapidan to whip Lee and take Richmond. Lee drove him in the first battle, and then he executed what your people call a 'brilliant flank movement,' and fought Lee again. Lee drove him a second time, and then Grant made another 'flank movement;' and so they kept on—Lee whipping, and Grant flanking—until Grant got where he is now. And what is the net result? Grant has lost seventy-five or eighty thousand men, *more than Lee had at the outset,*—and is no nearer taking Richmond than at first; and Lee, whose front has never been broken, holds him completely in check, and has men enough to spare to invade Maryland and threaten Washington! Sherman, to be sure, is before Atlanta; but suppose he is, and suppose he takes it? You know that the farther he goes from his base of supplies, the weaker he grows, and the more disastrous defeat will be to him. And defeat may come. So, in a military view, I should certainly say our position was better than yours.

"As to money: we are richer than you are. You smile; but admit that our paper is worth nothing,—it answers as a circulating medium, and we hold it all ourselves. If every dollar of it were lost, we should, as we have no foreign debt, be none the poorer. But it is worth something; it has the solid basis of a large cotton crop, while yours rests on nothing, and you owe all the world. As to resources: we do not lack for arms or ammunition, and we have still a wide territory from which to gather supplies. So, you see, we are not in extremities. But, if we were, if we were without money, without food, without weapons,—if our whole country were desolated, and our armies crushed and disbanded,—could we, without giving up our manhood, give up our right to govern ourselves? Would *you* not rather die, and feel yourself a man, than live, and be subject to a foreign power?"

"From your standpoint there is force in what you say," replied the colonel. "But we did not come to argue with you, Mr. Davis. We came hoping to find some honorable way to peace, and I am grieved to hear you say what you do. When I have seen your young men dying on the battle-field, and your old men, women, and children starving in their homes, I have felt I could risk my life to save them. For that reason I am here; and I am grieved — grieved — that there is no hope."

"I know your motives, Colonel Jaquess," said Mr. Davis, "and I honor you for them; but what can I do more than I am doing? I would give my poor life gladly, if it would bring peace and good-will to the two countries; but it would not. It is with your own people you should labor. It is they who desolate our homes, burn our wheat fields, break the wheels of wagons carrying away our women and children, and destroy supplies meant for our sick and wounded. At your door lies all the misery and the crime of this war, and it is a fearful, fearful account."

"Not all of it, Mr. Davis; I admit a fearful account, but it is not all at our door. The passions of both sides are aroused. Unarmed men are hanged, prisoners are shot down in cold blood by yourselves. Elements of barbarism are entering the war from both sides that should make us, — you and me, — as Christian men, shudder to think of. In God's name, let us stop it. Let us do something, concede something, to bring about peace. You cannot expect, with only four and a half millions, as Mr. Benjamin says you have, to hold out forever against twenty millions."

Again Mr. Davis smiled, saying, "Do you suppose there are twenty millions at the North determined to crush us? I do not so read the returns of your recent elections. To my mind they show that fully one-half of your people think we are right, and would fight for us if they had the opportunity."

"You are mistaken, Mr. Davis. A small number of our

people, a very small number, are your friends, — Secessionists. The rest differ about measures and candidates, but are united in the determination to sustain the Union. Whoever is elected in November, he must be committed to a vigorous prosecution of the war."

Mr. Davis still looking incredulous, I remarked, "It is so, sir; whoever tells you otherwise deceives you. Not one in fifty of our twenty millions would consent to any peace that involved disunion. I think I know Northern sentiment, and I assure you that it is so.

"The majority are in favor of Mr. Lincoln, and nearly all of those opposed to him are so because they think he does not fight you with enough vigor. The radical Republicans, who go for slave-suffrage and thorough confiscation, are those who will defeat him, if he is defeated. But if he is defeated before the people, the House will elect a worse man, — worse I mean for you. It is more radical than he is, — you can see that from Mr. Ashley's reconstruction bill, — and the people are more radical than the House. Mr. Lincoln, I know, is about to call out five hundred thousand more men, and I don't see how you can resist much longer; but if you do, you will only deepen the radical feeling of the Northern people. They would now give you fair, honorable, *generous* terms; but let them suffer much more, let there be a dead man in every house, as there is now one in every village, and they will give you no terms, — they will insist on hanging every rebel south of — Pardon my terms, I mean no offence."

"You give no offence," replied Mr. Davis, smiling pleasantly, "I wouldn't have you pick your words. This is a frank, free talk, and I like you the better for saying what you think. Go on."

"I was merely going to add that, let the Northern people

once really feel the war, — they do not feel it yet, — and they will insist on hanging every one of your leaders."

"Well," said Mr. Davis, "admitting all you say, I can't see how it effects our position. There are some things worse than hanging and extermination. We reckon giving up the right of self-government one of those things."

"By self-government you mean disunion, — Southern independence?"

"Yes," he answered.

"And slavery, you say, is no longer an element in the contest?"

"No, it is not. It never was an essential element. It was only a means of bringing other conflicting elements to an earlier culmination. It fired the musket which was already capped and loaded. There are essential differences between the North and the South, that will, however this war may end, make them two nations."

"You ask me to say what I think. Will you allow me to say that I know the South pretty well, and never observed those differences?"

"Then," he said, "you have not used your eyes. My eyes are poorer than yours, but I have seen them for years."

The laugh was upon me, and Mr. Benjamin enjoyed it.

"Well, sir, be that as it may, if I understand you, the dispute with your Government is now narrowed down to this, union or disunion."

"Yes," said Mr. Davis, "or, to put it in other words, independence or subjugation."

"Then the two governments are irreconcilably apart. They have no alternative but to fight it out. But it is not so with the people. They are tired of fighting, and want peace, and, as they bear all the burden and suffering of the war, is it not right that they should have peace, and have it on such terms as a majority of them shall elect? This you certainly can't object to, if you are sincere in saying that a majority in the North think you are right. You have the entire South with you, and if the South were reinforced by even a large proportion of the North, you would have a large majority for your views. The Constitution expressly says that it was made by 'the people of the United States.' If they had power to make it, they have power to unmake it, or so to modify it as to suit your views. Thus, if the majority think as you do, you will have accomplished your end, without the firing of another gun or the death of another combatant."

"I don't understand you; be a little more explicit."

"Well, suppose that the two governments should agree to something like this: To go to the people of the whole country with two propositions, say, peace with disunion and Southern independence as your proposition; and peace with union, emancipation with compensation for the slaves, no confiscation, and universal amnesty, as ours. Let the citizens of all the United States (as they existed before the war) vote 'Yes' or 'No' on these two propositions, at a special election within sixty days. If a majority vote 'Disunion,' our Government to be bound by it, and to let you go in peace. If a majority vote 'Union,' yours to be bound by it, and to stay in peace. The two governments can contract in this way, and the people, though constitutionally unable to decide on peace or war, can elect which of any two propositions shall govern their rulers. Let Lee and Grant, meanwhile, agree to an armistice. This would sheathe the sword, and if once sheathed it would never again be drawn by this generation."

"The plan is altogether impracticable," said Mr. Davis.

"If the South were only one State it might work, but as it is, if one Southern State objected to emancipation it would nullify the whole thing, for you are aware the people of Virginia cannot vote slavery out of South Carolina, or the people of South Carolina vote it out of Virginia."

"But three-fourths of the States can amend the Constitution. Let it be done in that way, — in any way, so that it be done by the people. I am not, like you, a statesman, and I do not know just how such a plan could be carried out; but you get the idea, — that the people shall decide the question."

Said Mr. Davis, "That the majority shall decide it, you mean. We seceded to rid ourselves of the rule of the majority, and this would subject us to it again."

"But the majority must rule finally, either with bullets or ballots."

"I am not so sure of that," said Mr. Davis. "Neither current events nor history show that the majority rules, or ever did rule. The contrary, I think, is true. Why, sir, the man who should go before the Southern people with such a proposition — with any proposition which implied that the North was to have a voice in determining the domestic relations of the South — could not live a day! He would be hanged to the first tree, without judge or jury."

"Allow me to doubt that. I think it more likely he would be hanged if he let the Southern people know that the majority could not rule," I replied, smiling.

"I have no fear of that," rejoined Mr. Davis, also smiling most good-humoredly. "I give you leave to proclaim my sentiments from every housetop in the South."

"But, seriously, sir," I said, "you let the majority rule in a single State; why not let it rule in the whole country?"

"Because the States are independent and sovereign. The country is not. It is only a confederation of States, or rather it was; it is now *two* confederations."

"Oh, yes!" I rejoined, "I have heard of your doctrine of 'State Rights,' which, translated into plain English, is that a part is greater than the whole, and we Americans are not a people, but merely a political partnership."

"That is all," he answered, smiling.

"Your very name, sir, ' *United* States,' implies that," said Mr. Benjamin. "But tell me, are the terms you have named — compensated emancipation, no confiscation, and universal amnesty — the terms which Mr. Lincoln authorized you to offer us?"

"No, sir, Mr. Lincoln did not authorize me to offer you any terms. But I think that both he, the Congress, and the Northern people, for the sake of peace, would assent to some such conditions."

"They are *very* generous," replied Mr. Davis, showing, for the first time during the interview, some angry feeling. "But amnesty, sir, applies to criminals. We have committed no crime. Confiscation is of no account unless you can enforce it; and emancipation! you have already emancipated nearly two millions of our slaves, and if you will take care of them you may emancipate the rest. I had a few when the war began. I was of some use to them; they never were of any to me. Against their will you emancipated them; and you may emancipate every negro in the Confederacy; but we will be free! We will govern ourselves! We will do it, if we have to see every Southern plantation sacked, and every Southern city in flames."

"I see, Mr. Davis," I said, " that it is useless to continue this conversation; and you will pardon us if we have seemed to press our views with too much pertinacity. We love the old flag, and that must be our apology for intruding upon you at all."

"You have not intruded upon me," he replied, resuming his usual manner. "I am glad to have met you both. I once loved the old flag as well as you do. I would have died for it; but now it is to me only the emblem of oppression."

"I hope the day may never come, Mr. Davis, when I say that," said the colonel.

A half hour's conversation on other topics — not of public interest — ensued, and then we rose to go. As we did so the Confederate President gave me his hand, and, bidding me a kindly "good-by," expressed the hope of seeing me again in Richmond in happier times, — when peace should have returned; but with the colonel his parting was particularly cordial. Taking his hand in both of his, he said to him, "Colonel, I respect your character and your motives, and I wish you well, — I wish you every good I can wish you consistently with the interests of the Confederacy."

The quiet, straightforward bearing of our "fighting parson" had evidently impressed Mr. Davis very favorably.

As we were leaving the room, he added, " Say to Mr. Lincoln from me, that I shall at any time be pleased to receive proposals for peace on the basis of our independence. It will be useless to approach me with any other."

When we went out, Mr. Benjamin called to Judge Ould, who had been waiting in the hall during the entire interview of nearly three hours, and we passed out of the front entrance together. As I put my arm within that of the judge, he said to me, " Well, what is the result?"

" Nothing but war, war to the knife."

"Ephraim is joined to his idols; let him alone," added the colonel.

We now had "drawn Mr. Davis's fire." He certainly had been explicit enough to convince the dullest intellect that there could be no peace with the Southern Government without the acknowledgment of Southern independence. Colonel Jaquess still clung to the idea of some honorable peace on some terms short of disunion; but I did not, and was merely anxious to get out of the Confederacy at the earliest possible moment, in order to spread far and wide the Southern ultimatum, that every Northern voter might go to the polls at the November election with full knowledge that, if he did not cast his ballot for Abraham Lincoln, he would be voting for the dismemberment and ruin of his country. With these thoughts in my mind, I joined Judge Ould in the hall of the old United States Custom-house at Richmond, on that July night in 1864.

It was not far from midnight when, arm in arm with Judge Ould, we took our way through the silent, deserted streets, to our elevated quarters in the Spotswood Hotel. As we climbed the long stairs which led to our room in the fourth story, I said to Judge Ould, "We can accomplish nothing more by remaining here. Suppose you allow us to shake the sacred soil from our feet to-morrow."

"Very well," he answered. "At what hour will you start?"

"The earlier, the better. As near daybreak as may be,—to avoid the sun."

"We can't be ready before ten o'clock," he said. "The mules are quartered six miles out of town."

This sounded strange, for Jack, our ebony Jehu, had said to me the night before: "Dem is mighty foine mules, massa. I tends ter dem mules myself. *We keeps 'em right round de corner.*" Taken together, the statements of the two Confederate officials had a bad look; but Mr. Davis had just given me a message to his niece, — a lady from whom I had brought a letter of introduction to him, — and Mr. Benjamin had just entrusted Colonel Jaquess with a letter to a Northern friend to be mailed within the limits of the " United States," therefore the discrepancy did not alarm me, for these facts seemed to assure us a safe deliverance from Dixie. Merely saying, " Very well, — then ten o'clock let it be," we bade the judge good night at the landing and entered our apartment.

We found the guard, Mr. Javins, stretched at full length on his bed, and snoring like the Seven Sleepers. Day and night, from the first moment of our entrance into the Confederate dominions, that worthy, with a revolver in his sleeve, our door-key in his pocket, and a Yankee in each one of his eyes, had implicitly obeyed his instructions, — " Keep a constant watch upon them," — but overtasked nature had at last got the better of him, and he was sleeping on his post. Not caring to disturb him, we bolted the door, slid the key under his pillow, and followed him to the land of dreams.

When I awoke in the morning, breakfast was already laid on the centre-table, and an army of newsboys were shouting under our windows, " 'Ere's the *Enquirer* and the *Dispatch.* Great news from the front. Gen'ral Grant mortally killed, — shot with a cannon."

We opened the papers, and there, sure enough, General Grant was killed, — and laid out in dingy sheets, with a big gun firing great volleys over him. Breakfast over, I resumed the papers, and was deep in their flaming editorials, when ten o'clock struck from a neighboring steeple, and I laid them down and listened for the tread of the judge on the stairway. I had heard it before, but had not listened for it till that moment. General Butler had told us we would find him a courteous gentleman and a most agreeable companion, and said to us, as we were coming away, " You are going in without a safeguard, and so, technically, you are spies, therefore you must use the utmost prudence, for your most innocent remarks may be misrepresented and get you into trouble. My advice to you is to hold no communication with any one except Davis, Benjamin, and Judge Ould, and to be sure to win the confidence and goodwill of the judge. You can do this by being perfectly frank and outspoken with him."

We had acted on this suggestion, and he had spent nearly the whole of Sunday with us in what seemed to be to him most enjoyable intercourse. But now he came not, though we waited for him as those " that watch for the morning." One hour, two hours, three hours went slowly away, and still he came not. Why was he thus late, that prompt man who was always " on time," who had put us through the streets of Richmond the night before on a trot, lest we should be a second late at our appointment with Jeff Davis? Did he mean to bake us brown with the mid-day sun? Or had the mules overslept themselves, or their quarters been moved still further out of town? I did not know, and it was useless to speculate, so I lighted a cigar, and took up again the morning paper. But the stinging editorials had lost their sting, and the pointed paragraphs, though sharper than a meat-axe, fell on me as harmless as if I had been encased in a coat of mail. For slowly it began to dawn upon me that the Confederate officials had probably made up their minds to detain us in Richmond, — not, perhaps, to hold us as spies, but to keep us under lock and key until our presidential election had been decided; for the astute

Mr. Benjamin had concluded that Mr. Davis had expressed himself altogether too freely the night before, giving me — an editorial writer on the New York *Tribune* — just the ammunition that was needed to kill the Peace party and reëlect Mr. Lincoln, which meant no compromise with the South until the Confederacy was utterly destroyed.

Ten days in Castle Thunder in my then state of health would have ended my mortal career; and I had looked at this alternative before setting out. But then I had seen it afar off; now I stood face to face with it; and I thought of home, — of the young responsibilities who were accustomed to look for me there, — and I said to Javins, "Will you oblige me by stepping into the hall? My friend and I would have a few words together."

As he passed out, I said to the colonel, "Ould is more than three hours late! What does it mean?"

All this while he had sat, his spectacles on his nose, and his chair canted against the window-sill, absorbed in the newspapers. Occasionally he would look up to comment on something he was reading, but not a movement of his face, nor a glance of his eye had betrayed that he was conscious of Judge Ould's delay, or of my extreme restlessness. As I said this he took off his spectacles, and, quietly rubbing the glasses with his handkerchief, he replied: "It looks badly, but — I ask no odds of them. We have tried to serve the country. That is enough. Let them hang us if they like. But if they do, — if they ill-treat two men who have come to them with the olive-branch of peace, — their rotten Confederacy won't hold together for a fortnight: the civilized world will pray for its destruction."

I opened the door, and called Javins into the room, and then kept on smoking for another two hours. Then, just as three o'clock sounded from a near-by church, Judge

Ould entered the room, saying, with decided curtness, "Good evening."

When we had returned his salutation he said, "Well, gentleman, if you are ready, we'll walk around to the Libby."

The curtness of his tone should have made me perceive that he was playing upon us a practical joke; but not stopping to reflect, I jumped to the conclusion that my worst apprehensions were realized. And this, which seemed then a certainty, was a positive relief from the suspense I had undergone during those harrowing five hours of waiting. Saying, "We are ready," we took up our portmanteaus, and followed him down the stairway. At the outer door we found Jack, our ebony driver of the previous day, and the ambulance drawn up to the sidewalk. Their presence was assurance of our speedy exit from Dixie, and I gave expression to my feelings somewhat as follows: "How are you, Jack? You're the best-looking darkey I ever saw."

"I's bery well, massa, bery well. Hope you's well," replied Jack, grinning until he made himself uglier than nature had intended. "I's glad you tinks I's good-looking."

"Good-looking! You're better-looking than any white man I ever met."

"You've odd notions of beauty," said Judge Ould, smiling. "That accounts for your being an Abolitionist."

"No, it don't;" and I added, in a tone too low for Jack to hear, "It only implies that, until I saw that darkey, I doubted our getting out of Dixie. Tell me, why are you so long behind time?"

"I'll tell you," he said, "when the war is over. Now I'll take you through the Libby and the hospitals, if you'd like to go."

We expressed the desire, and, ordering Jack to follow with the ambulance, the judge led the way down the principal thoroughfare. A few shops were open, a few negro women were passing in and out among them, and a few wounded soldiers were limping along the sidewalks; but scarcely an able-bodied man was anywhere visible. A poor soldier, who had lost both legs and a hand, was seated at a street corner, asking alms of the colored women as they passed! Pointing to him, the judge said, "There is one of our arguments against reunion. If you'll walk with me two squares I'll show you a thousand."

"All asking alms of colored women! Is it not an argument for reunion?"

He made no reply; but after awhile, scanning our faces as if he would detect our hidden thoughts, he said, in an abrupt, pointed way, "Grant was to have attacked us yesterday. Why didn't he do it?"

"How should we know?" I answered, with equal abruptness.

He said, "You came from Foster's only the day before. That's where the attack was to have been made."

"Why was it not made?"

"I don't know. Some think it was because you came in, and were expected out that way."

"Oh! that accounts for your being five hours behind time! You think we are spies, sent in to survey, and report on the Newmarket route!"

"No, I do not," he answered, earnestly. "I think you are honest men, *and I've said so.*"

"That shows you are worthy of the national reputation you won as district attorney of the city of Washington. We *are* honest men; nevertheless, we sincerely thank you."

By this time we had reached a dingy brick building, from

one corner of which protruded a small sign, bearing, in black letters on a white ground, the words

LIBBY AND SON,
SHIP-CHANDLERS AND GROCERS.

It was three stories high, and about a hundred and thirty feet in width by a hundred and ten in depth. In front, the first story was on a level with the street, allowing space for a tier of dungeons under the sidewalk; and in the rear, the land sloped away till the basement floor rose above ground. Its unpainted walls were scorched to a rusty brown, and its sunken doors and low windows, filled here and there with a dusky pane, were cobwebbed and weather-stained, giving the whole building a most uninviting and desolate appearance. A flaxen-haired boy in ragged "butternuts" and a Union cap, and an old man in gray regimentals, with a bent body and a limping gait, were pacing to and fro before it, with muskets on their shoulders; but no other soldiers were in sight. Turning to the judge, I said: " If Grant or Ben Butler knew that Richmond was defended by only such men, how long would it be before they took it ? "

"Several years," he answered. "When such men give out our women will fall in. Let them try it."

Opening a door at the right, he led us into a large, high-studded apartment, with a bare floor and greasy brown walls, hung around with battle-scenes and cheap lithographs of the Confederate leaders. Several officers in Secession gray were lounging about this room, and one of them, a short, slightly built, young-looking man, rose as we entered, and in a half-pompous, half-obsequious way said to Judge Ould, " Ah, Colonel Ould, I am very glad to see you."

The judge returned the greeting with a stateliness that was in striking contrast with his usual frank and cordial manner, and then introduced the officer to us as "Major Turner, keeper of the Libby." I had heard of him, and it was with some reluctance that I took his proffered hand. However, I did take it, and at the same time inquired, "Are you related to H. M. Turner, of Fayetteville, N. C.?"

"No, sir," he answered, "I'm of the old Virginia family" (I never met a negro-whipper or negro-trader who did not profess to belong to that family). "Are you a North Carolinian?" he asked.

"No, sir, — " Before I could add another word Judge Ould said: "No, major; these gentlemen hail from Georgia. They are strangers here, and I'd thank you to show them over the prison."

"Certainly, colonel, most certainly; I'll do it with great pleasure."

Then the little man bustled about, put on his cap, gave a few orders to his subordinates, and led us through another outside door, into the prison. He was a few rods in advance with Colonel Jaquess, when Judge Ould said to me: "Your prisoners have belied Turner. You see that he's not the hyena they have represented."

"You've given evidence of your remarkable penetration in detecting that we are honest men, but allow me to say that you are at fault as to Turner. These cringing, mild-mannered men are the worst of tyrants when they have the power."

"But you can't think him a tyrant!"

"I do; I can believe every word that has been said against him. He's a coward and a bully, or I can't read English. It is written all over his face."

The judge laughed boisterously, and called out to Turner: "I say, major, our friend here is painting your portrait."

"I hope he is making a handsome man of me," said Turner, in a sycophantic way.

"No, he isn't," answered the judge, still laughing; "he is drawing you to the life, as if he had known you for half a century."

We had entered a room about forty feet wide, and a hundred feet deep, with bare brick walls, a rough plank floor, and narrow, dingy windows, to whose sashes only a few broken panes were clinging. A row of tin wash-basins, and a wooden trough which served as a bathing vessel, were at one end of it, and half a dozen cheap stools and hard-bottomed chairs were littered about the floor, but it had no other furniture. And this room, with eight others of similar appointments, and three basements floored with earth and filled with débris, composed the famous Libby Prison, in which, for months together, thousands of the best and bravest men that ever went to battle were allowed to rot and to starve.

At the date of our visit, not more than a hundred prisoners were in the Libby, its contents having recently been emptied into a worse sink in Georgia; but almost constantly during the war, twelve, and sometimes thirteen hundred Northern soldiers were hived within those desolate rooms and filthy cellars, with a space of only ten feet by two allotted to each for all the purposes of existence!

Overrun with vermin, perishing with cold, breathing a stifled, tainted atmosphere, no space allowed them for rest by day, and lying down at night "wormed and dovetailed together like fish in a basket," their daily rations only two ounces of stale beef and a small lump of hard corn-bread, and their lives the forfeit if they caught but one streak of

God's blue sky through those filthy windows!—they endured there all the horrors of the "middle-passage," which was the disgrace of the slave-trade. My soul sickened as I looked on the scene of their wretchedness. If the liberty those men achieved for us were not worth even so fearful a price, if it were not cheaply purchased with the blood and agony of those many brave and true souls, who went into that foul den, only to die, or to come out of it the shadows of men,—living ghosts, condemned to a wretched life, and to fade away before the daybreak of the universal freedom that has come, who would not have cried out for peace,—for peace on almost any terms?

While these thoughts were in my mind, the cringing, foul-mouthed, brutal, contemptible ruffian who had been the zealous agent for the infliction of all this misery, stood within two paces of me! I could have stretched out my arm, and, with half an effort, have crushed him, and — I did not do it!

"This is where that Yankee devil, Streight, who raised hell so among you down in Georgia, got out," said Turner, pausing before a jut in the wall of the room. "A flue was here, you see, but we've bricked it up. They took up the hearth, let themselves down into the basement, and then dug through the wall, and sixty feet underground, into the yard of a deserted building over the way. If you'd like to see the place, step down with me to the basement."

"We would, major. We'd be right glad ter," I replied, adopting, at a hint from Judge Ould, the Georgia dialect.

We descended a rough plank stairway, and entered the basement. It was a damp, mouldy, dismal place, and even then—in hot July weather—as cold as an ice-house. What must it have been in midwinter!

The keeper led us along the wall to where Col. A. D.

Streight and more than sixty of his officers and men had broken from the prison, and then said, "The wall is three feet thick, but they went through it, and all the way under the street, with only a few case-knives, a chisel, and a dustpan."

"Wal, they war smart! But, keeper, whar was yer eyes all o' thet time? Down our way, ef a man couldn't see sixty Yankees a-wuckin' so fur six weeks, in a clar place like this yere, we'd reckon he warn't fit ter 'tend a pen o' niggers."

The judge whispered, "You're overdoing it. Hold in, and talk better English." Turner winced like a struck hound, but, smothering his wrath, he smilingly replied, "The place wasn't clear then. It was filled with straw and rubbish. The Yankees covered the opening with it, and hid away among it when any one was coming. I caught two of them down here one day, but they pulled the wool over my eyes, and I let them off with a few days in a dungeon. But that fellow Streight would outwit the devil. He was the most unruly customer I've had in the twenty months I've been here. I put him in keep, time and again, but I never could cool him down."

"Whar is the keep?" I asked. "Ye's got lots o' them, I reckon."

"No, — only nine. Step this way, and I'll show you."

"Talk better English," said the judge, laughing, as we fell a few paces behind Turner. "There are some school-masters in Georgia."

"Not in the part I cum from," I answered, also laughing. "That fellow has swallowed me body and boots. Let us alone, and I'll have all he knows out of him, and something besides."

The dungeons were low, close, dismal apartments, about

twelve feet square, boarded off from the remainder of the cellar, and lighted by only a narrow grating under the sidewalk. Their floors were encrusted with filth, and their walls stained and damp with the rain, which had dripped down from the street.

"And how many does ye commonly lodge yere, when yer hotel's full?" I asked of Turner.

"I have had," he said, "twenty in each, but fifteen is about as many as they comfortably hold."

"I reckon! And then the comfort moughtn't be much ter brag on."

The keeper soon invited us to walk into the adjoining basement. I was a few paces in advance of him, taking a straight course to the entrance, when a sentinel, pacing to and fro in the middle of the apartment, levelled his musket, so as to bar my way, saying, as he did so, "Ye carn't pass yere, sir. Ye must go 'round by the wall."

This drew my attention to the spot, and I observed that a space about fifteen feet square, in the centre of the basement, and directly in front of the sentinel, had been recently dug up with a spade. While in all other places the ground was trodden to the hardness and color of granite, this spot seemed to be soft, and had the reddish-yellow hue of the "sacred soil." Another sentry was pacing to and fro on its other side, so that the spot was completely guarded. Why was it so closely protected? The reason flashed upon me, and I said to Turner, "I say, how many barr'ls has ye in thar?"

"Enough to blow this old shanty to h—," he answered, curtly.

"I reckon! Put 'em thar when that feller Dahlgren wus agwine ter rescue 'em,— the Yankees?"

"I reckon," was his only answer; but that was enough,

with the lately upturned earth, to establish as a fact what has been persistently denied by all Confederate writers. The powder stored there was, in case of outside attack, to have blown to atoms hundreds of unarmed and innocent men.

In this room, seated on the ground or leaning listlessly against the walls, were a dozen poor fellows, who were held as hostages for a like number held under sentence of death by our Government. Their dejected, homesick, weary look disclosed some of the horrors of imprisonment.

"Let us go," I said to the judge. "I've had enough of this."

"No," said Turner, "you must see the up-stairs. It ain't so gloomy up there."

It was not so gloomy, for some little of God's sunlight did come in through the dingy windows; but the few prisoners in the upper rooms wore the same sad, disconsolate look as those we had seen in the basement. "It is not hard fare, or close quarters, that kills men," said Judge Ould; "it is homesickness; and the strongest and bravest succumb to it first."

In the sill of an attic window, I found a Minie ball. Prying it out with my knife, and holding it up to Turner, I said, "So, ye keeps this room fur a shootin'-gallery, does ye?"

"Yes," he answered, laughing. "The boys practise once in a while on the Yankees. You see, the rules forbid their coming within three feet of the windows. Sometimes they do, and then the boys take a pop at them."

"And sometimes hit 'em. Hit many on 'em?"

"Yes; a heap."

As we passed out of the entrance door, Judge Ould said, "Now, tell me, what do you think of the Libby?"

"I think it is that place Saint John speaks of in the

Revelation, 'the habitation of devils and the hold of every foul and unclean thing.' I can't conceive of any worse hell than such a place, presided over by such a miscreant as that man Turner. You have had it 'swept and garnished' to pull the wool over our eyes, — just as you strung that army of pickets along the Newmarket road; but this Minie ball," holding it out to him, " and that guarded spot in the basement tell its entire history. The men that planned and control such a den are no better than devils, and are not fit associates for such an upright, high-minded man as you are. I have taken a strong liking to you, — I never met a man for whom, on so short an acquaintance, I conceived so kindly a feeling, — so let me beg of you to wash your hands of these scoundrels; if you feel that you should fight us, do it in man fashion, at the head of your regiment, but not in concert with such a cowardly, hellish set of miscreants as control your prisons."

"You are very indiscreet, my Yankee friend," said Judge Ould, his face flushed, and speaking in a low tone. "I've kept you out of one scrape to-day; don't oblige me to get you out of another."

"If you have done that, I thank you; but it's no more than I expected of you. Butler told us that he knew you well, — that you were a square, honorable man, and we could depend on you in all circumstances."

"Did Butler say that?" asked Judge Ould, smiling. "Give him my compliments, and tell him that I think the devil is not so black as he is painted. Now I'll take you through Castle Thunder and the prison hospitals, on the condition that you address all your censorious remarks to me privately. Doubtless the places will be fixed up a little, for they know a couple of Georgians are coming, but you can see below the whitewash."

We then visited Castle Thunder and the hospitals for the Union wounded, and, about six o'clock, were ready to take our seats in the ambulance which was to convey us to the headquarters of General Foster, at Deep Bottom. As we were about to take our seats in the ambulance, Judge Ould drew me a short distance aside, saying: " I have a favor to ask of you."

The favor was that I should obtain from Mr. Lincoln permits for some half-dozen persons to pass, to or fro, through the lines. I assured him that, beyond question, Mr. Lincoln would give the desired permissions, and then I said: "Now, judge, explain to me your delay of this morning."

He then said that at nine o'clock he had gone to Mr. Davis's house for the official permit to take us out, and had found there Secretary Benjamin, who was impressing upon Mr. Davis the necessity of placing us in Castle Thunder until the Northern election was over. He insisted that while Jaquess was sincerely desirous of opening the door for peace, I had no expectation of doing so, and was solely bent on drawing them out on points that would prejudice them with Northern voters.

Mr. Davis hesitated, — he thought they could not honorably detain men who had come to them on a peace errand. While the judgment of Davis was in suspense, Ould had entered the room, and Davis appealed to him for his opinion. Ould assured him that I was so frank a man that he should have discovered any political purpose if I had one; that I had expressed myself with the utmost freedom — and not always in a complimentary manner — about Southern men and Southern principles; and as an instance of my very uncommon frankness he mentioned my exposure of the ruse they had attempted to play upon us with the

Sibley tents and the overgrown picket-stations. Davis adjourned the discussion by asking Ould to call on him at two o'clock, when he would decide the matter. At that time he gave Ould the permit, with the remark, "This is probably a bad business for us, anyway; but it would alienate many of our Northern friends should we hold on to these gentlemen."

We arrived near the Union lines at Deep Bottom soon after sunset, and the waving of a white flag brought to us a young officer from the nearest picket-station. He went at once to General Foster for a couple of horses, and in half an hour we entered the general's tent. It was after his dinner-hour, but he proposed to kill for us the fatted calf. "For," he said, "these, my sons, were dead, and are alive again; were lost, and are found." We let him kill the calf, — it tasted wonderfully like salt pork, — and then again mounting his horses, we were at ten o'clock that night at General Butler's headquarters.

At General Grant's invitation, Colonel Jaquess remained a few days at City Point, but I took the first boat for Washington. On the way down the river, and while the facts were fresh in my mind, I wrote out the interview with Davis and Benjamin, which I proposed to read to Mr. Lincoln, to avoid the omissions and inaccuracies that might occur in a verbal recital. Arrived in Washington, I hurried to the White House. Mr. Sumner was closeted with the President, but my name was no sooner announced than a kindly voice said, "Come in. Bring him in." As I entered his room he rose and, grasping my hand, said: "I'm glad you're back. I heard of your return two nights ago, but they said you were non-committal. What is it, — as we expected?"

"Exactly, sir," I answered. "There is no peace without

separation. Coming down on the boat, I wrote out the interview to read to you when you are at leisure."

"I am at leisure now," he replied. "Sumner, too, would be glad to hear it."

When I had finished the reading, he said, "What do you propose to do with this?"

"Put a beginning and an end to it, sir, on my way home, and hand it to the *Tribune*."

"Can't you get it into the *Atlantic Monthly?*" he asked. "It would have less of a partisan look there."

"No doubt I can, sir," I replied; "but there would be some delay about it."

"And it is important that Davis's position should be known at once," said Mr. Lincoln. "It will show the country that I didn't fight shy of Greeley's Niagara business without a reason; and everybody is agog to hear your report. Let it go into the *Tribune*."

"Permit me to suggest," said Mr. Sumner, "that Mr. Gilmore put at once a short card, with the separation declaration of Davis, into one of the Boston papers, and then, as soon as he can, the fuller report into the *Atlantic*."

"That is it," said Mr. Lincoln. "Put Davis's 'We are not fighting for slavery; we are fighting for independence' into the card, — that is enough; and send me the proof of what goes into the *Atlantic*. Don't let it appear till I return the proof. Some day all this will come out, but just now we must use discretion."

As I rose to leave, Mr. Lincoln took my hand, and while he held it in his said, "Jaquess was right, — God's hand is in it. This may be worth as much to us as half a dozen battles. Get the thing out as soon as you can; but don't forget to send me the proof of what you write for the *Atlantic*. Good-by. God bless you."

The "card" appeared in the Boston *Evening Transcript* of July 22, 1864, and two or three days afterwards Mr. James T. Fields handed to me the proof of the *Atlantic* article, which I at once forwarded to Mr. Lincoln. He retained it seven days, and thereby delayed the issue of the magazine considerably beyond the usual period; and when the proof came back from him it was curtailed a full page and a half of its original proportions. He had stricken out the terms he was willing to grant to the Rebellion, and all reference which I had made to compensation for the slaves. I had intended the article not only as a declaration of Mr. Davis's position, but also as a manifesto to the Southern people of the liberal conditions on which they could return to the Union. I thought a knowledge of those conditions would create a rebellion within a rebellion, and so much deplete the Southern armies as to shorten the war materially.

Mr. Lincoln told me subsequently that he held the proof under consideration for a few days because, while he was at first tempted to let the article stand as I had written it, fuller reflection convinced him that the publication of his terms would sow dissension in the South, and he was unwilling that his words should have any such effect. Had these terms been accepted, the South would have come out of the war in a better financial position than the North, and the revolted States would have been saved the long agony of reconstruction.

Oliver Wendell Holmes wrote[1] me soon afterwards that beyond any question the *Atlantic* article had a larger number of readers than any magazine article ever written. It was republished by nearly every leading newspaper in the North,

[1] The letter is in the library of Johns Hopkins University.

and was copied entire by the London *Times*, *News*, and *Telegraph*. It was doubtless read by not less than one-half of the four millions of men who voted in the presidential election of 1864; and it may have turned from the "error of their ways" the comparatively small number that were needed to give McClellan the popular, and, perhaps, the electoral vote for the presidency.

E. A. Pollard, in his "Southern History of the War," says: "No doubt can rest in history that, at the time of the Chicago Convention [which nominated McClellan], the Democratic party in the North had prepared a secret programme of operations, the final and inevitable conclusion of which was the acknowledgment of the independence of the Confederate States." Commenting on this declaration in the *Tribune*, Horace Greeley said: "We have always supposed that there was a general understanding arrived at between the rebel commissioners in Canada, and their Democratic visitors from this side, as to what should be said and done at Chicago, and that it was spoiled by Jeff Davis's peremptory declaration to Jaquess and Gilmore that he would consent to no peace that did not recognize the Southern Confederacy as henceforth independent. We believe that visit of Jaquess and Gilmore to Richmond saved the vote of this [New York] State to Lincoln, though Sherman's capture of Atlanta, and Sheridan's victories in the Valley doubtless coöperated with the semi-treasonable follies of the Chicago Convention and Platform to render the general triumph of Lincoln more complete and overwhelming."

President Lincoln recognized the political character, and estimated the importance of our "mission" in a letter which he addressed to Abram Wakeman, postmaster at New York City, directly after the interview that is just recorded. The letter may be found in Volume II. of "The Letters and Speeches of Abraham Lincoln," by John Hay and John G. Nicolay. In the same work may be found the draft of a message to Congress that was prepared, some few months later, by Mr. Lincoln, recommending an appropriation of three hundred million dollars for payment for the slaves who had been manumitted by his proclamation, and which was not delivered or published, because it was objected to by his Cabinet.

In this connection I am reminded to state that when the Hon. Robert J. Walker returned in the fall of 1864, from his visit to Europe in the service of the Treasury Department, he questioned me as to the "true inwardness" of the "Peace Mission to Richmond," remarking that I was certainly too well informed to expect that peace would result from the journey. After disclosing — as was my habit with him — the whole inner history of the transaction, I remarked, "But, Governor, was it not very magnanimous in Mr. Lincoln to so urgently seek the counsel of Mr. Chase when he had so recently been obliged to request him to 'step down and out' from his Cabinet, and was aware that he harbored towards him intensely bitter feelings?"

Mr. Walker laughed as he answered, "Can you not see an elephant without using your glasses? Mr. Lincoln was about to offer compensation for the slaves, and he knew that the Abolitionists and radical Republicans would make 'Rome howl' over the proposition. What would so effectually silence their clamor as a statement by their great leader, Mr. Chase, that he had helped to form, and fully assented to, those propositions? Have I not often told you that Mr. Lincoln was the shrewdest of all living politicians?"

It is incontestable that our visit to Richmond bore fruit

to the "healing of the nation;" but, had I been asked to repeat the visit under similar circumstances, I think I should have answered in the words of the young Quakeress, who, against the rules of the society, had married a military man, and was called up before the elders to receive the penalty of excommunication, but was told by the tender-hearted brethren that she would be forgiven if she said that she was sorry. "I can't," she answered, "truly say that I am sorry; but I will say that I will not do so again."

CHAPTER XVIII.

THE GREAT CONSPIRACY.

As early as the summer of 1863 rumors were prevalent in the North of the existence at the West of a treasonable organization under the various names of "Sons of Liberty," "American Knights," and "Knights of the Golden Circle," the object of which was to effect a disruption of the Northern States, and thus afford efficient aid in the establishment of the Southern Confederacy. There was at the time no positive proof of the truth of this rumor, and it was altogether discredited by Secretary Stanton, but it was so far believed by President Lincoln, as early as July, 1863, that he declined to appoint Judge Edmonds to investigate into the origin of the New York riots, lest he should thereby disturb a hornets' nest, and find himself with two rebellions on his hands — as I have shown in the chapter on "The *Tribune* in the Draft Riots."

The first trustworthy evidence of this formidable organization was obtained by General Rosecrans in February, 1864, — soon after he had been appointed to the command of the Department of the Missouri; and the full discovery he made of this conspiracy is one of the most important of the many great services he rendered to the country. His spies joined the treasonable order, and were admitted to its secret conclaves, where they learned that it was a gigantic organization, overspreading nearly all of the Western

States, and having as its commanders-in-chief, C. L. Vallandigham, of Ohio, and General Stirling Price, of Missouri. It had a military organization, with general and subordinate officers, and claimed five hundred thousand enrolled members, all bound to a blind obedience to the orders of their superiors, and pledged to "take up arms against any government found waging war against a people endeavoring to establish a government of their own choice." Its immediate objects were a general rising in Missouri and a similar rising in Ohio, Indiana, Illinois, and Kentucky, in coöperation with Confederate forces which were to invade the last-named State and Missouri. A part of its programme was the liberation of the Confederate prisoners of war at Camp Douglas, Camp Morton, Johnson's Island, and other Northern prisons, and the supplying of them with arms that were being secretly brought into the country.

The time was auspicious for the enterprise, Missouri and the other Western States having been denuded of troops, for service elsewhere, and all the prisons being insufficiently guarded by soldiers of the Veteran Reserve Corps, many of whom were totally unfit for military duty. When all was in readiness, Jacob Thompson, of Mississippi, who had been Mr. Buchanan's Secretary of the Interior, appeared at the Clifton House, Niagara Falls, with, it was said, a large sum of money, to take direction of the operations. This made it evident that, if the organization had not been planned by the Richmond authorities, it was under their direct control, and was to be made to serve as an auxiliary force in their war upon the union.

The first movement was by Stirling Price, against Missouri, which State he invaded late in September with nearly twenty thousand men, expecting to be joined by twenty-three thousand American Knights in the counties bordering on Arkansas; but by the superb strategy of Rosecrans, Price's plans were frustrated, and he was driven, by a much inferior force, from the State by the middle of November.

Thus the snake was scotched, but not killed. Before Price's rear-guard was safely over the line into Arkansas, Thompson was ready for another spring at Camp Douglas, in the suburbs of Chicago. And this spring was to be more deadly than the other, — a blow struck at the very heart of the great West, and calculated to paralyze the energies of the entire North. The eight or nine thousand prisoners at Camp Douglas were to be joined by the four thousand Canadian refugees, and Missouri "Butternuts" to be engaged in their release, and the five thousand American Knights who were resident in Chicago. This force of about eighteen thousand men would be a nucleus around which the conspirators in other parts of Illinois might gather; and being joined by the prisoners liberated from other camps, and members of the order from other States, they would soon form an army a hundred thousand strong. So fully had everything been foreseen and arranged for, that the leaders expected to gather and organize this vast body of men within the space of a fortnight.

The Union Government could bring into the field no force to withstand the progress of such an army. The consequence would be that the entire character of the war would be changed; its theatre would be shifted from the border to the heart of the Free States, and Southern independence, and the beginning at the North of that process of disintegration so confidently counted on by the Confederate leaders at the outbreak of hostilities, would have followed.

As I have said, the nucleus for this great hostile gathering of American Knights was to have been the body of Confederate soldiers who were to be liberated from the various Northern prisons. How many they numbered at this period cannot be stated with accuracy, but estimating the entire force by the number confined at Camp Douglas, it could not have varied much from forty thousand; and if we call to mind that all the prisons were insufficiently guarded, and none were constructed with a view to resisting attack from an outside enemy, it will be seen that the danger was not only imminent, but absolutely appalling. Jacob Thompson had rightly said that, Camp Douglas once in his hands, the most populous cities of the West, and every one of its loyal citizens, would be altogether at the mercy of his Confederate soldiery.

What saved the West from being engulfed in this whirlpool of ruin? Nothing but the cool brain, sleepless vigilance, and remarkable sagacity of one man, — a young officer never read of in the newspapers, removed from field duty because of disability; but specially commissioned, I verily believe, by the Providence that guards our country, to ferret out and foil this deeper-laid, wider-spread, and more diabolical conspiracy than any that darkens the pages of history. On the roll of atrocious villainy, not even Catiline is worthy to rank with Jacob Thompson. Others than this young man were instrumental in dragging the dark iniquity to light; but they failed to fathom its deep enormity or to discover its point of outbreak. He did that, and he throttled the tiger when it was about to spring, and so he is deserving of the lasting gratitude of the country. How he did it I now propose to tell. It is a marvellous tale; it will sound more like romance than history, but its every word is true as I heard it from the lips of the young officer himself, and his chief subordinates in Camp Douglas, during the week immediately following the crowning event of the remarkable story. Moreover, every fact in the account was verified to me by official documents, or credible witnesses, during the three days that I was occupied in the investigation.

There was nothing remarkable in the appearance of this young officer. He was about thirty years of age, nearly six feet in height, with an erect, military carriage, a frank, manly face, and he looked every inch a soldier, such a soldier as would stand up all day in a square hand-to-hand fight with an open enemy; but the keenest eye would detect in him no indication of the crafty genius that delights to follow the windings of wickedness when burrowing in the dark. But if not a Fouché or a Vidocq, he was certainly an able man; for in a section where able men are as plenty as apple-blossoms in June, he was elected State Senator before he was twenty-seven, and, entering the volunteer army as a subaltern officer, he had risen before the battle of Perryville to the command of a regiment. At that battle a Confederate bullet entered his shoulder, and crushed the bones of his right elbow. This disabled him for field duty, and thus it came about that he assumed the light blue of the Veteran Reserves, and, on the second day of May, 1864, was appointed to the command of the prison camp near the city of Chicago.

Camp Douglas stood on the shore of Lake Michigan, about three miles from the business centre of Chicago. It contained twenty or more acres of flat, sandy soil, and was surrounded by a close board fence, an inch thick, and fourteen feet high, which a score of men, armed with heavy axes, might easily have battered down in less than an hour. This fence was its sole exterior protection. Along the front of the enclosure ran the public highway that led to Chicago, and opening on this highway was the front gateway, built of plank somewhat thicker than the fence, but no protection against the blows of a stout axeman. Near the gateway were the offices of the commandant of the prison, and directly in their rear was a plot of about four acres, occupied as a parade-ground and by the barracks of the guard. Adjoining this was another space devoted to the hospital buildings, the bakery, and the dispensary, which last was in charge of a Confederate surgeon, who had been an apothecary at his home.

In the rear of these various buildings, and abutting on the rear fence of the prison enclosure, were the barracks of the prisoners, — sixty-four long, low buildings, ranged in rows of sixteen, divided by wide streets, and capable of comfortably housing ten thousand prisoners. At the time of my visit there were in these barracks 8,308 private soldiers of the Confederate army, and, as these were the very men whom Jacob Thompson intended to serve as the fiery nucleus of the force that was to devastate the West, I may as well expend upon them a few words of description. I passed a large portion of three days among them, conversing with them freely, and sharing their rations, and, but for their "butternut" garb and Southern lingo, I might have taken them for a gathering of back-country Yankees. Some few were what are commonly styled "gentlemen," but much the larger number were workingmen, accustomed to some form of mechanical or agricultural labor. Not many of them could read or write, and they lacked the refinement of manner that comes from contact with cultivated society, but they were essentially Yankees, differing from the Northern Jonathan only as they had been warped by slavery, or kept down by slaveholders.

Whittling and swapping are counted Yankee peculiaritics. That number of Englishmen, hived within the limits of a dozen acres, would have taken to grumbling, Germans to smoking, and Irishmen to brawling, but those eight thousand Southerners had taken to whittling, thus showing themselves to be Yankees,—and no amount of false education and bad politics will ever make them anything else. One had whittled a fiddle from a pine shingle; another, a clarionet from an ox-bone; a third, a meerschaum from a corn-cob; a fourth, a water-wheel—which, he said, would propel machinery without a waterfall—from half a dozen sticks of hickory; a fifth, with no previous practice, made gold rings from brass, and jet from gutta-percha; and, to crown all, a sixth had actually whittled a whistle—and a whistle that would blow—out of a pig's tail.

And they displayed the trading as well as the inventive genius of Yankees. One had swapped coats until he had got entirely out at the elbows, another trousers until his came scarcely below the knees, another hats until he had only part of a rim and the "smallest showing" of a crown, and yet every time—so he said—he had got the best of the trade; and another regularly bought out the old apple woman and *peddled* her stock about the camp at the rate of a dollar "a grab," payable in greenbacks. With these striking peculiarities,—whittling, swapping, and peddling,—no one could deny that those men were Yankees; perhaps not descended from Plymouth Rock, but coming by a more direct route from the British Islands.

The town-meeting is said to be the most striking peculiarity of New England society, and it is reckoned by some as the very bulwark of Yankee liberty. It does not exist in the South, because it has been repressed by more than two centuries of slavery. But it must be in the Southern blood, for it burst forth in full flower at Camp Douglas. I was informed of it by Captain Sponable, the gentlemanly inspector of the prison, with whom one evening I attended one of the meetings. It was held in the long hall of a barrack, a room about eighty feet in length, with three tiers of bunks on either side, and furnished with a stove and a number of hard-bottomed benches. The lamps had been lighted and something more than a hundred natives were assembled, a few of whom, seated on tomato boxes, were engaged at euchre or "seven-up;" but much the larger number were squatted on the floor or leaning against the bunks, listening to an impassioned speaker who was "fighting his battles over again," and knocking the "rotten Union inter everlastin' smash."

He was followed by "your feller citizen, Jim Hurdle, sir," who during the other's speech had stood nursing his coat-tails before the stove, but at the conclusion extended his right arm, and pitched into the previous speaker as if he meant to give us ocular proof of the possibility of annihilation.

A glance was enough to convince me that Mr. Hurdle was a "character" and a "genius" of the first order. His coat was decidedly seedy, his hat much the worse for wear, and his trousers so out at the knees that one might suppose he had spent his entire life in religious devotions; but he was a "born gentleman," above work and "too proud to be beholden to a kentry he had fit agin." He knew a little of everything under the sun, and had a tongue that could outrun any railway engine in the universe. The opposing orator had devoted his energies to knocking the rotten Union into forty thousand flinders. Mr. Hurdle expended his upon the Confederacy. "The Confederacy, sir," he shouted, "ar' busted,— gone all ter smash. It ar' rottener nor any egg that ever was sot on, and dedder'n any door nail that ever was driv."

" But it bites a leetle yit, Jim," said some one from among the audience.

" Bites," echoed Mr. Hurdle; " of course it do. So do a turtle arter his head ar' cut off. I know'd one of them critters onc't that an old nigger man decapitated. The next day he was amusin' himself pokin' sticks at him, and the turtle was bitin' at him like time. Then I says ter the old feller: ' Why, Pomp, I thought the turtle was dead.' ' Well, he am dead, massa,' says Pomp, ' but the critter doan't know enough ter be sensible ob it.' And so, feller citizens, the Confederacy ar' dead, but Jeff Davis and them sort o' fellers don't know enough to be sensible of it."

But at nine o'clock " lights out " rang through the camp, and the captain and I retired to his quarters. Seated there, he told me of Mr. Hurdle's escape not long before from the prison. I do not remember how he managed to elude the guard, but he did so and got safely into Chicago. There he wandered about the streets till he was nearly famished, when at last he came upon a baker's wagon standing in front of a provision store. There being no one in sight, and deeming it better to steal than to starve, he thrust his hand into the wagon to confiscate a loaf of bread; but before he had secured one, a dog sprang out of the wagon and seized him by the slack of his trousers. In the struggle that followed both he and the dog rolled over in the gutter together, and then Mr. Hurdle tried to pull up a paving-stone to brain the animal. The stone refused to come up, but he managed finally to get away with badly damaged trousers. Then, taking a straight course back to Camp Douglas, he applied to the commandant for readmission to his former quarters, saying it was not safe to be at large in a country "where they let loose the dogs and tie up the paving-stones."

Wendell Phillips used to say that if you scratched a Yankee you would come at once upon a savage. With the Southern Yankees in Camp Douglas it would not be necessary to go below the cuticle to come upon the untamed animal. About fifteen hundred of them were the rough riders of John Morgan, — men who feared neither God, man, nor the devil; as many more were Texas rangers, — wild, reckless characters, fonder of a fight than of a dinner, and ready for any enterprise, however desperate, that held out the smallest prospect of freedom. The remainder were the equals — every man of them — of any of our Northern soldiers, and better by half than the foreign mercenaries whom we had bribed by bounties to fill the Southern graveyards.

Against such an army, well equipped and ably led, whether with or without outside aid, what force could be opposed by the new commandant? Precisely seven hundred and ninety-six maimed veterans, stiff with wounds and racked with rheumatism, and posted behind a slender board fence that would tumble to the ground sooner than did the walls of Jericho before the trumpets of Joshua. At once he called upon his commanding general for reinforcements, though as yet he knew nothing of the disclosures. Rosecrans had already sent to the War Department. But no reinforcements could be had; every able-bodied man was needed at the front, for the country was then in the supremest crisis of the great struggle. Seeing then that he must rely altogether upon his own resources, he resolved at once to make himself master of the situation, — to repair by vigilance his deficiency in numbers. He had already discovered that the prison was in charge of the prisoners; that they served out rations and distributed clothing to their comrades, dealt out ammunition to the guards, and even kept the records in the quarters of the commandant. This state of things underwent a sudden change. With the exception of a very few, whose characters recommended them to peculiar confidence, all were at once placed where they belonged, on the inner side of the prison fence.

A post-office was connected with the camp, and this next received the commandant's attention. Everything connected with it seemed to be entirely regular. A vast number of letters came and went; but they all passed unsealed, and appeared to convey nothing contraband. However, many of them were short epistles on long pieces of paper, a curious circumstance among correspondents with whom stationery was scarce and greenbacks were not overplenty. One hot day in June the commandant builded a fire, and gave some of the letters a warming; when lo! presto! prestissimo! the white spaces broke out into dark lines, breathing thoughts blacker than the fluid that wrote them, revealing the fact that the prisoners were in constant communication with outside friends, and expected to join in a grand celebration on the coming Fourth of July, when they would burn an "all-fired sight of powder," and "go up like a rocket," if they did have to come down like a stick.

The commandant called to mind that the National Convention of the Peace party was to assemble at Chicago on the Fourth of July; that a vast concourse of people would come together on the occasion, and that, in so great a throng, it would be easy for the "clans to gather," attack the camp, and liberate the prisoners. He acted promptly. Instantly Prison Square received a fresh instalment of prisoners, genuine "Butternuts," but loyal men, who fraternized with the Confederates, and soon learned that the commandant's suspicions were well founded. The prisoners were to salute the old flag on Independence Day, but not with blank cartridges.

But the loyal Butternuts failed to discern who were to join in the outside celebration, and the commandant set his own wits to working. Soon he heard of the "Society of the Illini," whose object, as set forth by its constitution, was "the more perfect development of the literary, scientific, moral, physical, and social welfare of the 'conservative citizens' of Chicago." The commandant knew a "conservative citizen" whose development was not altogether perfect; him he induced to join the organization, and he was soon deep in the outer secrets of the order. He could not penetrate its inner mysteries, but he learned that the Society numbered some thousands of members, all fully armed and impatiently waiting the signal for an attack on Camp Douglas.

However, the assembling of the Chicago Convention was postponed to the 29th of August, and the Fourth of July passed away without extraordinary fireworks.

But the commandant did not go to sleep. He still kept his wits a-working; the loyal Butternuts still ate prisoners' rations; and the red flame still brought out black thoughts on the white letter paper. Quietly the garrison was reinforced; quietly increased vigilance was enjoined upon the sentinels; and the tranquil, assured bearing of the commandant told no one that he was playing with hot coals on a barrel of gunpowder.

So July rolled away into August, and the commandant gave his views of the state of things to his commanding general. This letter came into my hands, and its contents stated as facts, that five thousand armed traitors were then domiciled in Chicago; that they expected to be soon joined by a considerable body of Confederates from Canada; that the object of the combination was the release of the prisoners at Camp Douglas, and that success in that enterprise would be the signal for a general uprising of the disloyal elements throughout Indiana and Illinois, — all this information being the result of two months' persistent burrowing in the dark!

At last the loyal Democrats came together to the great Peace Convention, and with them came Satan also. Bands of ill-favored men in bushy hair, bad whiskey, and seedy homespun staggered from the railway stations and hung about the street corners. A reader of Dante might have taken them for delegates from the lower regions, had not their clothing been plainly perishable, while devils are supposed to wear indestructible raiment. They had come, they announced, to make a Peace President, but they brandished bowie-knives and bellowed for war even in the sacred precincts of the Peace Convention. But, war or peace, the commandant was prepared for it.

For days reinforcements had poured into Camp Douglas until it actually bristled with bayonets. On every side it was guarded with cannon, and day and night mounted men patrolled the avenues to give warning of the first hostile gathering. But there was no gathering. The conspirators were there, three thousand strong, with five thousand Illini to back them. From every point of the compass — from Canada, Missouri, Southern Illinois, Ohio, Indiana, New York, and even loyal Vermont — red-handed men had come to give the Peace candidate a bloody baptism. Not long afterwards one of the leaders, whom I met as a prisoner in Camp Douglas, said to me, " We had spies in every public place, — in the telegraph office, the camp itself, and even close by the commandant's headquarters, and knew every hour all that was passing. From the observatory, opposite the camp, I myself saw the arrangements for our reception. We outnumbered you two to one, but our force was badly disciplined. Success in such circumstances was impossible; and on the third day of the Convention we announced from headquarters that an attack at that time was impracticable. It would have cost the lives of hundreds of the prisoners, and, perhaps, the capture or destruction of the whole of us."

Thus the storm blew over, without leaden rain, and its usual accompaniment of lightning and thunder.

A dead calm followed, during which the Illini slunk back to their holes; the prisoners took to honest ink; the loyal Butternuts walked the streets clad like Christians, and the commandant went to sleep with only one eye open. Thus the world rolled round into November.

The presidential election was near at hand, the great contest on which hung the fate of the Republic. The commandant was convinced of this, and desired to marshal his old constituents for the final struggle between Union and Disunion. He obtained a furlough to go to his Wisconsin home and mount the " stump " for President Lincoln. He was about to set out, his private secretary was ready, and the carriage waiting at the gateway, when an indefinable feeling took possession of him, holding him back with a presentiment of coming danger. It would not be shaken off, and reluctantly he postponed his journey until the morrow. Before the morrow facts were developed which made his presence in Chicago essential to the safety of the city and the lives of its citizens. The scotched snake had come to vigorous life, and was preparing for another and a deadlier spring.

It was not long before a St. Louis detective, professedly a Secessionist, but secretly in the service of the Government, called at his office, requesting a private interview. The detective informed him that he had just met, in hiding in Chicago, Colonel Marmaduke, of St. Louis, a brother of General Marmaduke, and a son of a former governor of Missouri, who had told him that he, and several other Confederate officers, were then in Chicago to coöperate with other persons in releasing the prisoners of Camp Douglas and other prisons, and in inaugurating a rebellion at the North. The movement, he said, was under the auspices of the American Knights (to which order the Society of the Illini belonged), and was to begin operations by an attack on Camp Douglas on election night.

The detective, as he related this interview to me, said, "The young man rested his head upon his hand, and looked as if he had lost his mother." And well he might! For, lulled into a false security, he had allowed himself to be stripped of his reinforcements, and again had but eight hundred men in garrison to resist the attack which had been so long in preparation. Only seventy hours were left to him! What would he not give for twice that number? In that time he might secure additional troops. The detective left him pacing the floor, his face pale, but his manner cool and collected, as if he were gathering together all his resources for what was to be the great crisis of his life. He was still pacing the floor when, two hours later, a stranger was ushered into his private office. From the lips and pen of this stranger I had what followed, and I think it may be relied on.

He was a slim, light-haired young man, of apparently

twenty-seven or twenty-eight years, with fine, regular features, and the indefinable air that denotes good breeding. Recognizing the commandant by the eagle upon his shoulder, he said, "Can I see you alone, sir?"

"Certainly," answered the Union officer, motioning to his secretary to leave the room. As the door closed the other said: "My name is Langhorn, Maurice Langhorn, of Kentucky. I am a colonel in the Rebel army, and have put my life into your hands to warn you of the most hellish plot in history."

"Your life is safe, sir," replied the commandant, "if your visit is an honest one; I shall be glad to hear what you have to say. Be seated."

The Confederate officer took the proffered chair, and sat there till the small hours of the morning. In the limits of a single chapter I cannot attempt to recount all that passed between them. My interview with the Confederate officer on this subject lasted five hours, and the statement of it, which he subsequently wrote out for me, occupies fourteen pages of closely written foolscap. That statement is now in the historical library of the Johns Hopkins University, at Baltimore, and may be seen by any one who makes the proper application.

Colonel Langhorn began by saying that, sixty days previously, he had left Richmond with verbal despatches from the Confederate Secretary of War, to Jacob Thompson, the director of the disloyal operations in Canada. These despatches had relation to a vast plot designed to wrap the West in flames, to sever it from the East, and so secure the independence of the South. The plot had been concocted months before at Richmond, and in the previous May Jacob Thompson, supplied with two hundred and fifty thousand dollars in sterling exchange, had been sent to Canada to superintend its execution. This money was lodged in a bank at Montreal, and had furnished the funds which had already fitted out the abortive expeditions against Johnson's Island and Camp Douglas. The plot embraced the order of American Knights, which was spread all over the West, and numbered five hundred thousand men, three hundred and fifty thousand of whom were armed. A force of twelve hundred Canadian refugees and bushwhackers from Southern Illinois and Missouri was to attack Camp Douglas on Tuesday night, the 8th of November, liberate and arm the prisoners, and sack the city of Chicago. This was to be the signal for a general uprising throughout the West, and for a simultaneous advance by Hood upon Nashville, by Buckner upon Louisville, and Price upon St. Louis. Vallandigham was to lead the movement in Ohio, Bowles in Indiana, and Walsh in Illinois. The forces were to rendezvous at Dayton and Cincinnati in Ohio, at New Albany and Indianapolis in Indiana, and at Rock Island, Chicago, and Springfield in Illinois, and those gathered at the last-named place, after seizing the arsenal, were to march to the aid of Price in taking St. Louis. Prominent Union men and officers were to be seized, placed in irons, and sent South, and the more obnoxious of them were to be assassinated. All cities captured were to be sacked and burned, and a band of a hundred desperate men had been organized to burn the larger Northern cities, which were not included in the field of active operations. Two hundred Confederate officers, who were to conduct the military movements, had been in Canada, but were then stationed throughout the West, at the various points to be attacked, waiting the outbreak at Chicago. Captain Hines, who had been second in command to John Morgan, and had won the confidence of Jacob Thompson by his successful management of the escape of the famous partisan leader from the Ohio penitentiary, had control of the initial movement against Camp Douglas; but Colonel Grenfell, — a brother of the noted major-general of the British army, — assisted by Colonel Marmaduke, of Missouri, and other able Confederate officers, was to manage the military part of the operations in Chicago. All these officers were at that moment in the city, waiting the arrival of the men, who were to come in small squads, over various railroads, during the following three days.

Colonel Langhorn had known of the plot for months, but its atrocious details of burning and assassination had come to his knowledge only within a fortnight. They had appalled him; and though he was betraying his friends and the South that he loved, the humanity in him would not let him rest till he had washed his hands of the horrible iniquity.

The commandant listened with nervous interest to the whole of this recital; but when the Southern officer uttered this last remark he almost groaned out, "Why did you not come to me before?"

The answer was, "I could not; I gave Thompson my opinion of this diabolical thing, and have been watched. I feel sure they have tracked me here. My life on your streets to-night would not be worth an ounce of powder."

"That is no doubt true," said the commandant; "but what must be done?"

"Arrest the Butternuts as they come into Chicago," replied the Kentuckian.

"That I can do," responded the commandant; "but the leaders are here; I must have them, — do you know them?"

"I do; but not where they are quartered," was the answer.

At two o'clock the commandant showed Colonel Langhorn to a bed, but went back himself, and paced the floor till sunrise. In the morning his plan was formed. It was a desperate plan; but desperate circumstances require desperate expedients.

In the prison was a young officer of the Texan rangers, who had been a member of Bragg's staff, but had resigned from it to take service as a private under John Morgan, and had been captured on his unfortunate expedition into Ohio. He was, therefore, well acquainted with Hines, Grenfell, and the other Confederate officers then in Chicago. He was a believer in the doctrine of States' Rights, but was an honest man, who, when his word had been given, could be fully trusted. One glance at his open, resolute face showed that he feared nothing; that he had, too, the rare courage which delights in danger, and courts heroic enterprise from pure love of peril. Moreover, he was a cultivated man, of prepossessing appearance and winning address, which, with his frank, outspoken character, had so won upon the previous commandant of the prison that he made him chief clerk in the medical department, where his reports, written in a hand that might pass for copper-plate engraving, were the admiration of all beholders.

It was the custom at that period to allow citizens free access to the camp, and among the many good men and women who came to visit and befriend the prisoners was a young lady, the daughter of a well-known resident of Chicago. She met the Texan, and a result as natural as the union of hydrogen and oxygen followed. But since Adam fell in love with Eve, who ever heard of courting going on in a prison? It is not exactly the thing, thought the commandant, and he said to the Texan, " Had you not better pay your addresses to the lady at her father's house, like a gentleman?"

A guard accompanied the prisoner on his wooing expeditions, but it was surmised that he remained outside, or bestowed his attentions upon the girls in the kitchen.

This was the state of things when the commandant of whom I am writing — Colonel Benjamin J. Sweet, of the 21st Wisconsin Volunteers — took charge of Camp Douglas. He learned the facts, scanned the Texan's face, and called to mind that he, himself, once went a-courting. As he paced his room that Friday night he bethought him of the Texan. Did he love his State better than he loved his affianced wife? The commandant resolved to test him, and with the first streak of day he sent for him. He opened to him the whole atrocious plan, laying stress upon its features of burning and assassination. Then he said, "I can attend to the rank and file, but I want your help to ferret out and apprehend the leaders."

The Texan had listened with undisguised horror to the bloody details of the conspiracy; now he looked into the eyes of the commandant, and said, slowly : " But I shall betray my friends! Can I do that in honor?"

" Did you ask that question when you betrayed your country?" answered the commandant.

" Let me go from camp for an hour," said the Texan; "then I will give you my decision."

" Very well," replied Colonel Sweet; and unattended by a guard, the prisoner left the prison.

I did not question the Texan as to what passed between him and his affianced during that hour, for all such things are sacred; but he told me that her last words to him were, " Do your duty. Blot out your record of treason."

On his return to the camp, the Texan merely said to the commandant, "I will do it," and then the details of the plan were talked over between them. He was to escape from the prison, so as to give the Confederate leaders no suspicion of the part he was playing, and also to thus win the confidence of their friends, so they would disclose to him their hiding-places. How to manage the escape puzzled the Texan, but the commandant had a brain fertile in expedients, and equal to any emergency. An adopted citizen in the scavenger line made daily visits to the camp in the way of his business, and him the commandant sent for, and told that he must help the Texan to get out of the prison.

"Arrah, yer Honor," said the old Irishman, "I hain't a tr-raitor. Bless your beautiful sowl! I love the country; and, besides, it might damage me good name, and me purty profession."

He was assured that his name would be all the more honorable if he should fare for a few weeks on prison rations; and then he assented to his part of the programme. Half an hour before sunset he came into the camp with his wagon. He filled it with dry bones, broken bottles, decayed food, and the rubbish of the prison; and down underneath he stowed away the Texan. A hundred prisoners crowded around to shut off the gaze of the guard; but outside the prison fence was the real danger. There he had to pass two gates, and run the gauntlet of half a dozen sentinels. His wagon was fuller than usual, and the late hour — it was now after sunset — would of itself excite suspicion. It might test the pluck of a braver man, for the bayonets of the sentries were fixed, and their guns at the half trigger. But he reached the outer gate in safety. Now Saint Patrick must help him, for he will need all the impudence of an Irishman. The gate was rolled back; the commandant stood nervously by; but the sentry cried out, "You can't pass; it's agin orders. No wagons kin go out arter drum-beat."

"Arrah, don't ye be a fool, — don't be after obstructing an honest man's business," answered the Irishman, pushing on into the gateway.

The sentinel was vigilant, for the commandant's eye was on him. "Halt," he cried, " or I'll fire."

"Fire! Waste yer powder on yer friends, like the bloody-minded spalpeen that ye are," said the scavenger, cracking his whip and moving forward. It was well that he did not look back. Had he done so, he might have been melted to his own soap-grease, for the sentry's musket was levelled, and he was about to fire, — but the commandant roared out, "Don't shoot!" and the old man and the old horse trotted off into the twilight.

Not fifteen minutes later two men in slouched hats and seedy butternuts emerged from the commandant's quarters. With muffled faces, and hasty strides, they made their way over the dimly lighted road into the city. Pausing after awhile before a large mansion, they crouched down among the shadows. It was the home of the Grand Treasurer of the order of American Knights, and into it very soon they saw the Texan enter. The good man knew him well, and over his escape he greatly rejoiced. He ordered up for him the fatted calf, and soon it was on the table, steaming hot, and done brown in the roasting. When the repast was over they discussed together a bottle of champagne and the situation. The custodian of Confederate funds said the Texan must not remain in Chicago, for there he would of a certainty be discovered. He must be off to Cincinnati by the first train, and he would arrive there in the nick of time, for warm work was daily expected. Had he any money about him?

No; the Texan had left it behind, with his Sunday clothes, in the prison.

Well, he must have funds; but the worthy gentleman could give him none, for he was a loyal man; of course he was, for was he not the " people's " candidate for governor of Illinois? But it was never known that a woman was hanged for treason. With this the worthy Treasurer nodded to his wife, who opened her purse and tossed the Texan a roll of greenbacks. As she did so, the good man said: " The Cincinnati train does not leave till midnight. Meanwhile, you will have time to see Hines and Grenfell, — they are at the Richmond House."

At the end of an hour " good night " was said, and the Texan went out to find the leaders of the conspiracy. Down the dimly lighted street he hurried, the long, dark shadows following close at his heels.

He entered the private door of the Richmond House, spoke a magic word, and was conducted to a room in the upper story. Three low, prolonged raps on the wall, and he was among them. They were seated around a small table, on which was a plan of the prison enclosure. One was about forty-five, — a tall, thin man, with a wiry frame, a jovial face, and eyes which had the wild, roving look of the Arabs. He was dressed after the fashion of an English sportsman, and his dog — a fine gray bloodhound — was stretched on the hearth-rug near him. He looked a reckless, desperate character, and had an adventurous history.[1] In battle he was said to be a thunderbolt, lightning harnessed, and inspired with the will of a devil. He was just the character to lead the dark, desperate en-

[1] See Fremantle's " Three Months in the Southern States," page 148.

terprise on which they had entered. It was St. Leger Grenfell.

At his right sat another tall, erect man of about thirty, with large, prominent eyes, and thin, black hair and mustache. He was of dark complexion, had a sharp, thin nose, a small, close mouth, a coarse, high voice, and a quick, somewhat boisterous manner. His face bore traces of dissipation, and his dress betokened the dandy; but his deep, clear eye, and pale, wrinkled forehead denoted a cool, crafty intellect.[1] This was the noted Captain Hines, the right-hand man of John Morgan, and the soul and brains of the Chicago enterprise. The others were the meaner sort of villains. I do not know how they looked, and if I did know, they would not be worth describing.

Hines and Grenfell sprang to their feet, and grasped the hands of the Texan. He was a godsend, — sent to take the post of honor and of danger; to lead the attack on the front gateway of the prison. So they said with great oaths as they sat down, spread out the map, and explained to him the plan of operations, which to all human appearance would have been successful, had they been allowed to put it into execution.

Two hundred Confederate refugees from Canada, and a hundred Butternuts from Fayette and Christian Counties, they said, had already arrived; many more from Kentucky and Missouri were coming; and by Tuesday they expected that a thousand or twelve hundred desperate men, armed to the teeth, would be in Chicago. Taking advantage of the excitement of election night, they proposed with this force to attack the camp and prison. The force would be divided into five parties. One squad, under Grenfell, would be held in reserve a few hundred yards

[1] Detective's description.

from the main body, and would guard the large number of guns already provided to arm the prisoners. Another — command of which they offered the Texan — would assault the front gateway, and engage the attention of the eight hundred veteran reserves quartered in Garrison Square. The work of this squad would be dangerous, for it would encounter a force four times its strength, well armed and supplied with artillery; but it would be speedily relieved by the other divisions. Those under Colonel Marmaduke and Robert Anderson, of Kentucky, and Brigadier-General Charles Walsh, of Chicago, Commander of the American Knights, would simultaneously assail three sides of Prison Square, break down the prison fence, liberate the prisoners, and, taking the garrison in the rear, compel a general surrender. This accomplished, small parties would be despatched to cut the telegraph wires and hold the railway stations, and then the whole body would march into the city, and rendezvous in Court Square.

The insurgents having then been reinforced by the five thousand Illini, and provided with the arms of the city — six brass field-pieces — and the arms and ammunition stored in private warehouses, would begin the work of destruction. The banks would be robbed, the stores gutted, the houses of loyal men plundered; the railroad stations, grain elevators, and all public buildings would be set on fire, and the city itself burned to the ground. To facilitate this, the water plugs had been already marked, and a force detailed to set the water running. In brief, the war would be brought home to the North; Chicago would be treated like a place taken by assault, and given over to the torch, the sword, and the brutal lust of a drunken soldiery. On it would be wreaked all the havoc, the desolation, and the agony which three and a half years of most bloody and disastrous war had heaped upon the South, and its up-going flames would be the torch that should light a score of other Northern cities to a like destruction.

It was a diabolical plan, conceived far down amid the thick darkness, and brought up by the archfiend himself, who, doubtless, sat there in that grim circle, toying with the hideous thing, and with his cloven foot beating a merry tattoo on a death's head and cross-bones, under the table.

As he concluded, Hines turned to the Texan, and said: "Well, my boy, there will be, for awhile, eight hundred against your two hundred. What do you say? Will you take the post of honor and of danger?"

The Texan drew a long breath, then through his barred teeth he blurted out, "I will."

On those two words hung thousands of lives, and millions upon millions of property.

Soon Hines and another man announced that their time was about up. "Fielding and I," said Hines, "never stay in this d—d town after midnight. You are fools or you wouldn't."

Suddenly, as these words were uttered, a slouched hat, listening at the key-hole, sprang up, moved softly through the hall, and stole down the stairway. Half an hour later the Texan opened the private door of the Richmond House, looked cautiously about for a few moments, and then stalked away towards the heart of the city.

The moon was down, the street-lamps burned dimly, but after him glided the shadows.

In a room at the Tremont House, at this late hour, the commandant was pacing the floor, as was his habit, when the door opened and a man entered. The man's face was flushed, his teeth were clenched, his eyes were flashing.

He was stirred to the depths of his being. Could he be the self-contained Texan?

"What is the matter?" asked the commandant.

The other sat down, and in an abstracted way, as if talking to himself, he recounted the whole of that diabolical interview, which had swept away for him the fallacies of a lifetime. In conclusion he said, "Hitherto, this night, I have acted from love for a pure and true woman, but now, sir, I see that it is my duty to humanity to balk this most hellish plot of the century."

The first gray of the morning was streaking the east, when he went forth to find a hiding-place. The sun was not up, and the dawning light came dimly through the misty clouds, but after him still glided the long dark shadows.

Meanwhile, the escape of the Texan had been reported to the commandant by Captain Wells Sponable, the inspector of the prison. "Make a thorough search," said the commandant, "a great hue and cry, and ransack the house of every rebel sympathizer in Chicago, but let not a man go near the home of the lady to whom Shanks is affianced."

Sponable took the hint, and made a search of exceeding thoroughness. Hand-bills were gotten out, a reward was offered, and by that Sunday noon the name of the Texan was on every street corner. Squads of soldiers and police invaded every disloyal asylum. Strange things were brought to light, — arms enough to equip half a dozen regiments, — and strange gentry were dragged out of dark closets; but nowhere was found the Texan, for he was safely housed in the dwelling of his affianced, who was preparing for him such a disguise as soon would deceive the commandant himself.

Just at dark, a person giving his name as Burlingham called at the private entrance of the Tremont House, and asked for Colonel Sweet, of Camp Douglas. He was shown to his room, the usher wondering what the commandant could have to do with such a dandy. He sported a light rattan, wore a stove-pipe hat, a Sunday suit, and was shaven and shorn of every hirsute adornment. The commandant scanned him from head to foot, and said, impatient at the interruption, " What can I do for you, sir ? "

The Texan sank into a chair, laughing heartily and saying, " I see you do not know me."

The commandant did not so much as smile; he merely said, " You are well disguised; but tell me how goes it ? "

The Texan answered that the plot thickened. More Butternuts had arrived, and the blow would be struck on Tuesday night, certain. He had seen his men, — two hundred picked, and every one of them clamoring for pickings. Hines, who carried the bag, was to give him ten thousand greenbacks, to stop their mouths and stuff their pockets, at nine o'clock the next morning.

" And to-morrow night we will have them sure! And how say you, — shall I give you shackles and a dungeon ? " asked the commandant, his mouth wreathing with grim wrinkles.

" Anything you like," answered the Texan ; " anything to blot out my record of treason."

The Texan gone, up and down the room went the commandant as was his fashion. He was playing a desperate game. The stake was awful. He held the ace of trumps, — but should he risk the game upon it ? At half past eight he sat down and wrote a despatch to his general, in which he said, " My force is, as you know, too weak, and much overworked, — only eight hundred men, all told, to guard between eight and nine thousand prisoners. I am certainly not justified in waiting to take risks, and mean to arrest these officers, if possible, before morning."

The despatch goes off, but still he is undecided. If he strikes that night, Hines may escape, for the fox has a hole out of town, and may keep under cover until morning. Besides, the Texan would go out of prison a penniless man among strangers; and those ten thousand greenbacks were lawful prize, and should be the country's dower with the maiden. But, republics are grateful, and the country would deal generously by the Texan. This thought decided him, and he went back to Camp Douglas, sent for the police, and got his bluecoats ready. At two o'clock that Monday morning, they swooped to the prey, and within an hour a hundred strange birds were in the talons of the eagle. Such another haul of buzzards and night-hawks never was made since Michael subdued the great dragon and the dark angels. When they were all gathered in, the commandant sat down and wrote another despatch to his general. It was dated Camp Douglas, Nov. 7th, four o'clock A. M., and said:

Have made during the night the following arrests of rebel officers, escaped prisoners of war, and citizens in connection with them:

Morgan's Adjutant-General, Colonel G. St. Leger Grenfell, in company with J. T. Shanks, an escaped prisoner of war, at the Richmond House, Colonel Vincent Marmaduke, brother of General Marmaduke, Brigadier-General Charles Walsh, of the Sons of Liberty, Captain Cantrill, of Morgan's command, and Charles Traverse. Cantrill and Traverse arrested in Walsh's house, in which were found two cartloads of large-size revolvers, loaded and capped, two hundred stands of muskets, loaded, and ammunition. Also seized two boxes of guns concealed in a room in the city. Also arrested Buck Morris, treasurer of Sons of Liberty, having complete proof of his assisting Shanks to escape and plotting to release prisoners at this camp. . . . There are many strangers and suspicious persons in the city believed to be guerrillas and rebel soldiers.

In the same report the commandant writes as follows of the general operations:

Adopting measures which proved effective to detect the presence and identify the persons of the officers and leaders, and ascertain their plans, it was manifest that they had the means of gathering a force considerably larger than the little garrison then guarding between eight and nine thousand prisoners of war at Camp Douglas, and that, taking advantage of the excitement and the large number of persons who would fill the streets on election night, they intended to make a night attack on and surprise this camp, release and arm the prisoners of war, cut the telegraph wires, burn the railroad depots, seize the banks and stores containing arms and ammunition, take possession of the city, and commence a campaign for the release of other prisoners of war in the States of Illinois and Indiana, thus organizing an army to effect and give success to the general uprising so long contemplated by the Sons of Liberty.

At the Richmond House the Texan was captured when lying in bed with Grenfell. They were put into irons, and driven off to Camp Douglas together. A few days later the Texan, in relating these details to me, while the commandant sat near by at his desk writing, said: " Words cannot describe my relief when those handcuffs were put upon us. At times before, the sense of responsibility almost overpowered me. Then I felt like a man who had just come into a fortune. The wonder to me now is, how the colonel could have trusted so much to a rebel."

" Trusted!" echoed the commandant, looking up from his writing; "I had faith in you; I thought you wouldn't betray me; but I trusted your own life in your own hands, that was all. Too much was at stake to do more. Your every step was shadowed, from the moment you left this camp till you came back to it in irons. Two detectives were constantly at your back, sworn to take your life if you wavered for half a second."

"Is that true?" asked the Texan in a musing way, but without moving a muscle. "I didn't know it, but I felt it in the air."

In the room at the Richmond House, and on the table around which was discussed the diabolical plan, was found a slip of paper on which was scrawled in pencil marks:

Colonel:—You *must* leave this house *to-night.* Go to the Briggs House. J. FIELDING.

Fielding was the assumed name of the officer who burrowed with Hines out of town, where even his fellow conspirators did not know. The tone of the note indicates that Hines suspected danger from the Texan. Beyond a doubt he did. Another day and his life might have been the forfeit, and had not Colonel Sweet acted that very night, Camp Douglas might have been sprung upon a little too suddenly. So he was not an hour too soon; and he was justified in his prompt action, though it cost the Texan the dower he was anxious he should receive with his affianced wife.

A shiver of genuine horror passed over Chicago when it awoke on the following morning. From mouth to mouth the tidings ran; fathers clasped their children in their arms, mothers pressed their babes to their bosoms, appalled at the fearful catastrophe from which they had so narrowly escaped. And well they might be affrighted, for no imagination can picture the horrors that would have followed the falling of such an avalanche upon the sleeping city. "One hour of such a catastrophe would destroy the creations of a quarter of a century, and expose the homes of nearly two hundred thousand souls to every conceivable form of desecration." [1] The event would have had no parallel in savage history.

On the following day the men of Chicago went to the polls and voted for Abraham Lincoln and the Union, and thus told the world what honest Illinois thought of the miscreants who had devised this diabolical plot to aid in the destruction of their country.

But the danger was not entirely over. Hines and other leaders of the conspiracy were yet at large, and thousands of armed men were still ready for an outbreak at a signal from these leaders. It was election day. Excited crowds thronged the streets, and mingled among them were the armed and lawless bushwhackers. A spark only was needed to start a conflagration; but the commandant was equal to the occasion. The merchants had spontaneously come together in the Exchange, to consider the peril of the situation, and hearing of this, he sent them word to arm themselves, and to give a musket to every man who could be trusted. On the instant two hundred volunteered, and before noon of that day probably not less than a thousand were patrolling every avenue and by-way of the city. All that day, and all that night, and all the following day, they made the weary rounds, — young men and old, some on foot, some on horseback, and among the latter many who had not been in a saddle for a twelvemonth, until at last Chicago went to its slumbers in security.

Meanwhile, searches were going on, and arrests being made hourly. To the "birds" already bagged was soon added another flock of two hundred. The sorrier sort, in butternut brown, were emptied into an old church, where they might bewail their sins, and pray for their country.

[1] Chicago *Tribune*, Nov. 8, 1864.

Those of gayer plumage were caged in the dark cells of Camp Douglas. Rare " birds " they were: an embryo Semmes, a city attorney, a would-be sheriff, and a would-be governor, — would-be assassins, all of them.

The president and secretary of the Illini were arrested, and then the lodges of the worshipful order were invaded. The members had met often since the first arrests were made, but they had come together with greater secrecy, redoubled their vigilance, changed their passwords, and subjected to closer questioning every one who was admitted. They were biding their time, swearing in new members, and preparing to strike under other and, perhaps, abler leaders; but these visits of the crippled veterans of Camp Douglas disturbed their dreams, and they scattered like wolves chased by firebrands.

On the Friday night following the election the loyal men and women of Chicago came together to rejoice over the presidential victory which had saved the life of the nation. Thousands upon thousands had come together, and Colonel Sweet, the commandant, had been urgently pressed to be present on the occasion. When he appeared, cheer after cheer went up from the vast assemblage, till the very walls of the huge building echoed the enthusiasm of the people. In response to a universal call, he arose, and when the tumult of applause had somewhat subsided, he said: " I thank you for this cordial greeting. I came here to celebrate with you our great victory. Four years ago, when I entered the army, I cast aside politics, and now I know only loyal men and traitors. The loyal men have triumphed, but our victory is not complete. We must crush out every vestige of treason in the North; and, if the Government give me power, I will do my part in the work of subjugation."

Colonel Sweet was a man of only moderate means, and in employing detectives to shadow the newly arrived Butternuts, and to unearth the hidden conspirators, he had been obliged to expend about a thousand dollars from his own slender resources. Hearing of this, the patriotic ladies of the First Baptist Church in Chicago collected that sum of money, and, investing it in a United States bond, caused it to be presented to him by the Hon. George C. Bates, at a meeting called for the purpose. In response to the remarks of Mr. Bates on the occasion, the commandant modestly said:

"Sir, I thank you for the gracious and eloquent manner in which you have made this presentation, and the fair ladies of the First Baptist Church, in whose behalf you have spoken.... In whatever has been done here of late to foil the enemy and protect Chicago, the officers and enlisted men of the small, patient, willing garrison of Camp Douglas, rather than myself, deserve gratitude and commendation.

"I accept this thousand-dollar bond in the same spirit in which it is given, and gratefully hope to be able to send it as an heirloom down through the generations which shall come after me, gaining traditional and intrinsic value as the story of this war is told, and the Government now assailed, and by which it was issued, stands firm and proudly against all assaults of hatred or foreign intrigue from without, or of faction or insurrection from within, growing in wealth, prosperity, population, freedom, and national glory, grandeur, and power through the ages.

"Sir, your kind words and the manifestations of this audience make me feel that henceforward I have two homes: one in my own beloved and true State of Wisconsin, in the little county of Calumet, which to-night nestles my loved ones from the cold, under its mantle of snow; where every rivulet and old rock are dear to me, — among a brave, honest, and patriotic people, where there are whole towns in which scarcely an able-bodied man remains who has not volunteered, been clothed in blue, and taught the use of arms in defending those free institutions around which the hopes of mankind cluster; and another home in the hearts of the noble-minded and generous men and women of this marvellous metropolis of the Northwest, the munificent and loyal city of Chicago."

As soon as he had read the newspaper accounts of the suppression of the attempted outbreak at Camp Douglas, Mr. Stanton, the Secretary of War, telegraphed Colonel Sweet, "Hold your prisoners and arms captured at all hazards. Your energetic action meets with the approval of this Department." And soon afterwards President Lincoln promoted him to a brigadier-generalship in the volunteer army.

But J. T. Shanks, the Texan, without whose help the commandant could not have apprehended the leaders of the conspiracy, was cast upon the world with not a friend or a dollar; and, worse than that, he was left in daily danger of assassination, and for safety was forced to shelter himself, day and night, within the enclosure of Camp Douglas. The important part he had taken in arresting the chief conspirators gradually leaked out, and it soon coming to the ears of the agents of the conspiracy in Canada, they offered a thousand dollars in gold to whoever should take his life, as the due reward for his treachery to the Southern cause. This led to the banding together of a number of assassins in Chicago, pledged to accomplish that object, and to divide the reward between them.

These men went boldly about the work, even seeking for

the Texan within the walls of Camp Douglas; but in this they were foiled by the astuteness of the Commandant, who, anticipating some such design, had given strict orders against the admission of any stranger within the prison grounds without a written pass from himself, or his chief subordinate, Captain Sponable. Then he proposed to secure for Shanks some appointment in the Union army, where his pay would suffice for the support of himself and the young lady to whom he was betrothed. This kindly proffer the Texan felt obliged to decline for the reason that he could not fight his native State, or come in conflict with his life-long friends and associates.

In these circumstances the Texan wrote to me, stating his situation, and requesting that I would use my influence to secure for him a position in some commercial house in New York or Boston, where his clerical knowledge might enable him to give a decent livelihood to the noble woman who was content to share his fortunes, whatever they might be. I at once made personal application to such business friends as I had in both cities, but to no avail. All were full-handed, and several of them were holding their old employees on at reduced pay to keep the wolf from the door. At the end of a week of this fruitless effort, I wrote to Shanks of the result, and said that I would go direct to President Lincoln, of whom I had never asked a favor, and I thought that in the goodness of his heart he would find a respectable position for him in some one of the departments, with an income sufficient to his requirements.

Accordingly, that night I went on to Washington, and early on the following morning called upon Mr. Lincoln. I found him in excellent spirits, and I soon got him in decidedly good-humor by opening to him the budget of laughable stories I had gathered since our last interview,—a thing he was always sure to call for on every convenient occasion. At last I broached the real object of my visit by asking if he had seen any full account of the suppression of the attempted outbreak at Camp Douglas.

He had seen, he said, Colonel Sweet's report, and what had been published about it in the Chicago newspapers, but for a long time he had believed in the existence of the treasonable organization. That was the real reason he had neglected to appoint Judge Edmonds to investigate the New York riots. Both outbreaks were fruits of the same tree, and if we shook the tree we might get more of its fruit than we could conveniently handle. Did I know anything more of the outbreak than had been published?

"Yes," I answered, "I know all about it,—all its inside history, and it is one of the most dramatic episodes of the war. During the week after election I lectured for three successive nights before the Young Men's Christian Association of Chicago, and all of the intervening days I passed in Camp Douglas, where Colonel Sweet opened everything to me. He is a rare and true man, exactly fitted for the work he had to do, and his services deserve the recognition you have given them; but, after all, it was a woman who saved Chicago, and rolled up that tremendous vote the city gave you at the election."

"A woman!" he said. "How was that? Tell me."

"'Tis a long story, and you haven't time now; a half-dozen were waiting for you when I came in."

He ran his eye over a number of cards that lay before him on the table, and said, "Not one of them has any special business with me, so go on; I can give you the whole forenoon. But tell me, have you seen the Governor since he got back?"

"Yes. I met him by appointment in New York, and he made me tell all that I knew, — as you do usually; and he told me of all his transactions in Europe, and besides a little thing about yourself that I had not so much as suspected."

"And what was that?" he asked, smiling.

"I had told him that I thought it was a magnanimous thing in you to invite Mr. Chase to confer with you about the terms to be offered to the Confederacy, when you knew he was sadly disgruntled over your having so recently asked him to step down and out from the Treasury; at which he laughed, saying he had thought I could see an elephant without an eyeglass; that you had invited Chase because you intended to offer compensation for the slaves, and you wanted his approval of it, because that would shut the mouths of the Abolitionists, who would be sure to censure you fiercely for any such proposal."

"Then you are not so astute as the Governor. I fear it won't do to send you on another mission to Richmond. But, now, Mr. Envoy Extraordinary, let me have the Camp Douglas story."

I then went on with a detailed account of the entire event, laying special stress on the part that Shanks took in it, and repeating the words his affianced used to him, — "Do your duty. Blot out your record of treason."

At this, he said, "She is a noble woman, and he must be a good deal of a man to have won the love of such a woman."

"I judge him to be so, and he turned himself inside out to me during our three days' intercourse. I received a letter from him about ten days ago that is the finest specimen of chirography I have ever seen. I have it in my pocket. Would you not like to see it?"

He expressed the desire, and I handed him the letter in which Shanks explained his circumstances, and requested me to assist him. He glanced casually at it, saying, "It certainly is beautifully written, and with all the ease of ordinary penmanship;" then, as if something special had caught his eye, he asked, "Do you mean that I shall read it?"

"Yes, if you please; that is why I have brought it with me."

The letter was a long one, but before he had read through the first page he said, "Ah, I see why you have shown me this; you think a wink is as good as a nod to a blind horse."

"Yes, but either is more effective if the horse is not blind."

"Well, he is not — not entirely so; but let me read the rest of this."

This done, he said, "He says Sweet has proposed to get for him a captaincy in some Union regiment. What do you think I ought to do for him?"

"I have thought you might find a suitable place for him in some one of the departments."

"What! A mere clerkship for a man who has the nerve to take his life in his hand, and do a great deed for such a woman? No, he has the right stuff in him, and she will keep him straight. He should be where he will have a chance for promotion. Suppose I make him captain in one of the Western regiments, where there will be no possibility of his coming in conflict with his old friends?"

"That would do beautifully. May I write him that you will do that?"

"Yes, and say that if there is any position he would like

better, he must let you know; that I will do all that I can for him on the condition that he marries that young lady. And ask him to tell her that I hope God will bless her for what she has done for the country."

The Texan married the young lady, and gratefully accepted a captaincy in a Union regiment stationed in the far West. Several of his letters to me are in the historical library of the Johns Hopkins University; the only one I have now at hand is dated Camp Rankin, Colorado Territory, August 5, 1865, and it so well expresses the spirit of the man that I am tempted to quote a portion of it. In it he says:

> The assistance I rendered the military authorities in detecting the rebel officers was prompted solely by patriotic principle, and not by the hope of any future aggrandizement. By doing what I did, I have incurred the ill-will of many thousands whom I regard as worse enemies than the bitterest rebels ever confined at Camp Douglas. I feel very grateful for the honor conferred on me,— the commission of captain in the United States Army,— and also proud that I again possess the confidence and good-will of the best government that ever existed, and my pride and ambition will ever be to show, *by my acts*, that I merit its confidence.

One day, during the Civil War, I met on a railway in Michigan a man who said to me, "Sir, I used to be an atheist, but watching the progress of the war, and seeing how all its events have worked together to secure the freedom of all men, I have become convinced that there is a Great Intelligence who governs the universe, and has this country in his especial keeping." I never doubted this great truth, but an inside knowledge of some of the pivotal events of the war confirmed my belief in it, and satisfied me that Abraham Lincoln was His selected instrument to conduct this nation in its onward career to a great destiny.

INDEX.

Adams, Colonel Julius W., 191.

Allston, ex-Governor of South Carolina. His declaration of the purposes of the Confederacy in the spring of 1861, 231, 232.

Benjamin, Judah P., Confederate Secretary of State, 258; receives us at the State Department in Richmond, 259-272, 287.

Butler, General Benjamin F., 247. First meeting with him, 250; a visit at his headquarters, 250-253.

Cameron, Simon. The author introduced by him to Abraham Lincoln, 13; communicates account of the first Cabinet session after fall of Fort Sumter, 23-29; his plan for subduing the revolted States, 25-26.

Carleton, George W., declines to publish the book "Among the Pines," 71; subsequently assumes its publication at a royalty of twenty-five per cent., 73.

Carpenter, Inspector, 188, 189.

Chase, Salmon P., 29, 50. In conference with President Lincoln, 242-247, 292.

Conspiracy, The great Western, 294-333. Its extent and connection with the Richmond leaders, 294-295; its outbreak to be the capture of Camp Douglas and other military prisons; suppressed by Colonel Benjamin J. Sweet; description of him and of Camp Douglas, 298-303; Colonel Sweet's watchfulness and sagacity, 303-310; he employs J. T. Shanks, a Texas ranger, to detect and apprehend the leading conspirators, 312-324; he saved Chicago from destruction, 325-326; President Lincoln rewards Shanks by a commission in the United States Army.

Davis, Jefferson, 17, 30. Interview with him, and his views on "self-government," 261-272.

Davis, Jeff C., 127.

Ducat, Arthur C., 124, 125.

Edmonds, Judge John W. An article of his in the *Continental Monthly* commented on by President Lincoln, 80; consents to investigate the origin of the New York riots, 198.

Garesche, 129, 130.

Garfield, General James A. A description of him, 118; Rosecrans's estimate of him, 123; camp-meeting in his quarters, 125-131; his opinion of Rosecrans, 145, 222-226.

Gay, Sidney Howard, managing editor of the New York *Tribune*, 81, 89-90, 94, 151. His heroic devotion to duty during the New York riots of 1863, 169-200.

Grant, General U. S., 90, 97, 156. He defeats the Wilmington expedition, 226-228; his personal appearance, 249; refuses to pass the writer into the Confederate lines, but alters his decision on hearing from President Lincoln, 252, 253.

Great Uprising, and great meeting in New York City, 33-35.

Greeley, Horace, the author's first interview with, 39-48; regrets his nomination of President Lincoln, 42; doubts the ability of the North to subdue the Southern States, and questions if it were not wise to let them depart in peace, 46; his proposal to secure advance news of governmental policy, 46; opinion of Robert T. Walker, 55; his feeling towards President Lincoln, 63; his dissatisfaction with him, 82, 90-92, 97, 101; his emotion on hearing of the battle of Chancellorsville, 103, 151, 167; forbids the arming of the *Tribune* building during the riots, 170; the arming of the *Tribune* to resist the rioters, 173, 174, 181-185; his reckless bravery in the riots, 193-194; his opinion of them, 199; his character and characteristic anecdotes of him, 200-205.

Grenfell, Colonel St. Leger, 311, 316-323.

Hall, A. Oakey. His zealous patriotism, 51; writes for the *Continental Monthly*, 68.

Hines, Captain, 310, 317-319, 322-324.

Hooker, General, 95, 96, 103.

Jaquess, Colonel James F. First interview with him, 137-141; General Garfield's letter about him, 164; President Lincoln's anxiety for his safety, 165; his reception within the Confederate lines, 165, 233-241, 246-291.

Javins, Charles, 255-259, 274-276.

Kidder, Edward, 208-218.

Kidder, Frederic. His plan for subduing the South, 21, 22; writes for the *Continental Monthly*, 68; notice of him and of his plan for the conquest of the revolted States, 206-229; meets General Grant with Governor Andrew, 228.

Kirkland, Caroline M. (Mary Clavers), suggests the book "Among the Pines," 65.

Langhorn, Colonel Maurice, 309-312.

Leland, Charles Godfrey, editor of the *Knickerbocker*. His great ability as a political writer, 37; chosen editor of the *Continental Monthly*, 38; his enthusiastic work on the *Continental Monthly*, 68; brief sketch of him, 69; the important work done by him in arousing the public to the necessity of emancipation, 86, 87.

Lincoln, Abraham. The author's first interview with him on April 13, 1861, 13-22; his personal appearance, 14; expresses a readiness to emancipate the slaves as a war measure, in obedience to the overwhelming sentiment of the North; is struck by the plan of the British Cabinet for subduing the revolted colonies in the Revolution, 21, 42, 43; letter of his to Robert J. Walker, to be shown to Horace Greeley, 54; his course in the *Trent* affair stated by himself, 55; his first conception of an Emancipation Proclamation, November, 1861, 57-62; circumstances attending the issue of "The Emancipation Proclamation," 75, 76, 84, 85; his remarkable memory, 78; combination among the Republican leaders in opposition to his administration, 97-102; declines any conversation respecting the visit of Colonel Jaquess to the Confederate leaders, 150; forbids army aid to a negro insurrection, 151; interview with him about Jaquess, 156-162; his view of compensate emancipation, 158, 159; declines to investigate the origin of the New York riots, 199; dictates a letter to Governor Vance, of North Carolina, in reference to peace proposals, 215, 216; recommends communications to pass through General Garfield, 222; his view of the war, 228, 229, 235; outlines the terms of peace he would grant the Confederacy, 242-245; advises publication in the *Atlantic Monthly* of a report of the "Peace Mission" of 1864, 289; rewards J. T. Shanks for his services in defeating the intended attack upon Camp Douglas by a commission in the United States Army, 332.

Longstreet, General, 165.

Marmaduke, Colonel, 308, 311-318, 322.

McClellan, General, 75, 82, 232.

Negley, General, 128.

Ould, Robert, Confederate Commissioner of Exchange, 249, 251; his gentlemanly treatment of us in Richmond, 255-288.

Palmer, General, 127.

Parton, James, 168. His account of the New York draft riots, 171-177.

Peace Mission of 1864. Preliminaries to it, 229-247; report of same, 248-291.

Pope, General, 128.

Porter, William, 131.

Price, General Sterling, 295, 296.

Richmond, Our visit to, in July, 1864, 248-293.

Rosecrans, General William S., 91, 97, 100-103, 114-125; declines a nomination for the Presidency, 145-147; approves of Colonel Jaquess visiting the Confederate leaders, 140, 141; his dissatisfaction with Secretary Stanton, 141, 142; refuses to sanction a proposed negro insurrection, 142-144; an estimate of him, 153, 294.

Seward, William H., 20, 24. His opposition to coercive measures applied to the South, 29, 33, 34, 42, 43; his waning influence with President Lincoln, 50, 51; disapproves of the *Continental Monthly*, 69-91.

Shanks, J. T., 312-324, 328-333.

Sheridan, General Philip H. Rosecrans's estimate of him, 124; an interview with him, 128-130.

Stanley, General, 126, 127, 131.

Stanton, Secretary, 91, 92, 125, 141, 154-156.

Stevens, Alex., 17.

Streight, Colonel A. D., 282, 283.

Sweet, Colonel Benjamin J., 297-332.

Thomas, General George H. A description of him, 121; invites Union men to meet the writer, 213.

Thompson, Jacob, 295-299, 309, 311.

Travel in war time, 104-113; at the receipt of custom, 106, 107; alarm from guerillas, 108, 109; a strange passenger, 110-113.

Tribune (New York) in the draft riots, 168-197.

Turchin, General, 127.

Turner, Major, the notorious keeper, conducts us through Libby Prison, 279-286.

Van Cleve, General, 126.

Vance, Governor, 209, 227.

Walker, Robert J. The author's meeting him in Washington, D. C., April 13, 1861, 9; his personal appearance and remarkable career, 10-12; predicts a long war, but the future union and greatness of this country, 29-32; his opinion of slavery, 35-36; his great speech in New York City, 34, 35, 40, 41, 49-51; declines the position of Secretary of State in President Lincoln's Cabinet, 51; advises President Lincoln's course in the *Trent* affair, 56; his pleasure at the first appearance of the *Continental Monthly*, 67; his statement of the country at the close of 1862, 87, 88; he goes to Europe as financial agent for the Government in March, 1863, where he negotiates two hundred and fifty millions of the United States 5-20 bonds, 88; estimate of him as a financier, 89, 222, 223.